RALLY

RALLY

MAURICE HAMILTON

PARTRIDGE PRESS

Designed by Graeme Murdoch

Text copyright © 1987 by Maurice Hamilton
Photographs copyright © 1987 as credited

Published in Great Britain by
Partridge Press
Maxwelton House
Boltro Road
Haywards Heath
West Sussex

(Partridge Press is an imprint of
Transworld Publishers Limited
61–63 Uxbridge Road, London W5)

Printed in Great Britain by
BAS Printers Limited
Over Wallop
Hampshire

ISBN 1-85225-029-1

All photographs in this book are by
Quadrant Picture Library except for the
following:
Private Collection: 58, 214
Colorsport: 60, 169, 189, 195, 213
LAT: 62, 71, 76, 83, 86, 113, 131, 138,
    139 (inset), 147, 158, 159, 166, 171, 215
    (Aaltonen), 216 (Salonen), 217 (McRae
    and Rohrl)
Sporting Pictures UK: 129 (top), 132, 140,
    142, 144, 154, 207, 217 (Alen and
    Kankkunen)
All-Sport: 129 (bottom), 130, 133, 134,
    173, 178, 179, 184
Mark Leech: 143
Colin Taylor Productions: 94, 152, 163

CONTENTS

INTRODUCTION

THE VILLAGE of Ardmillan sits on the western shore of Strangford Lough in County Down. It's a long way, both geographically and physically, from the terrain used for the RAC Rally. But it was here, while sitting on the wall outside the Orange Hall, that I was mesmerised by the sound and fury of a rally car in full cry.

Northern Ireland may have more than its fair share of anomalies which may, at times, appear sad and senseless. But, from a motor sport enthusiast's point of view, the ability to close public roads, more or less at the drop of a hat, represents a sound piece of legislation which is strangely lacking elsewhere in the United Kingdom.

Ardmillan may have just one narrow street, fed at one end by a ninety-degree left-hand bend but, on a still night on Good Friday 1968, this was part of a Special Stage on the Circuit of Ireland Rally.

One of the first cars through was the Ford Escort Twin Cam of Roger Clark and Jim Porter. There are certain sights and sounds in motor sport which you never forget. This was one of them.

The villagers, gossiping casually outside their front doors, stopped their idle chatter as the muffled beat of the Twin Cam orchestrated the sudden bursts of light sweeping the nearby hillocks. There were moments of quiet, interrupted by the urgent stabbing of the throttle as Clark worked his way down the narrow road leading to Ardmillan. Another lull, followed by a volley of sound as the Escort rushed across a causeway 400 yards from the village, it's slashing lights illuminating the buildings at the end of the street. Where there had been murky darkness and muffled conversation before, there was now a sea of expectant faces, transfixed by the violent change in tempo.

The Ford was hurled into the heart of the village. The car's broadside attitude lit up the grey façades which now reverberated to the engine's beautiful bellow. Caught momentarily in the spread of six dazzling spotlights, the villagers stepped back defensively into the sanctuary of their homes. Five seconds later, Clark and Porter were gone, not into the front parlour of the terraced house opposite, but into the next bend. And into the memories of those who saw it.

The recall may be embellished by the rose-tinted tricks of time – but I don't think so.

It is the sort of mental picture which more than a million spectators carry home in November each year after an encounter with the RAC Rally. It is the effect of watching a driver take his car close to the limit, retreat momentarily, only seemingly to return to the edge of disaster at the very next corner. The impact on the senses is the same, be it on a rocky road in Greece, a snow-covered pass in France, the uneven camber of a village street in Ulster, or a gravel track in a British forest.

The RAC Rally may not be able to use the public roads in England, Scotland and Wales, but the Forestry Commission provide a more than adequate substitute. It is here that the rally cars are driven flat out, against the clock and without the benefit of pace notes. This is what makes the RAC Rally one of the toughest motoring events in the world; one which ranks alongside the Monte Carlo and Safari rallies in terms of prestige.

It wasn't always so. The first major rally in Great Britain, held in March 1932, was something of an adventure. The 'treasure hunt' image remained until the emphasis was switched from the map-reading skills of the navigator to the fluency and concentration of the driver. Once the RAC Rally moved off the highways and into the forests, the growth in both the stature and the depth of challenge was inevitable.

Now, the RAC Rally, supported loyally by Lombard, remains a highlight of the international calendar even though the substance of rallying in general has been diluted, supposedly in the interests of safety, in line with the demands of the sport's governing body.

A detailed account of each RAC Rally would require a couple of volumes, such is the complexity and change which has attended the event during the past 50 years. The purpose of this book is to trace the metamorphosis from the gentlemanly era to the present day when rule books and horsepower have superceded rugs and hampers as essential tools of the trade.

Along the way, we follow progress on the international scene and measure the transition of a sport from three-piece suits and trilbys to four-point harnesses and flame-proof overalls; record the growth in power from 10 hp to 500 bhp. And, more important perhaps, measure the *effect* of such rapid technical development.

The story is told, not through my observations alone, but with the collaboration of those who are more intimate with the sport than I. And, for that, I am deeply grateful to the following people who found time to look back while busily forging rallying's future:

I would like to thank Jack Kemsley, Jim Porter, Dave Whittock, Malcolm Neill, Bob Evans and Graham Robson for their detailed accounts of running various aspects of the RAC Rally; Stuart Turner, Peter Browning, John Davenport, Fred Gallagher, Terry Harryman and Chris Serle for their views on managing drivers and/or teams, either from the co-driver's seat or the team manager's chair; Erik Carlsson and Roger Clark for their memories of winning the RAC Rally; Denis Jenkinson, Peter Foubister, Barry Hinchliffe, Trudy Wybrott and Scott Brownlee for their varied but vital assistance. And, above all, I owe a debt of gratitude to Mike Greasley for his words of encouragement and discreet guidance.

Thanks are also due for the many sources of reference; to Chris Leftley and the RAC for the use of facilities at the splendid library in Pall Mall; *Autocar* magazine, without whose delightful pre-war reports this book would not have been possible; *Autosport*, for comprehensive coverage of the post-war period; David Tremayne, for allowing me to delve into back issues of *Motoring News*; Eoin Young's Specialist Book Broking Service for archive material and out-of-print titles; Peter Duke of Duke Marketing for his generous supply of videos to add vivid pictures to the hours of research; Quadrant Picture Library for their excellent service and superb store of photographs from the early editions of *The Autocar*. And, lastly, to the RAC Motor Sports Association's Derek Tye, Jo-Ann Lynch and, in particular, Martin Whitaker for his valued assistance both before and after the book reached fruition.

The following story is a tribute to the graft and sweat endured by the drivers and co-drivers; to the detail planning of the teams as they try to defeat the meticulous efforts of the RAC MSA. But, ultimately, it must be dedicated to the 12,000 volunteers who, in November of each year, work with unselfish perseverence in frequently atrocious conditions. Without them, there would be no RAC Rally; no indelible memories.

Maurice Hamilton

1

THE EARLY DAYS

A Sign of the Times

AT THE BEGINNING of December 1931, a motorist lost a sack of almonds somewhere between London and Ipswich. The incident was reported to the weekly magazine, *The Autocar*, for inclusion in the 'Lost and Found' column. A typical week would include the discovery of a wallet containing £2 on the roadside near Brighton, and the finding of 'three lady's hats in a cardboard box: Southampton to Salisbury'.

Those were honest times when motoring was still a novelty and nothing was spared to return wayward items to their rightful owners. Judging by the action of the motorist bound for Ipswich, this was also a period of financial constraint. A lost sack of almonds, apart from the obvious hazard to other motorists, was not to be dismissed lightly.

Unemployment was high and, with Britain in the grip of a vicious recession, the government called for a temporary halt to the spending of sterling abroad. That may have been only a severe handicap for the enterprising businessman; for the sporting motorist it was a disaster. It meant the end of British participation in the Monte Carlo Rally for instance – assuming the average motorist had a conscience. But, since vehicle ownership was usually the privilege of the few, it seems the majority of motorists felt duty-bound to heed the government's suggestion.

Picking up the cudgels on behalf of their readers, *The Autocar* published a strong editorial on November 20 1931. Under the heading 'A Rally at Home? Combining Sport with the National Economy' it said:

> For many years past one of the most popular of the annual international motoring fixtures has been the Monte Carlo Rally. Quite a number of British competitors have taken part, with no little credit to themselves and to their cars, and the whole affair has provided good British propaganda on the Continent. In the present economic emergency, however, we have to consider whether or not the results, from the point of view of increasing the demand for our products abroad, justify the very considerable sums of money that the British participants spend in France and Monaco.
>
> Frankly, we think that, however sporting a trip the great rally may have been, it was only worthy of support so long as the pound sterling was valued in France at about 124 francs. Recent events have put a very different complexion on the subject. A request not to spend money abroad has been issued to the nation, and the appeal applies to motorists just as much as to other travellers. Is there, then, no way

End of the road; beginning of a motor sporting classic. H. J. Gould's Lagonda leads the AC of Miss Caulfield across the finishing line at the end of the 1,000-mile run to Torquay in 1932. For 4d (1.6p) you could read a comprehensive report in 'The Autocar'.

9

in which the fun of the Monte Carlo Rally can be enjoyed without doing anything which is deprecated by the Government?

The answer, we think, is in the affirmative. A rally is good for trade, and a rally should be held and widely supported; but why not keep the course within the boundaries of our own country? This subject was discussed at the Scottish Motor Show last week, and it was considered that a very attractive rally at home could be organised. Several of our South Coast resorts would be suitable rallying points – Torquay was one which was favoured – and the starting points could be any towns in England, Scotland, Wales or Northern Ireland, marks being given for distance covered, just as is the case in the Monte Carlo Rally.

If, in addition to the rally proper, there were to be a *concours d'elegance*, the appeal of the event would be widened, and it might be decided that the cars should be sent over a supplementary reliability course on Dartmoor.

The idea is well worthy of serious debate.

That is a revealing insight into the purpose and format of rallying at the time, but the plea for a major event within Britain should not create the impression that the sport – if it could be called that – was unheard of in the United Kingdom.

Indeed, 31 years earlier, a wonderful collection of snorting, clattering vehicles had gathered in the Agricultural Hall in London before setting off on a 1,000-mile trial. This 18-day run through England and Scotland required a great deal of courage on the part of the 65 entrants. Not only were they asking much of their machinery, some of them were setting out for such far-flung places as Sheffield and Edinburgh in vehicles running on solid tyres and steered by a device resembling a boat's tiller. It was a pioneering event which, to put it in perspective, preceded Louis Bleriot's flight across the Channel by several years.

The fact that they actually managed to reach their destination did much to increase the popularity of the motor car. With confidence in the horseless carriage knowing no bounds, motoring outings – generally known as trials – became a popular pastime. It was the shrewd Monegasques, however, who, first introduced the word 'Rally' to the world of the automobile.

A Stroll South

With trade in Monaco being somewhat slack in the winter months, it was decided that an international rally, starting from various points in Europe and finishing in the Principality, would do much for the balance of payments. Thus, in 1911, the *Rallye Automobile vers Monte Carlo* was born.

Described at the time as a 'comfort race through Europe', the event attracted visitors with the desired credentials. They had not been under the slightest pressure during the runs from Paris, Geneva, Boulogne, Vienna, Brussels and Berlin since the generous time allowance called for an average speed of around seven miles-per-hour. Barring mechanical misfortune they were able to eat and sleep in a civilised manner on the adventure.

Having arrived safely – although not always in comfort since one or two of the vehicles were open-topped – a prize was awarded for the best decorated motor car, the winner triumphantly posing by a machine festooned with flowers and garlands.

The latter-day image of Roger Clark grinning from a Ford Escort decked in Freesias is difficult to imagine, as is also a driver of Clark's calibre tackling a section of a rally as *slowly* as possible. But that is exactly what was required when *The Autocar* editorial was heeded and Britain's first RAC Rally got under way.

According to Graham Robson, the eminent rallying historian and a long-time contributor to *The Autocar*, the magazine was, in a manner of speaking, a front for the Royal Automobile Club. It was not surprising, therefore, that Commander F. P. Armstrong R.N., the Secretary of the RAC, gave his full approval in a letter to the magazine. He wrote:

> The RAC would gladly give its support to the scheme and undertake the organisation of the competition. I am confident that any proposals which have for their objects the retention in this country of money which would ordinarily be spent abroad, and the drawing of the public attention to the attractions of British coastal resorts, would greatly appeal to the governing body of motoring sport in this country.

Sounding a note of caution, however, the 'Disconnected Jottings' column in a subsequent issue of the same magazine said:

> Participants in the Monte Carlo Rally keep the flag flying abroad. . . . It must not be forgotten that there are many people to whom the warmth of the Riviera is a real necessity rather than a luxury. Townsend Brothers' Ferries have succeeded in making arrangements with certain hotels on the Riviera to agree for all payments for hotel accomodation to remain in this country and to be invested in British funds.

The columnist then argued that rather than being seen as a substitute for the Monte Carlo Rally, the British event should be considered separately and could not aspire, for the first year at least, to being more than a 'jolly all-British affair'.

Winning as Slowly as Possible

Once the nod of approval had been given, the prime motivating force turned out to be Captain A. W. Phillips M.C., a mercurial man with a sharp eye for detail.

With the date set for 1–5 March 1932, Torquay was selected as the finishing point since the boost to the resort's trade would be welcomed. (In fact, the event was officially known as the Torquay Rally.) Edinburgh, Newcastle-on-Tyne, Liverpool, Harrogate, Buxton, Leamington, Norwich, Bath and London were chosen as the starting points.

Each route covered 1,000 miles – but that was not as severe as it may seem since the RAC's main objective was to make sure *everyone* reached Torquay, where a series of tests would decide the winner. At the end of the rally there would be also a *Concours d'Elegance*, an essential part of any motoring event and for many entrants the sole purpose of taking part.

The routes, then, were something of an ambitious venture without overtaxing the competitors unduly – at least, not by modern standards, although at the time a 45-mile trip to Brighton was considered to be the limit of reasonable endurance.

The slogan 'Enter the Rally and see Britain' said it all. Three hundred and sixty-seven motorists responded. There were Lords and Earls, Dukes and Countesses, racing drivers and record-breakers. Three hundred and forty-one cars took the start – and only 47 were penalised en route to Torquay, an indication of the straightforward nature of the road sections, where an average speed of 22 mph for 1,100cc cars and 25 mph for those with a larger engine was required.

None the less it was not all plain sailing. There were no overnight halts and opportunities for rest were limited. One competitor fell asleep at the wheel and rammed a telegraph pole near Exeter. Another skidded on ice – of which there was thankfully very little – and overturned, while a similar fate befell Miss R. H. Grimsley when her car collided with a horse. She had travelled a mere eight miles from the Leamington starting point. *The Autocar*, in its 12-page report, noted:

> During the night, near Cambridge, a rabbit committed suicide beneath A. G. D. Clease's Jaguar SS1, and in the early morning a partridge did likewise near Chester while a few minutes later a pheasant just cleared the windscreen. R. M. V. Sutton killed a pheasant with his Lea-Francis and sent it home to his wife.

Realising that the rally could not possibly be decided on the road, the RAC laid on a series of three tests along the Torquay promenade. For the first, cars had to be driven for 100 yards in top gear – as *slowly* as possible. Then followed an acceleration test, at the end of which the distance taken to bring the car to a standstill was measured.

The last two results were clear-cut, Donald Healey accelerating his Invicta along the 100-yard straight in 7.6 seconds. However, a complex formula had been dreamed up in an effort to equate the enormous variety of cars taking part and, in the event, it soon became clear that a very slow performance on the first section would count favourably. And one or two cars could move at a pace barely perceptible to the eye.

This was achieved thanks to a fluid flywheel* which allowed the cathedral-like limousines to transport their occupants with the minimum of fuss and vibration. The winner, by a considerable margin, turned out to be Col. A. H. Loughborough, his lofty Lanchester ticking

*A fluid flywheel should really have been called a fluid clutch. It was in place of the friction clutch as we know it today, and, in simple terms, consisted of a sealed drum attached to the end of the crankshaft and filled with a thick oil. This fluid was the only contact between the engine and the remainder of the transmission. As a series of vanes on the flywheel (inside the drum) began to gather speed, drag would be created. The movement would slowly begin to turn vanes on the end of the outgoing transmission shaft and, at a predetermined speed, this specially-prepared oil would become solid, thus finalising the link between engine and gearbox. By now, the car would have slowly gathered speed and purred gently into the distance. Since the Lanchester had a pre-selector gearbox, there was no need for a clutch pedal.

The slowest shall be first. Col. A. H. Loughborough (with pipe in hand) poses with his travelling companions alongside his Lanchester. Col. Loughborough enjoyed the best individual performance on the Torquay Rally in 1932, effectively the forerunner of the RAC Rally.

over gently to inch serenely along the prom at an average of 0.66 mph! Indeed, once the good Colonel and his passengers were under way, there was almost time for the judges to take tea before the finish.

As it turned out, the judges were kept on their toes by the devious thinking of some competitors as means fair and foul were employed to keep their cars at a crawl. The feathering of the clutch was strictly forbidden and observers were forced to watch the back seat passengers as well as the driver since at least one entrant was found to be receiving assistance by means of trap doors in the rear footwell area!

The inevitable *concours*, or coachwork, competition on the final day did not affect the result. In theory, there was not an outright winner of the event but Colonel Loughborough enjoyed the best individual performance to become, with the mellowing effect of time on statistics, the winner of the first RAC Rally.

Up and Running

The scene had been set. The competitors enthused over the event and the RAC and Captain Phillips were congratulated on their success. The parameters of rallying at the time were clear. Competitors raced against the clock rather than each other and the emphasis was on reliability and the adherence to a time schedule, albeit a generous one. The results would be decided by a series of tests once the final destination had been reached. Along the way, a spirit of adventure, a dash of fortitude – and narry a protest at the end of it.

It was 'gentlemanly' in every respect. The competitors wore suits and waistcoats, their trilby hats consigned to the rear parcel shelf. Colonel Loughborough, his double-breasted jacket correctly buttoned, held his pipe while posing alongside the Lanchester with his three male travelling companions and ladies in smart coats and feather boas stood beside their cars for the benefit of the cameras.

It was reminiscent of a society wedding, and certainly the dinner at the Imperial Hotel, Torquay, later that evening had all the pomp and glitter which the occasion demanded. *The Autocar* reported:

> The brilliance of the scene bore testimony to the fact that the thousand people of both sexes who had journeyed so far had by no means travelled light, for even if the evening toilette of the modern woman may be carried in the door pocket of the modern car, a man's dress suit requires a certain amount of space in the luggage equipment.

Such unbridled chauvinism was mild when compared with the comments made by the magazine's 'Vagrant' contributor as he surveyed the scene that evening. The reason for the sobriquet becomes clear as you reach the end of his report:

> At this point the Town Clerk seemed to catch my eye, and, taking it as a cue, I was on the point of rising to add my contribution to the non-existent speeches when His Worship (the Mayor) forestalled me by pushing back his chair and leaving the dining room, followed by all the others. However, despite this disappointment, for I really speak very nicely indeed, I can give the evening full marks.

Clearly, the Mayor of Torquay was no fool . . .

The Ladies Award in Class 1 had gone to Lady de Clifford, even though her Lagonda was actually driven by Paddie Naismith in the final test. Her Ladyship, apparently, had been taken ill but since Miss Naismith was a driver of some standing, the switch was akin to a professional rider taking over for the jump-off in a competition on the village green.

The ladies were to play an attractive and important part in years to come. Fashion, as ever, had its say although expediency dictated that one or two ladies actually dared to wear, whisper it, trousers. *The Motor*, reporting on the event the following year, noted:

> Not a few of the women drivers found trousers warmer than skirts and there were a few amusing cases of mistaken identity due to this cause. At the final control, for instance, an official was expressing his view of the appalling weather in no uncertain terms, imagining that the flannel-trousered legs protruding from the door of a small car belonged to a man. Judge his confusion when the wearer of the trousers turned out to be a girl!

As can be gathered, the weather in 1933 was less than favourable, an unfortunate setback for Hastings, the host town. Once again, the routes measured approximately 1,000 miles from each of the nine starting points. The tests, rather stiffer than before, decided the class winners.

In the early days, results were decided by a series of tests at the finish. Kathleen, Countess of Drogheda, takes the brake test in her SS1 on the prom at Torquay in 1932.

It was the same the following year when the 'rallying point' switched to Bournemouth and only 14 of a colossal 351 finishers lost time on the road. Class results were decided by speed and manoeuvring tests around pylons on the prom, but again no outright winner was declared.

Indeed, in 1935, not even the class winners were signified and this lack of recognition brought a deterioration in the size and quality of the entry list – a 'mere' 192 taking the start in 1937. Even so, the RAC Rally was seen abroad as nothing more than a national event; a motoring jolly in the true British tradition. Elsewhere, rallying was gathering pace in every sense of the word.

If you were a serious competitor, the Monte Carlo Rally was the event to relish. The organisers had long since abandoned the comfort image and by the late 1920s simply reaching the Principality was an achievement in itself since the rally was run in January when Europe was usually in the grip of severe weather.

A report on the 1929 Monte Carlo Rally spoke of a competitor, making his way from Stockholm, rolling into a field, from where his battered car was retrieved by a team of horses. The organisers had developed a handicap system based on the mileage from the various starting points and, frequently, those opting for John O'Groats had a job reaching the North of Scotland, never mind taking the start and then battling south once more!

British participation was high and, in 1931, Donald Healey won the Monte Carlo Rally at the wheel of his familiar 4.5-litre Invicta, the two-seater open sports car being a brave choice for the 2,000-mile run from Stavanger to the Cote d'Azur.

Healey's success against strong opposition – including Grand Prix drivers J.-P. Wimille and Louis Chiron – did much for the image of the Monte Carlo Rally at home. With entries of around 200 cars, and a required average speed of between 30 and 40 mph, the rally attracted the interest of the media. And that, in turn, caught the eye of the manufacturers. There were no works teams as we know them today, but support was always forthcoming for respectable and serious private entries.

Elsewhere in Europe, international rallying was developing powerfully through the incredibly demanding Alpine Rally and the Liege–Rome–Liege; events which would have made the average entrant for the RAC Rally blanch. The Alpine Trial, as it was known before World War I, was considered to be the ultimate test for those brave enough to tackle the mountain passes in the most fundamental of cars. When it was revived, the route encompassed tortuous mountain passes in Austria, Italy, Switzerland and France. This was real, hairy-chested motoring for those willing to urge their cars to the limit with sheer drops beckoning from the edge of the unprotected roads.

The Liege–Rome–Liege was something else again. Here, competitors were expected to motor from Belgium to Rome and back without rest. The uncompromising route called for swift progress along mountain roads. It was not necessary to hold speed tests in Liege to decide the winner: rarely did anyone return without having incurred a time penalty along the 3,000-mile route. And if they did, the organisers would consider themselves derelict in their duty; the event had been too easy!

Small wonder, then, that Britain's motoring counterparts across the Channel looked upon the RAC Rally with amused indifference. The outbreak of World War II in 1939, however, turned everyone's attention to more serious matters.

'Parc Fermé' in every sense. In 1936, competitors parked overnight in a children's recreation ground in Torquay, an early, more relaxed example of the Parc Fermé in which cars are impounded during lengthy halts on modern-day rallies.

2

SOCIAL TO PROFESSIONAL

Post-War Revival

THE DISRUPTION caused by the War to motor sport was total. Economy had taken a battering; cars and spare parts were in short supply; the very roads were, in places, beyond immediate repair. Two neutral countries, Portugal and Switzerland, were the first to pick up the pieces of competition in 1947.

Two years later, the 'Monte' was back. The format was very much as before with long runs from Glasgow, Lisbon, Florence, Stockholm, Oslo, Prague and Monte Carlo itself preceding the competitive tests in the Principality. While the likes of the Alpine and the Liege–Rome–Liege set new standards in toughness, the Monte Carlo remained very much a social event.

The same could be said of the RAC Rally. True, it was granted International status on its return to the calendar in 1951 but, in effect, it was no more than a national tour with the results decided by brief tests.

Of the 266 entries, only a handful came from abroad. Following the change brought into force in 1939, only four starting points (Brighton, Harrogate, Cheltenham and Skegness) were used, with the finish in Bournemouth. And the date was switched to June, a move which was likely to dilute rather than strengthen what little challenge remained during the six-day tour to Scotland, back to Cornwall and on to Hampshire. Also for the first time the tests were spread along the routes rather than being concentrated at the end. All four routes converged on the Silverstone circuit in Northamptonshire and the final task, to complete a given number of laps on the club circuit at a minimum average speed according to class, was simple enough. The result was a shambles.

Ingenious methods employed by competitors to count off the number of laps included marbles, children's counters, cherries, a book of matches, chalk marks on the facia and, in one case, clothes pegs on the sun visors. Even then, one or two crews got their arithmetic wrong. But that was not the main bone of contention.

There was confusion over the starting and finishing points since the entrance and exit to the track were a few yards apart. Rather than leave the circuit at the appropriate 'out' sign, many drivers felt they should complete their last lap by crossing the line at the point where they entered – a reasonable assumption. The extra lap meant they were credited with a slower time.

Several crews failed the speed test completely – a terrible state of affairs at such an early stage! Even though the timing was carried out by the august Bentley Drivers' Club, there were voluble protests. At the end of the rally, the Stewards, in keeping with the event's rather wet image, simply wiped the Silverstone test from the final results. This, of course, upset drivers who had completed the test quickly and in the prescribed manner!

In a stubborn refusal to break with tradition, there was no outright winner but the best performance was put up by a Jaguar XK120 driven by Ian Appleyard. With Morgans occupying the next two places and further XK120s filling out the top six, it was clear that a fast sports car was ideal when it came to negotiating the all-important tests. The days of slow driving and the lumbering limousine were over.

In Europe that realisation had dawned some time before. The Liege–Rome–Liege was dominated by Lancias, Ferraris, Jaguars, Porsches and Mercedes-Benz although, of course, this event had everything to do with endurance and reliability and bore no resemblance whatsoever to the RAC Rally. Neither, for that matter, did the Alpine Rally. Speed continued to be the criterion here and Appleyard, driving his XK120, won this magnificent event in 1950 and 1951.

The Monte Carlo Rally, meanwhile, continued at its own pace. Which was very slow. While the Alpine and the Liege brought high speed and pressure, the 'Monte' continued to place the emphasis on navigation across Europe and time-keeping. And in mild weather the runs to the South of France could be tedious in the extreme. On the other hand, only five cars reached Monte Carlo without penalty in 1950 when severe conditions blanketed Europe.

Ian Appleyard's highly successful Jaguar XK120.

The RAC, realising that the warmth of June was hardly likely to produce the conditions which would test car and driver, returned to March for the 1952 rally and, in a move which probably did not seem significant at the time, the event was sponsored by the *Daily Telegraph*.

There was a fair amount of snow encountered on the run to Scotland but the event boiled down to nothing more than a 'Rally of the Tests'. The following year, for instance, the 194 starters had to tackle a standing start at Silverstone; manoeuvring in and out of garages at Castle Combe in Wiltshire; a hill climb at Prescott; a time test at Llandrindod Wells; a speed test at Blackpool; more hill climbs in the Lake District; more manoeuvring at Turnberry; a speed test at Goodwood, in Sussex, and, of course, the final acceleration and driving test at Hastings.

And, at the end of it for the first time an official winner was declared, appropriately the redoubtable Ian Appleyard and his trusty Jaguar XK120, 'NUB 120'.

1954 was considered to be a memorable year. Apart from marking the first victory for a Triumph TR2 (driven by John Wallwork), there was an increased emphasis on navigation, thanks to night work in Wales and Derbyshire. At the end of the 2,000-mile run, only 164 of the 229 starters reached Blackpool, with a mere seven of those having the benefit of a clean score sheet. But if 1954 represented a pat on the back for the RAC, the following year marked the beginning of a serious decline as the British event fell behind the times in more ways than one.

Hunting for Lost Treasure

The ingredients were as before; a date in March, starts from Hastings and Blackpool, an overnight halt in Blackpool and the finish in Hastings. In between, night navigation in the Lake District, the West Country, Wales and Yorkshire, with 11 special tests scattered along the route to determine the result. Or, at least, they should have done. In the event, dreadful weather was to play a major part and highlighted inadequacies in the route and the organisation.

Many of the 229 starters crashed which, of course, was not the fault of the organisers. Indeed, the RAC moved heaven and plenty of snow to keep the special tests in condition but, in between, there was mayhem on the narrow roads and lanes.

At Hay-on-Wye, crews were delayed for up to two hours as the route became hopelessly blocked by slithering cars. Because of the tight confines those drivers capable of dealing with the tricky surface were unable to by-pass those who could not. The inevitable loss of marks for a late arrival at the next control point upset the form book, not to mention the highly frustrated crews.

Robin Butterell, a marshal in Wales, wrote a revealing report, published in the following week's edition of *Autosport*. Butterell noted that a layer of snow had frozen hard, making the road extremely treacherous. His job was to man the time clock – a straightforward business on a night other than this:

Johnny Wallwork gave the Triumph TR2 its maiden victory in 1954.

> More people began to filter through now, all complaining bitterly about certain big motor cars that couldn't get up hills.
>
> It was obvious to us by this time that the icy conditions were causing most people to lose a lot of time – some took it philosophically, others blasphemed all the way from the car to the time clock and back again.
>
> Mr. Fotheringham-Parker (191) didn't look very happy and nearly put the Yorkshire end of the rally book in the machine. He was by no means the only one who did this – some competitors threw their books at us . . .
>
> While appreciating the stress and strain of the prevailing conditions, we did consider it remarkable that some had got as far as they had, taking into consideration their lack-a-daisical attitude. Mr. Burton (179), with a cheery smile, thought that '1$\frac{1}{2}$ hours late wouldn't make much difference'.
>
> Mr. Woyts (23) put his hand brake on as he approached and took a few minutes to get it off again. Mr. Grant (29) seemed in good heart

in spite of standing in a queue of cars for two and a half hours. Mr. Newsham (186) was something of an oddity as he professed to have time in hand, a truly amazing fact.

Just as amazing was the fact that Butterell had driven 80 miles from Worcester and been on duty from 8.20 pm until 5.40 in the morning, returning to Worcester in time to reach his office for a day's work. On such enthusiasm are rallies run.

Butterell and his colleagues were stationed near Ystradfellte. By the time competitors reached there, the fact that they could not pronounce, never mind spell, the name had ceased to be a joke. Many wished they had never seen the place – and one or two never did. It was not that they had retired; merely that they chose to bypass the control point. And this was another contentious issue.

Gregor Grant, the Editor of *Autosport* and a competitor in the 1954 rally wrote:

The penalty for missing a control was 300 marks, yet the maximum lost for 30 minutes lateness in the special stages controls (of which Ystradfellte was an example) was also 300 marks. As the 10 marks per minute penalty was doubled for main road controls, it paid many people to miss out the special stages altogether and merely clock in at the main road controls. Crews who set out to do the special stages were heavily penalized for lateness at main road controls. If the penalty for missing intermediate controls had been (say) 1,000 marks, then it would have been fairer to folk who at least attempted to follow the rally route proper.

This was, indeed, an absurdity. Not only did it make a mockery of the event in the eyes of the few foreign competitors but it also showed the status of the RAC Rally in its true light. On the Liege–Rome–Liege, for example, the penalty for any lateness at certain controls was immediate exclusion. And no argument.

While the British event did not wish to emulate its foreign counterparts, attempts could have been made to bring the RAC Rally into line with current, competitive thinking. To many, however, it was no more than a navigational treasure hunt.

The Road to Nowhere

Petrol rationing, a direct result of the Suez War in 1956, had forced the cancellation of the 1957 rally but all was well the following year. On paper at least.

The RAC had made a visible effort to attract entries from abroad. The emphasis, they said, would be on speed; navigation would not play a part in determining the results. And, as a token of encouragement, a starting point was planned for Le Touquet, in France.

The 'foreigners' were cautious. There was just one entry from abroad – and he was a Briton living in Sweden. The Le Touquet control was quietly scrapped.

The British competitors would have done well to follow the circumspection of their overseas colleagues. Taking the RAC at their word, the works Sunbeam team, for example, removed the spotlamps from the roofs of their Rapiers, the better to gain an extra ounce of speed. Les Leston, according to contemporary reports, even went so far as to strip the heater from his Riley 1.5. It was a move he would live to regret.

When the route card was issued on the night before the start, competitors were horrified to discover that they were to be dispatched into the wilds of Wales. Detailed one-inch maps would be the minimum requirement and yet most crews were hopelessly unprepared with their quarter-inch maps. There was worse to come.

By the time the cars had reached Wales for the first 'secret' section, the temperature had dropped below freezing. Lt. Col. Crosby spun his Jaguar and jammed it between the hedges of a narrow lane on a steep downhill incline a few yards before the start of a hill climb at Lydstep, near Tenby. The Jaguar was immovable for quite some time, resulting in a loss of points for those following, since they were unable to reach the control within the allotted period.

Snow began to fall on the run north. There were further speed tests with one hill climb requiring drivers to stop half-way up, reverse over a white line, and then continue the climb! By the time drivers reached northern Carmarthen, several had become hopelessly lost. Control points were inaccessible and those who had failed to reach them, turned around and came face to face with other drivers determined to see the rally through to the end.

Elsewhere, competitors in trouble with their map reading found themselves approaching high-speed tests from the wrong direction and wandering into the path of those motoring flat-out. All was confusion – and there was more.

The business of a trifling 300-point penalty for a missed control continued to cause havoc, but on this occasion crafty competitors were able to exploit the rule to a ridiculous degree. They were helped by Regulation 7, which stated:

> To be classed as a finisher, a car must arrive at the final control within half an hour of their time of arrival and must have covered at least half of the route.

Half of the route meant, for example, that the man merely looking for a finisher's medal could check out of the Blackpool rest halt, check in to a hotel and enjoy a night's rest before rejoining the rally at Scotch Corner as the stalwarts struggled in after a harrowing grind around the Lake District.

Indeed, as *The Autocar* reported, Edward Harrison lost several hours transferring the steering assembly from his father's Ford Zephyr to his crashed car. He missed 14 controls as a consequence but finished higher

Peter Harper's natural ability was summed up by a win for Sunbeam Rapier in treacherous conditions in 1958.

than competitors who had visited every control.

Ironically, while the severe weather made the event the toughest yet, the rules contrived to make it the silliest. The hotels and bars in Hastings fairly hummed with indignation at the finish as only seven of the 135 finishers managed to complete the entire route without penalty.

There was, however, some justice in that the Sunbeam Rapier of Peter Harper, one of the seven, was declared a most worthy winner, but as a final act of foolishness, the award for the best 'foreign' driver was presented to Paddy Hopkirk from Northern Ireland. Meanwhile, the motoring scribes were beating out their warnings.

'It's just not good enough!' fumed the banner headline in *Autosport*. 'Look back in anger?' chimed the leader in *Motor Racing and Motor Rally*. Marcus Chambers, Competitions Manager at BMC, wrote in his book *Seven Year Twitch*:

> The prizegiving took place at the 'White Rock' pavilion, but the party spirit was not the same as when the crews are abroad; perhaps it's the wine, perhaps it's the food, but we do seem to become less inhibited as soon as we cross the channel. Looking back on the event, it was saved from being a dull and uninteresting rally by the weather. It turned out to be the last of the series which followed the old pattern, and I don't think anybody was sorry. The prize money was poor and the trophies were rather traditional. Furthermore, English seaside resorts are not exactly amusing in winter, with the wind whistling around the boarded-up amusement arcades and the seas dashing over the promenade.

Never mind appealing to foreign competitors, the RAC Rally was clearly losing its attraction at home. Something had to be done.

It was obvious that the British-style navigation, where competitors drove from map reference to map reference, maintaining a set average speed and competing in tests along the way, had its place in the sport.

But not in a so-called International Event.

Crews from abroad were accustomed to difficult road conditions, foul weather, mountain passes. But they were not prepared for the British preoccupation with navigation. And they certainly could not expect to cope with the Ordnance Survey maps. An International rally was expected to follow the traditional pattern; driving from A to B along a set route in a given time, maintaining a set average speed between specified points. The emphasis, therefore, should be on endurance, reliability and driving skill.

The RAC accepted this. But they needed to find a route which was both challenging and, at the same time, relatively easy for the foreign crews to locate. It called for a total rethink by someone who had rallied, and understood the problems. The RAC contacted Jack Kemsley.

The Rally that Jack Built

When Col. Loughborough's Lanchester chuffed imperiously along the prom at Torquay in 1932, a 22-year-old motoring enthusiast was helping officials monitor the progress of the winner. The following year, the name J. H. Kemsley appeared on the entry list for the RAC Rally and thus began an association which, some 25 years later, would have a far-reaching effect on the elevation of the event onto a more serious plane.

'I have to be honest and say that, at the time, I don't think the RAC were in the slightest bit interested in the rally – at least, not when compared with the attention paid to motor racing,' recalls Kemsley. 'It had become obvious that you couldn't hold a rally without using private ground. People used to say "Close the roads!" but it wasn't as simple as that. The problem wasn't so much obtaining a Road Closure order; it was finding insurance. *That* was the problem. So, in the meantime, I did what I could to make the whole thing more challenging.'

The date was shifted to November and the accent on driving tests reduced. Kemsley devised an arduous route, taking competitors from Blackpool to the Highlands of Scotland, returning through Wales to the finish at the Crystal Palace motor-racing circuit in South London. The concept was excellent.

It was enough to tempt 16 foreign competitors, including Paul Coltelloni, winner of the Monte Carlo Rally. More important still, the RAC Rally would have a bearing on the European Touring Challenge. There were six works Fords and eight cars (including the recently-launched Mini-Minor) from BMC. Everything was set for an epic contest. But it was to be ruined by the weather – or, at least, the effects of snow in the Highlands.

Trouble arose as the cars made their way South from Nairn to Blairgowrie. The regulations stated that competitors were free to choose their own route from control to control. However, judging by the required 30 mph average, it was obvious that the distance was based on the shortest possible route which, in this case, took cars through Tomintoul, the highest village in Britain.

In the event, snow had completely blocked the road near Tomintoul. Competitors were faced with finding an alternative route and this placed them in something of a predicament. Because of the local geography, crews had to decide whether to head for the control at Braemar as before or, in view of the prospect of further disruption, head straight for Blairgowrie, thereby missing a control (the penalty for this offence had been increased – but exclusion had been considered to be too strong a punishment).

Sixteen drivers decided to stick to the book and visit Braemar. It meant a lengthy detour and an average of around 40 mph but 15 of them clocked in within the permitted lateness of one hour. Gerry Burgess, driving a Ford Zephyr, was the first to arrive. And among the Rileys, Austin Healey Sprites, Singer Gazelles and Morgans which followed was a DKW 1000, driven by Wolfgang Levy, who was in contention for the European Championship. Just as significant was the fact that the German was being navigated by R. S. Turner; a Briton who would have a major effect, not only on this rally, but the sport in general. We will return to Stuart Turner later.

Gerry Burgess recalled the 'trip of his life' when questioned by *Motoring News*:

It was fantastic. I knew I had to average somewhere around forty over the main mountain roads. On the lower parts there were floods, and the car would soar over the top of a rise, the headlights in the air, and we'd come down into a solid wall of water. Half of the time I couldn't tell where the road was. Then, when we got up to the snow line, there was dirty yellow fog too. Sam (Croft-Pearson, Burgess's navigator) was really on the ball. He managed to find minor roads to cut off corners and we finally steamed into Braemar at around 100 mph.

**Gerry Burgess:
the trip of his life.**

When the rally finished in London, Burgess was declared the winner since he had incurred the least number of penalty points. Auto Union (DKW) lodged a protest. They claimed that, since the road had been blocked, the control at Braemar should be scrubbed. Since Herr Levy – along with nine other drivers – had only lost road penalties at Braemar, the result would be decided on points lost in the speed tests. It was no surprise to learn that Levy had lost the least number of points in the tests and he would therefore be declared the winner.

The Thin End of the Wedge

Given the state of rallying today, when the rule book and protests are an unfortunate and integral part of the business, Auto Union's action hardly merits a second thought. But in 1959 . . .

> When rally-driving was more of a sport and less a 'win-at-all-costs' business, such things (the necessary route deviation) used to be accepted as part of the game,

thundered John Gott, Chief Constable of Northamptonshire and leader of the BMC team. Gott, writing in *Autosport*, went on:

> It was recognized that all crews had the same difficulties to surmount and an equal choice of how best to surmount them and no one questioned, on a technical point, that victory should not go to the crew who did surmount them best.
> This is clearly not the view of the Auto Union team . . .

Mike Carson, in a closely reasoned account in *Motor Racing and Motor Rally*, concluded:

> The Rally was won and lost in the amount of time one wasted at the blocked road and then how fast one could drive round to Braemar. . . . Levy and his co-driver, Stuart Turner, are both far from being novices at this game, and by the time they got to the blocked road (they were No. 139), there must have been some chaos going on. Consequently they were probably in a better position than Gerry Burgess to make their decision whether to go on or go round. In fact they must have wasted too much time, or made the wrong decision; in either case the fault is theirs, and it would have been better if they had not moaned about it.

Strong words, although Gregor Grant, a competitor who made the dash to Braemar, perhaps offered a more realistic viewpoint – certainly in terms of the way sport in general was heading – when he surmised in his editorial:

> Protests mar all motor sporting events, but with the European Championship at stake, it is not difficult to understand why these have been lodged.

It was a viewpoint which Jack Kemsley shared, even though it was souring his first attempt at steering the rally onto a more professional footing. 'Yes, but it was for that very reason that the protest was lodged,' he says. 'We are talking about a works team here. Agreed, it was all very unfortunate and the problem was that we had been faced with a lot of snow, but Stuart Turner had no alternative but to protest for the Germans. Of course he was going to protest! He was too shrewd to do otherwise!'

The effect was to create chaos at Crystal Palace. The protest was rejected by the Stewards of the Rally. Burgess was the winner. Levy took his protest to the RAC Stewards, of whom there were enough present at Crystal Palace to sit in session immediately. The protest was rejected.

Normally, that would have been the end of the matter. But since Levy and his team were from Germany, they had the right of appeal, through their national club, to the supreme body, the Federation Internationale de l'Automobile in Paris. News that this course of action was to be followed was not well-received.

Stuart Turner, acting on behalf of Levy, was not the most popular man in town, as he recalls: 'Going back to the actual rally itself, I remember lying on the bonnet of the DKW as we ploughed our way through the snow, trying to find a way through to Braemar. We came across Erik Carlsson stuck in the snow and the whole thing was pretty bizarre. Nobody seemed to know whether it was possible to get through. If I recall, the officals up there didn't have the power to change the route even though it was impassable.

'But, for whatever reason, there was a protest and Joe Muggins here was left to go before the tribunal – Wolfgang Levy couldn't speak a word of English. The protest totally screwed the prize-giving, as well as everything else, and there I was, standing before Lord Brabazon, Sir Hartley Shawcross and a Col. Short. I was representing the power of Germany, with all these Englishmen behind me muttering angrily. It was an incredible scene!'

In the end, Auto Union gracefully withdrew their protest, but a point had been made. The RAC Rally had finally emerged as a first-class event and, with it, came the grudging acceptance of a new word – 'rallymanship'. Like it or not, winning at all costs had become the creed. The Braemar Incident was the thin end of a very large wedge which would finally smash through a once-gentlemanly sport. Thankfully, the RAC and Jack Kemsley would keep pace with this new professionalism.

And Now for Something Completely Different

There was a delay of nearly an hour as cars queued up at the foot of the hill waiting their turn for this first speed test and the light was failing fast as the later numbers wended their way through the sombre majesty of the mountains to the first special stage, 'Monument Hill', a two-mile dash over the roughest and most stone-strewn unsealed road imaginable, which had to be covered in three minutes. *Autosport*, December 1960.

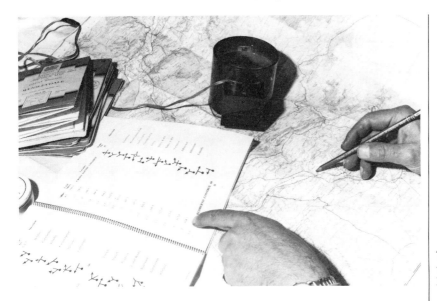

The Tulip Road Book
was introduced on the
RAC Rally in 1959.

Thus readers, in one breathless bound, were introduced to the fore-runner of the modern Special Stage. The RAC Rally was making its first tentative step away from the business of rushing from A to B on narrow minor public roads. Now they would rush from A to B on narrow private roads. And they would drive flat out – if they dared.

Jack Kemsley had included three such tests in the 2,064-mile route, the Monument Hill stage being located in Scotland, where the majority of serious motoring took place. Indeed, for the first time, Wales was not included on the itinerary. Not that anyone minded particularly since the route presented a challenge which would suit drivers from both home and abroad.

There was less navigation and crews had the benefit of a full 'Tulip Road Book' which, through a series of symbols and signs, gave precise directions keyed to the distance covered from the preceding control.

'The Tulip Road Book came from, not surprisingly, the Tulip Rally,' recalls Kemsley. 'The Dutch are such methodical people and they devised this scheme which, they claimed, meant competitors wouldn't even need a map to follow the route. And, strictly speaking, they were right. Bearing in mind all the problems we had had with foreign competitors struggling with navigation and reference points on our maps, it was only natural that we should introduce a Tulip-style road book to the RAC Rally. I had no compunction at all about doing that.'

Fifteen British and nine continental manufacturers entered the revised event which, significantly, would settle the European Rally Championship, although not in the manner which everyone hoped for. Within 100 miles of the start from Blackpool, Rene Trautmann crashed his Citroen in thick fog, thus handing the title to the Mercedes-Benz of Walter Schock and Rolf Moll; whereupon the German crew packed up and went home. This news was not greeted with enthusiasm, either by the organisers or, indeed, by Daimler-Benz in Stuttgart. But it was another sign of the times.

The most significant change, however, was the total domination of the 1960 rally by Erik Carlsson, of Sweden, and his funny little two-stroke, front-wheel drive Saab. It wasn't so funny, however, when the large Swede proved to be the only one of the 172 starters to finish without a single penalty on the road. And he completely annihilated the opposition on the Monument Hill special stage. Carlsson was immediately at home on the loose surface and the Saab, with its copious ground clearance, fairly skimmed across the bumps and ruts. If ever there was a pointer to the future, not only of the RAC Rally but the sport in general, then this was it.

Carlsson's penalty-free run was thanks to his commitment in the wet and foggy conditions and the guidance of his navigator, Stuart Turner. But when Carlsson lined up at the start of the first special stage, there was little Turner could do. Except pray.

'The stage was just over two miles long – a joke by today's standards,' recalls Turner. 'But it was typically rough and craggy and Erik, with this tiddly little engine, beat everyone. People kept asking me what it was like. I didn't know; I'd got my eyes shut! I'd never been driven so fast in my life. But there is no doubt that was the point at which the RAC Rally shifted from a traditional "Find Your Way" on the public roads rally to the type of event we know today.'

Carlsson remembers the stage and, at first, he thought the Saab would be at a disadvantage.

'It was narrow with long straights, but no fast bends. The few corners were quite sharp and I remember saying to Stuart: "Bloody Hell, the Healeys will beat us on those straights." But, in fact, it was quite rough and we were airborne quite a bit, which spoiled it for the Healeys and suited the Saab.'

At the time, Stuart Turner was writing the rally pages of *Motoring News* and he used his journalistic privilege to counter the muttering that Carlsson had enjoyed the benefit of practice on the special stage.

The surface was very loose and very rough, he wrote. One Rapier broke its sump. Carlsson showed just what a fabulous driver he is (and also what a suitable car the Saab is for rallying) by being the only one to do the section on time.

One of the inevitable rumours at the finish had it that Erik practised the stages 84 times! In actual fact, we 'recced' it once, and once only, in a very slow standard Minor which stopped halfway along with water in the electrics. The stage was so much like special stages on Swedish rallies that Carlsson simply commented 'is good for Saab' and would not go over it for a second time.

Meanwhile, Kemsley and his team had not been without their problems. An outbreak of Foot and Mouth disease in the Border region brought with it the threat of farmers patrolling the rally route with shotguns! The speed test (of which several remained on the schedule) at Charterhall was speedily cancelled and flooding elsewhere caused a certain amount of re-routing.

The fog, too, had presented problems. At one notorious T-junction in Yorkshire, several competitors left the road and disappeared into a field. It took 20 minutes or so to regain the road in some cases, but the unfortunate F. C. Brackett and navigator had to wait until daylight before they could find their way out.

There had been complaints, too, about a party of three in a Humber shooting brake. They were competing in the rally, but according to bemused eyewitnesses their vehicle was weighed down with cine cameras and bore a placard announcing their association with a film company. As they went about their alternative business, serious competitors were baulked badly but these pioneers of the celluloid were unabashed – to the tune of 3,764 road penalties at the end of the rally. On a more significant note, an 850cc Mini-Minor driven by David Seigle-Morris finished sixth overall. The funny little car, like the Saab, was no longer a joke.

As far as the rally was concerned, there were a number of wrinkles which obviously required smoothing – particularly the organisers' ill-advised requirement of a 30 mph average for the run along the A25 from Guildford to Brands Hatch in the rush-hour. Such an average is scarely possible on the M25 these days, never mind the old trunk road as it worked its way through Reigate, Redhill and the dreaded Westerham bottleneck.

The penalties on this section were duly scrapped but it was an unfortunate *faux pas* at the end of a rally in which strenuous efforts had been made to keep the cars quiet and unobtrusive as they passed through what Kemsley had termed 'Neutral Zones'. Indeed, as a deterrent against unruly behaviour, competitors for the first time had to display their entry numbers 'boldly painted on the sides of the car'. Previously the numbers had been confined to the small rally plates, although an earlier attempt to sport large numbers on a temporary basis during the tests ended in chaos when competitors found the specially prepared Speedwell numerals, not surprisingly, did not adhere to mud!

Generally speaking, criticisms were few. *Motor Racing and Motor Rally* moaned at length about minor points which Kemsley had already marked down for improvement. *Autosport* recalled the rally as 'a most enjoyable and sporting event. Quite the finest International event ever to be run in this country.'

At the end of the day, when the beetle-back Saab bearing 179 on its red flanks rose through the floor at the prize-giving at London's Talk of the Town theatre it marked more the promising beginning of a new era than the end of a commendable effort by the RAC.

The days when a motorist would lose a sack of almonds on the London to Ipswich road and expect to find them again were long gone.

3

A NEW PROFESSIONALISM

Commanding Respect

JACK KEMSLEY was already thinking about the following year's rally when Eartha Kitt took the stage at the Talk of the Town and entertained the winners in 1960; her song, 'Old Fashioned House', could not have been more timely. The RAC had just taken the first step towards ridding themselves of the dusty, parochial image which had settled on Britain's premiere rally during the previous decade. The 1961 RAC Rally would be the best yet.

The route covered some 2,000 miles, 200 of which were to be held on Forestry Commission land. It was a major step forward but the links with the past remained; the start would be in Blackpool, there would be speed tests at the Rest and Be Thankful hillclimb and both the Oulton Park and Mallory Park motor-racing circuits, with the final tests on the promenade at Brighton. In between, a 24-hour run to Inverness, a night's rest, and then over 48 hours of motoring through Yorkshire, the Midlands and the Welsh borders.

It was, by any standards, a tough schedule. In 1961, however, it was made worse by the terrain encountered on the special stages, making the previous year's dash over Monument Hill a mere cruise by comparison.

The rally dictionary suddenly had several additions: Kielder, Redesdale, Kershope, Staindale, Dovey and Radnor; names which would become a familiar and, at times, a ferocious part of the rally in years to come.

Kemsley started off as he meant to continue. To quote a popular saying at the time: 'The Rally of the Tests has become the Rally of the Forests.'

'Obviously, the forests were the answer,' says Kemsley. 'In fact, I had approached the Forestry Commission some years earlier but they didn't want to know. Then I think there must have been pressure from other Ministries and various sources because people were realising we had to get the rally off the public roads. So the forestry people said, rather reluctantly, that they would have another think about it. They said the roads were very rough and would be unsuitable for cars. I said that was exactly what I wanted!'

John Sprinzel tackles the Rest and Be Thankful hillclimb on his way to second place with the Austin-Healey Sebring Sprite shared with Richard Bensted-Smith in 1960.

For the first time competitors were seeded according to their experience in a bid to avoid unnecessary baulking. That was particularly important now that drivers were expected to average 43 mph on most of the stages; no way would anyone arrive in Brighton with a clean sheet this time. In fact, after the 7.2-mile Loch Lochy stage on the way to Inverness, the competitors could count themselves lucky to have a car capable of even *reaching* the Sussex coast: 'This was unbelievably rough and dangerous and caused a great deal of unnecessary mechanical failures,' wrote John Sprinzel in *Autosport*.

Kemsley did not need to be told; he knew the stage intimately, as he recalls:

'I always prepared the route myself – with the help of our chaps from each area of course. I'd always wanted to take the rally into those beautiful forests around Loch Ness and I remember going there with A. K. Stevenson, Secretary of the Royal Scottish Automobile Club. The bloke who met us was a whacking great forestry man; about six-foot four, ginger beard and a kilt. I explained about the rally and the fact that we were thinking of running cars through his forest. He just said "Aye," every now and again; nothing else. I seemed to be getting nowhere with this fellow.

'Then he excused himself; said he had a telephone call to make. I thought he was going to check up on us, and when he came back I asked if everything was in order. "Aye," he replied. "I've just been on the phone to my relatives, telling them to come and stay in November. I told them there's a rally coming through here and they should come and see the cars." He couldn't have cared less about permission!'

The forestry man and his relatives must have enjoyed watching cars struggle with tracks normally inhabited by massive lumber trucks but, elsewhere, the competitors were to find the going much easier, as Sprinzel reported in *Autosport*:

> Longest of the stages, in Staindale Forest, was a rather pointless exercise, with 21 miles of short straights between right-angled corners, where there was little chance to display skill and roadholding with only the brutal braking and acceleration in demand.
>
> Dovey Forest, during the Welsh night, was by far the finest and the most dramatic of the forestry roads, with 17 miles of the most wonderful sweeping climbs and descents, accompanied by what appeared to be very sharp drops into the Christmas trees.

Sprinzel, who had been sharing his local knowledge with the Porsche driver and European Champion, Hans-Joachim Walter, concluded that the tests were very much a waste of time now that the rally was being well and truly decided on the special stages. He did, however, make an interesting observation concerning the distribution of penalty points:

> The scoring this year was still a trifle unbalanced, as an error during the nights of navigation counted for very little and 10 minutes spent in a ditch was worth 10 penalty points and the same misadventure during a special stage cost 60 points.

Advance party from Sweden. Erik Carlsson became the first Scandinavian driver to win when, navigated by Stuart Turner, he took his Saab to a penalty-free victory in 1960.

It was, if anything, a pointer towards the increased significance of the special stages during the coming years. But, during 1961 at least, two of the stages were held on public roads (where the average was quite properly adjusted to 30 mph) and one forest stage in Yorkshire crossed an open road, straw bales being placed at the exit of the gravel track as a means of slowing competitors down.

Of the 150 starters, only 81 managed to finish. And leading them home was none other than Erik Carlsson in 'my little Sob'. Just as commendable, however, was an excellent second place for Pat Moss and Ann Wisdom in an Austin Healey 3000, a tingling beast of a motor car when compared with Carlsson's boxy screamer.

The professionals had nothing but praise for the new formula, although Carlsson, in his speech at the prize giving, asked Jack Kemsley for stages which were 'not so rough' for the following year. Rather than being interpreted as a harsh criticism, Carlsson's comment was seen as a charitable plea on behalf of competitors with machinery which was less robust than his Saab.

'The stages were very rough,' recalls Carlsson. 'But, yes, they really did suit the Saab. They also suited my driving style since I was used to Scandinavian roads. The Saab was strong and could keep up speed on the rough roads. Because it was such a small engine, you just kept flat out out and you didn't lose as much speed on the stages as the cars with more powerful engines.

'Also, I loved fog and bad weather! I had good eyesight but, more than that, the Saab with its less-powerful engine was at an advantage in these conditions. You didn't need to brake so much because you weren't going as fast as the other cars. But you could maintain a more consistent speed.

'In fact, the hardest part of the rally at that time was the road sections; these were very tight indeed. It wasn't easy, and with a small amount of power you had to push on all the time.'

There has since been the suggestion that Carlsson's co-driver, John Brown, arrived at the finish with a black eye as a testimony to frequent disagreements between driver and navigator.

'His left arm may have been badly bruised,' says Erik, 'but he certainly did not have a black eye. Although I would never hit anyone on the head, I did hit John on the arm quite a lot. I'm very stubborn – but he was worse! But, he's a nice boy; it was okay.'

The celebrations at Butlin's Ocean Hotel at Saltdean, near Brighton, saw Brown receive an award for navigating Carlsson, the trophy being donated by Optrex in recognition of the 'red-eye' work carried out by the occupants of the passenger seats. Ironically, navigation had not played a significant part on this occasion. Indeed, it was as much a sign of the times as the theft of valuable equipment from the Morley brothers' Healey, parked outside the hotel. But whatever the minor trials and tribulations, the RAC Rally had earned a new-found respect at home and, more important, abroad.

Narrowing of the Open Road

During a moment of enthusiasm, one competitor compared the 1961 RAC Rally with the Alpine and Liege marathons. It was a well-intentioned comment which reflected favourably upon the RAC although, in truth, the Alpine and Liege were in a different league from the British event – or any other international rally come to that.

If anything, the Liege had become even tougher than before. The 3,000-mile foot-to-the-floor epic had switched its turning point from Rome to Zagreb in 1956. The use of uncharted (by anyone, it sometimes seemed!) roads in Jugoslavia meant the emphasis moved from speed and reasonable durabilty to as much pace as you could muster on roads which made survival the simple criterion. That done, there were the usual mountain passes in the Dolomites and the French Alps to be crossed before heading all the way back to Belgium.

The ravages on the crew and machinery were appalling. In a summary of his captaincy of the BMC team, John Gott recalled the 1959 Liege: 'For the first and last time, the Liege that year had no general classification, but was split into touring and G.T. categories. To cover both, Marcus (Chambers, the BMC team manager) entered four Healey 3000s, and the girls (Pat Moss and Ann Wisdom) in their 'hot' A40, as we

Carlsson:
"I'm very stubborn".

reckoned that the combination was strong enough to beat any other ladies, whatever they drove.

'Our calculations were not too far out, for up to the three-quarter distance the girls were well ahead of their nearest rival. However, fatigue did them in the end, as it did for Jack Sears and Peter Garnier, both crews being just too tired to cope with unexpected patches of mist on the St. Jean circuit where both were excluded for a few minutes lateness under the Liege "sudden death" system which allows no lateness at all.'

The following year, however, Gott was able to report an outright win for Pat Moss and Ann Wisdom in an Austin-Healey 3000. The statistics say it was the first victory in an international championship rally for a ladies' crew and the first on the Liege by a British crew in a British car. Whatever interpretation the statistics may put on the result, they barely scratch the surface of this massive achievement by the English girls.

Along the way, the Liege traversed mountain terrain used by the Alpine Rally, which continued to be the apple in the eye of any professional rallyperson. Never mind the hype and razzamatazz surrounding the Monte Carlo Rally, a result on the Alpine was worth more in respect from your colleagues than any amount of media sensationalism for deeds of not-so-daring do on the way to Monaco.

In any case, the Alpine awarded its cherished *Coupe des Alpes* to competitors reaching the finish with a clean sheet – a tough assignment bearing in mind that just one minute over the time limit at any control along the 2,000-mile route meant a penalty. Do the impossible three years running and the competitor was presented with the *Coupe d'Or*. It says much for the skill of Stirling Moss and the lesser known brilliance of Ian Appleyard that they were the only two drivers to collect a *Coupe d'Or* in the Fifties. The wind of change during the next decade however would affect these classic events, just as it would the staunchly anachronistic Monte.

With a professional approach becoming *de rigueur*, Mercedes-Benz took matters one step further than the simple reconnaissance which factory teams saw as the limit of their route preparation for the Monte. The Germans realised the rally was likely to be settled on the final section – two laps of a 179-mile mountain circuit where regularity counted for more than speed since marks would be lost at six times the rate awarded on the 2,200-mile run to the Principality. They decided, therefore, to *practise*.

For six weeks, the works-supported Mercedes 220 SEs thrashed round the mountains. Come the day and they walked off with the first three places even though the crews had been well down the order when they first arrived in Monaco.

The gloves were off. No more would packing a shovel and sandwiches in the boot and hoping for the best be good enough.

As the RAC began their successful experiment with special stages in 1961, the *Automobile Club de Monaco* also introduced a series of stages on the run from Charbonnieres to Monte Carlo. But, unlike their British counterparts, they had to complicate matters in their unique style by producing a handicap which few people understood. Unless, of course, they were French: then they knew it meant a fair-to-reasonable chance of winning.

The formula was changed in detail from time to time but the Monegasques were unable to keep the irrepressible Erik Carlsson away from the victory podium in 1962 and '63. It was a sign that, like it or not, the Monte Carlo Rally was being swept along with the rallying revolution which was invading Europe from the direction of Scandinavia.

A Little Bit Sideways Now

The Brits were rather slow on the uptake. Carlsson's progress on the rough special stages was regarded with nothing more than mild curiosity; this strange Swedish fellow was doing all sorts of funny things with his odd little motor car. Whatever it was, it certainly wasn't to be found in the Police Manual on how to conduct an automobile at speed. And when further Scandinavians arrived in 1962, Gregor Grant tucked the following observation deep in his report in *Autosport*:

> Talk before the rally produced stories of the Swedish technique on special stages, where the clutch is not used for downward changes on loose and slippery surfaces, with front-drive machines. Finland's Rauno Aaltonen confirmed this, but stated afterwards that he did not use it on the RAC. However, it is significant that both Soderstrom (Morris Mini-Minor) and Trana (Cooper-Mini), were both eliminated with transmission troubles.

Grant's conclusion was logical, but he was merely touching on a technique which would totally transform rally driving. The clutch had become redundant, not through laziness on the driver's part, but because his left foot was heavily occupied with the brake pedal.

In simple terms, the driver was upsetting the balance of the car during cornering. Such a notion would have been considered perfectly outrageous a few years before. The accepted pattern for cornering was 'in slow and out fast'. The driver would run through the regimented routine of braking and changing down long before committing the car to the corner. Then followed the conventional line – clipping the apex and drifting towards the outside edge of the road at the exit.

This was all very well on the speed tests at Mallory Park and Brands Hatch but it soon proved a handicap when the rally switched to the forest special stages. Here the driver was faced with rough, loose surfaces where the grip was low. And, more to the point, the secret nature of the RAC Rally meant neither the driver nor his navigator had any idea which way the road went as they raced against the clock. The

Sunbeam Rapiers tackle a straw-bale chicane designed to slow competitors down at a point where the forest route crossed a public road in 1961.

'classic' line is all very well provided you know what to expect. With 'Kemsley's Law' on the RAC, competitors had come to anticipate the best and the worst of everything.

Given that many of the main routes in Scandinavia at the time were of loose surfaces, it was not surprising that the Swedes and Finns, also accustomed to continual sub-zero temperatures, were immediately at home in the forests.

Even so, Aaltonen, soon to become the 1965 Rally Champion of Europe, was not being unduly coy with Gregor Grant when asked about clutchless gear changing. He, too, was still learning the finer points of the art, as became evident in a subsequent interview with BMC Press Officer Wilson McComb, in the *Castrol Book of Achievements, 1966*:

> About four years ago, I heard a rumour that the big boys, like Erik Carlsson, were using left-foot braking, but it seemed impossible to get any details. I could find nobody who would explain it to me, and Erik himself said he was not using it. So I had to learn it for myself.
>
> Some people always throw the car sideways before the corner. It helps to reduce the speed quickly at the last moment, and of course it looks very impressive for the spectators! But when you are driving very fast over an unknown road, nine corners out of ten look slower than they really are. So my technique, quite simply, is to go into every corner a little *faster* than the speed which appears to be the maximum for each one.
>
> This means that in practice, nine corners go just right but on the tenth one I find I am going too fast. By the time I have realised this, it is much too late to throw the car sideways – there is no more time for that. I am going off the road – straight off with the front end, you understand.
>
> Now I keep the steering wheel position just the same, and I keep the accelerator still hard down, but very quickly I hit the brake pedal hard with my left foot – I don't keep it down, I just hit it. This causes the rear wheels to lock (the front wheels are being driven, Aaltonen referring to the Mini-Cooper S). Locked wheels have very little grip, so the tail begins to slide out, the car turns on its axis, and you can continue through the corner, on the road instead of using the ditch.

In fact, the advantages of this technique were to become obvious when, during the 1965 RAC Rally, sheet ice made the going treacherous, particularly without the benefit of studded tyres, which had been banned by the RAC to prevent unnecessary damage to the forest tracks. Paddy Hopkirk, also driving a Mini-Cooper S, had no alternative but to learn to adapt, as he recalled in his column 'From the Rally Seat' in *Autosport*:

> During this rally I learned to left-foot brake effectively. You use it to slow the car on long downhill sections, where to brake normally you would lock the wheels on the ice. But braking with the left foot, you keep the power on with the right and the wheels will not lock. You have to change gear without the clutch, of course, but that comes with very little practice. I still can't do it like a Finn, but I shall use it in future when faced with sheet ice sloping downhill when I have not got studded tyres.

On the flip side, for the service crews if not the drivers, left-foot braking on a tortuous mountain road tended to cause excessive wear and a dangerous increase in temperature. Timo Makinen, who was particularly hard on his brakes, had been known to reach the end of a long special stage and have his brakes catch fire once the car rolled to a standstill.

Going hand-in-hand with the new style of driving was a revision in thinking about the car required to cope with loose surface, secret stages. Fast sports cars may have had their place on tarmac events, and in the speed trials of the pre-Kemsley RAC, but from 1961 onwards, it had become clear that a more nimble, not to say robust, machine was required. And having the weight concentrated over the driven wheels would be of considerable benefit – which explains much about Carlsson's performance with the Saab and yet another win in the 1962 RAC Rally.

Rougher Than Ever

Into his stride now, Jack Kemsley produced 38 special stages that year and the increasing sophistication of this form of rallying saw a smoother operation all round. The 'Tulip' style route card continued to make life easier for the navigator and the introduction of more clearly defined arrows, supplied by Dunlop, in the special stages proved invaluable.

'We'd had a few problems in that area,' recalls Kemsley. 'The organisers in each region had different ideas about arrowing. Some were better than others, but it meant a lack of consistency. Drivers never knew whether an indicated ninety degree corner meant what it said. Some places it was spot on, others, the corner turned out to be a hell of a lot tighter. So we had to rationalise that and stop the areas trying to out-do each other with more and more extravagent arrowing.'

But, as *Autosport* reported, even the best laid plans . . .

> On one short section, someone had clipped an arrow post, and the sign had been reversed. To their astonishment, Edward and John Harrison (Ford) covered this section in around two minutes, the resultant short-cut producing an average speed of over 120 mph!

The required average continued to be between 40 and 50 mph and it was appropriate that the forests could provide an outlet for the increasing performance of the cars. Outside, on the public highways, the police and other motorists were becoming increasingly intolerant of their sporting colleagues. Indeed, in 1962, a radar trap was in operation at Falkirk. That in itself was nothing new, but in these days when 'leaks' and 'moles' are commonplace within the fabric of government and commerce, it is interesting to note Gregor Grant's bristling comment 25 years ago:

> There was something of a security leak at Falkirk, where the police were operating a radar trap. I am sure that it is not ethical for the

> constabulary to inform the Scottish press as to the competitors who were alleged to have exceeded the 30 mph limit, and I feel that the Chief Constable ought to make enquiries as to why this was done.

It is not recorded whether the Chief Constable plugged this extremely serious leak but, doubtless by the time the prize giving took place at Bournemouth, the matter had been forgotten by all but those poor unfortunates who had been nicked!

Praise continued to be heaped on the RAC and their organisation, with Jack Kemsley and his team going from strength to strength. (His 'team', incidentally, was largely made up of his wife, son and two daughters working month in and month out from their home.) Jack also relied heavily on the network of RAC officials spread across the country.

'I would say to them, "look, the route is going to be 2,000 miles, give or take. I want you to do 300 miles in your area, starting at A and ending at B. In that 300 miles, by May 1, find me ten forests. Link them up, and on May 5, I'll come along and we'll go round it together." That's how it started. In fact, that's more or less how it's done today.'

In 1963, they had unearthed 400 miles of special stages and it was reported that cars were reaching '100 mph in the Greystoke Forest'. It was also noted that by the time competitors reached the rest halt at Peebles, 13 of the first 20 places were filled by Scandinavian drivers. Indeed, they finished first, second, third and fifth, Tom Trana leading the way in his Volvo PV544. But, significantly, fourth place belonged to Paddy Hopkirk and the BMC Mini-Cooper S.

At Their Service

In retrospect, the growth in stature of the Mini-Cooper turned out to be as pervasive an influence on rallying as the man who, in October 1961, had become team manager at BMC. When Marcus Chambers announced his decision to retire from the post he had served so admirably, a young, myopic upstart took his place. If anyone in rallying had not heard about Stuart Turner by now, that would soon change.

'I was writing the rally column for *Motoring News*,' recalls Turner, 'and to go from that to running the BMC team was the most magical thing of my life. I was 27 or 28 at the time and when I went to a board meeting, there would be the accountant, who was about 44, and everyone else there was over 55. But the board was made up of people like Syd Enever, the Head of Development, Reg Jackson, the Chief Inspector, Alec Hounslow, who had been Nuvolari's riding mechanic. And, of course, there was Alex Issigonis. I mean, I was sitting beside *legends*!'

Having spent several years in the navigator's seat sitting beside mere drivers, Turner had seen at first hand the shortcomings of rallying and, more important perhaps, the loopholes. The organisers' regulations, in Turner's view, were not there simply to be looked at and then locked

The start of something small. Paddy Hopkirk and Henry Liddon, pictured at Lulworth in Dorset, take the Mini Cooper S to fourth place in 1963.

in the brief case for reference in the event of a protest. The rule book was there to be torn apart, clause by clause, from the moment it flopped onto his desk at BMC. This introduction of a 'new professionalism' shook the stalwarts rigid.

'I was dead keen,' he says. 'I had just won the rally (with Carlsson in 1960) and suddenly I was a team manager. I was besotted with rushing around. So, on the first RAC Rally I did with BMC (1962), I got a rally driver to drive me, with a mechanic in the back of the car, and we went round the entire route. We had these fluorescent service signs for the first time. So, of course, they appeared everywhere and it had a psychological effect on the opposition. They'd think "Christ, BMC are *everywhere*!" even though all we had was one bloke with, perhaps, a pair of pliers . . .'

Servicing had been part and parcel of rallying for more than a decade of course, but by today's standards it was like watching a mechanic approach a modern turbocharged car with nothing more than a screwdriver and a set of feeler gauges. Turner was about to shift the importance and efficiency of servicing onto a new plane entirely.

There had been a period in the Fifties when, on certain events abroad, servicing or 'organised assistance' was forbidden. Curiously, the rule did not apply if, say, Citroen used one of their dealers who happened to be on the rally route. This meant that Marcus Chambers was frequently hard-pressed to find a BMC dealer and had to resort to 'adopting' garages for the day, assuming, of course, that none of the French or German factory teams had got there first! If that was the case, the BMC mechanics would wait by the roadside and pretend they were tourists who just happened to have the tools necessary to fix this Morris Minor which appeared to have broken down beside them. This farcical situation lasted for one year.

Compare, too, Turner's frantic activity, dashing from pillar to post, with the rather more leisurely progress of Chambers just two years previously, as recorded in *Seven Year Twitch*:

> 'I left the mechanics to deal with both works and private entries at the "Hydro" (the rest halt in Peebles) and set off for the Rest and be Thankful hillclimb by a short cut. We arrived at the summit, where the drivers parked their navigators and surplus equipment before returning to the bottom of the hill for the timed climb, and immediately got our gas stove going, producing some very tasty sausages and buttered rolls, with choice of tea or coffee . . .'

The bulk of the major service work in the Fifties was carried out in the team's transporter which, for obvious reasons, could not always be located where it was needed. On many occasions, the servicing was 'played by ear'.

On the 1958 rally, for instance, the rear axle on Paddy Hopkirk's Standard Pennant began to emit serious noises as the Ulsterman made his way through Scotland. Diverting to a Standard agent in Kelso, a replacement was found by staff who, as Chambers relates, 'were sufficiently enthusiastic to remove an axle from a car in the showroom and Paddy had another axle fitted and was away in an hour and four minutes.' Such luxury.

At least Hopkirk had some form of back-up. Private entrants got by as best they could. It is much the same today, except that the 'privateer' knows it is fruitless to tackle the RAC Rally without some form of support, even if it is the lads from the pub following the route in a borrowed estate car.

In 1959, for example, Gregor Grant and his navigator Brian McCaldin had to use their initiative, not to mention a great deal of resilience: 'Although Shell and BP had done a wonderful job of locating petrol stations that would remain open, it was always a problem to ensure there was plenty of fuel, in case of unexpected diversions,' wrote Grant. 'We, of course, had spare containers, but one of them (plastic) burst and sprayed us with petrol. Fortunately,' he continued matter-of-factly, 'we found a pump open at Hawes.'

It may be surprising to learn that Erik Carlsson's victories in 1960 and 1961 were achieved without service support. 'I did everything myself,' explains Carlsson. 'We had no service support whatsoever and I remember doing things like changing brake linings. As I said earlier, the road sections in those days were very, very tight and you had to work quickly and then drive like hell to keep on schedule.

'In fact, the only help we had was from two old boys who worked for Saab. The two-stroke engine used a lot of petrol, and in 1960 Stuart Turner worked out the possible danger areas where we might run out and there would be no supplies. So he arranged that the boys would meet us, in a village or somewhere like that in Wales late at night, and give us petrol. It was not until 1962 that I had what you might call proper service.'

Self-service. Erik Carlsson, the winner in 1960, works on the brakes of his Saab. Compare this with the massive service support enjoyed by the works drivers today.

Forty years before, competitors in the Alpine Trial were also very much on their own, although matters were simplified by the rule which forbade them to open the bonnets of their machines during the event! Even so, that did not prevent punctures from occurring. Nowadays, of course, a polished crew can swap wheels in the middle of a special stage in a minute or so. Imagine the task which faced the occupants of the leviathans which had fixed rims, thereby demanding a change of tyre in-situ. Pass the tyre-lever, ol' boy . . .

In fact, it was not until the Fifties that the tyre companies began to give any form of consistent service. David Hiam, of Dunlop, set new standards of organisation; and as rallying became more professional and competitive, the need for a slick support system was imperative. The day was dawning when a competitor would require one combination of tyres for the loose surfaces of the forests, then a change for tarmac work and then immediately back to 'Weathermasters' for the forests again. The RAC Rally in 1954 was a good example, with the third stage being a timed descent of the old toll road at Porlock, followed swiftly by a return to loose surfaces in the Brendon Forest.

Dunlop were quickly followed by support from Castrol, Ferodo and other 'trade' companies and, by the Sixties, they were not afraid to shout about their achievements.

The Rise and Rise of BMC

On January 31 1964, *Autosport* carried no less than six full-page advertisements heralding Paddy Hopkirk's win on the Monte Carlo Rally. It said as much for the importance which continued to be attached to the event as it did about BMC's magnificent achievement. 'BMC Wins

Monte Outright!' trumpeted their ad and this was merely part of a nation-wide campaign, as Stuart Turner recalls:

'Before the advent of the Mini, when we couldn't really think about winning an event outright, we'd go for class wins. We'd enter an MG Midget in the 1300cc class, someone else would have an MGB and win such-and-such a class, someone else had a Healey 3000 and so on. So we would come back from the Monte with a cluster of class wins and that would be worth a quarter-page ad in the *Daily Express*.

'In fact, what with Rootes, Triumph, Ford and the rest active at the time, the biggest battle was to see who got the best ad in Monday's *Daily Express*! I think it's significant that there was a damned sight more coverage given to rallying in those days. Mind you, Basil Cardew (Motoring Correspondent for the *Daily Express*) used to be chauffeured down to Monte Carlo by Rootes. None of this Dan Air charter from Gatwick which you chaps get – if you're lucky!'

Helping out in the BMC Competitions Press Office at the time was a keen young lad by the name of Peter Browning. As secretary of the Austin Healey Club, his credentials were good enough to allow a gradual introduction to the rally team itself. Browning, later to take Turner's place as team manager, remembers the Competition Department's bold approach to success advertising.

'The confidence of the team took some believing. Before every rally, we sent a car out with a photographer and took the pictures for the success ads on the road. The copy would be written in advance and then the appropriate words slotted in after the rally was over. I remember, at the time, Raymond Baxter was the Publicity Director and we would meet with the advertising agency at his office in Piccadilly, talk about the designs and have the space booked for a rally victory. The audacity of it! If you win a rally now, everyone's scratching around at the last minute, looking for photographs, trying to book space . . .'

Stuart Turner's advertising in 1964 had included reference to winning the Manufacturers' Team Prize thanks to three Mini-Cooper Ss finishing in the first seven places. Hopkirk had beaten the lavish efforts of Ford of Detroit, with their equally massive Falcons, and it was clear that the spin-off generated by the Monte had, in the eyes of the Americans at least, no equal. Unfortunately, their efforts to march in and take over were to be negated by the impudent little Mini, which would go from strength to strength.

Development on Alec Issigonis's innovative car had been rapid. The 848cc Mini had become the 997cc Mini-Cooper, followed, in May 1963, by the 1071cc Mini-Cooper S. From here, BMC developed the 970cc and 1275cc versions, the latter providing the ideal tool for rallying on the varying surfaces which were now part of the European championship scene.

Stuart Turner recalls his days with Issigonis: 'I once went into his office and told him that there were certain things we needed on the cars for the Monte which were, say, pushing the regulations a shade. But he nearly stopped Longbridge to get these things changed for me. I once said "Paddy is complaining about such and such on the transmission". Issigonis pressed this button and some bloke came running in, damn nearly stood to attention, had a word and then left. I asked Alec who he was. "Oh, that was the Chief Engineer of transmission".

'To sit with Alec, in the Hotel de Paris in Monte Carlo, with his car, his "baby", winning the rally; that was a nice moment, a really nice moment.'

Timo Makinen took his Cooper-S to victory in the 1964 Tulip Rally, an event which found much favour in rally circles. The Dutch, in order to overcome the obvious geographical constraints of remaining within the flat and boring confines of their border, took the rally to the mountain passes of France, Switzerland and West Germany before bringing competitors back to Holland for what was, by all accounts, a popular end-of-rally celebration.

Stuart Turner: 'They would finish off the rally proper with a race at the Zandvoort circuit (near Amsterdam). Then it was off to the prize-giving at 7.30 or so in the evening. You got to bed at about 4 am. It was all happening in the hotel; a cabaret here, a buffet there, brass bands marching through the middle of it all. And the trophies would be a spray of three silver tulips; beautifully done. It was a great, great event.'

Don and Erle Morley added another bunch of tulips to the BMC collection that year by winning the Grand Touring Class in their Austin Healey 3000. Four months later, Rauno Aaltonen would take this thunderous beast to a splendid win on the Liege rally, or 'Marathon de la Route' as it was now known because competitors now drove from Spa to Sofia and back to Liege.

The Mini-Coopers won the team prize on the Alpine Rally for BMC but the event itself (or at least the Touring Car category, since there was not supposed to be an outright winner) was won by a highly talented young Briton, Vic Elford, at the wheel of the rapidly improving Ford Cortina GT. Elford won a *Coupe*, as did Erik Carlsson, a superb effort in an underpowered car on such an arduous rally. The days of the fast road events in Europe, however, were numbered.

In Britain, for example, the Motor Rallies Advisory Committee had issued a report giving guidelines for the organisation and policing of rallies. Competitive motoring in itself was not a sensitive issue; it was more a case of where and when.

Matters were not helped in June when the national press expressed outrage over the testing of an AC Cobra at 185 mph on the M1 in preparation for Le Mans. It was a wonderful story, particularly when accompanied by photographs of the beast resting alongside Ford Cortinas and heavy lorries outside a transport cafe while the drivers, Jack Sears and Peter Bolton, had a cup of tea.

It had nothing to do with rallying, of course, but such a fundamental point was of no interest to the vociferous minority objecting to any form of noisy, smelly, motorised sport. All the more gratifying, then, for Jack Kemsley to read in *Autosport* on 20 November:

> The 1964 RAC Rally was a good, straightforward, hard-fought event. It was decided well and truly off the public highway and can have caused a minimum of inconvenience to the public.

The start and finish had been moved to London, an idea which did not find much favour with competitors as they grappled with rush-hour traffic at the end of 2,525 miles and not much sleep.

At 7 am on a Sunday morning, Kemsley had taken competitors to Bristol and then to Wales. By 2 am the following day, they had reached Llandrindod Wells, and at 5.20 am there was the luxury of a 57-minute halt at the Devil's Bridge Hotel. Lunchtime meant Oulton Park and then north to the border and, by 4 am on Tuesday, the survivors were glad of a 90-minute halt at Turnberry.

A good night's – the only night's – sleep was to be had later that day in Perth. A reasonably civilised 9 am start on Wednesday was the prelude to loop north to Blair Atholl and then the run south, finishing in the Duke of York's barracks at 7 pm on Thursday.

In between, there had been over 400 miles of special stages and an excessive amount of fog. Indeed, the problem with visibility went hand-in-hand with a disastrous breakdown in communications, the weary competitors reaching Perth only to find that a much-vaunted results service was some 30 hours behind. At the end of the event, however, it was clear that Tom Trana and Volvo had won the rally for the second year in succession, and on this occasion Trana had taken the European championship into the bargain.

Interestingly, Trana's principal championship rival, Erik Carlsson, had lost his chance – and his way – when a misleading arrow on a stage in Wales sent Carlsson and his co-driver, Gunnar Palm, in the wrong direction. Carlsson remembers the incident all too clearly:

'I can remember exactly how the cross-road looked,' says Carlsson. 'The junctions ahead were like a very shallow Y. It was raining at the time and, whatever had happened – whether the arrow had been moved, I don't know – I'll swear the arrow was pointing clearly in one direction and that's the way we went. Unfortunately, the road we took did not have any turnings for quite some way so we did not suspect anything. Then, of course, when we realised at the next junction that there were no arrows, it was too late. We had gone a couple of miles. But it was enough. We lost the rally and the championship.

'It was the only time I protested on the RAC. I thought the stage would be cancelled. But it wasn't. Anyway, that's history now. The RAC Rally was always one of my favourite events.'

The Saab driver's error was compounded by the organisers' decision

Timo Makinen: second in 1964 with the 'Big Healey'.

Tom Trana and the Volvo
PV544 on the Loch Ard
stage in 1964.

not to supply competitors with Tulip diagrams for each special stage. This caused a fair amount of moaning and groaning but the RAC did not relent – a stance which they were to maintain for almost twenty years.

Inadequate signs were not to blame for a spectacular exit by a young Finnish driver in a Saab. If anything, Simo Lampinen or, more to the point his navigator, John Davenport, knew too much. Davenport takes up the story: 'I had met Simo not long before and, since he had earned a works Saab drive in the RAC as a reward for winning the 1000 Lakes Rally for the second time running, we joined forces. He thought I would be a great help to him, particularly because of my "local knowledge". That was a mistake.

'At the time, the Eppynt ranges in Central Wales were always a favourite spot for a special stage, so we went and had a look around and made a few basic pace notes before the rally started. Sure enough, when we got the road book, there was a stage which used Eppynt, and Simo started to think he had got good value from his co-driver.

'When we reached Eppynt, the dreaded black ice was very much in evidence, and it was clear as soon as we got out on to the tarmac from the forest that the only grip to be found was right on the edge of the road where the grass and gravel prevented it from being too slippery.

'It worked very well and we caught the Morley twins in an Austin Healey 3000 who had started in front of us. We whistled past them on a crest and I got so excited by the whole thing that I forgot to read that one from the notes.

'Consequently, we now had one too many crests still to read, and when I confidently said 'flat over crest', we were a bit surprised to find that the road veered quite considerably to the right! I think that in dry conditions, Simo could have made it even then, but on black ice we had no chance at the speed we were doing and shot off into the surrounding countryside.

'Again, all might not have been lost but the soft mud had been churned up into ridges by army lorries and had then frozen hard. The Saab tripped over these as one might trip over a step. It rolled once sideways and then once end-over-end for good measure and landed on its four wheels. We were perfectly okay but, among other things, the back axle had been torn from its location. It was a case of pace notes on this secret rally coming adrift!'

Somewhat surprisingly, perhaps, the partnership endured and matured into a highly successful combination, as we shall see. But, for now, Lampinen and Davenport were spectators.

Minis had led at various stages but none were destined to finish in the top ten. BMC looked to Timo Makinen as he made remarkable progress with the Healey 3000 but second place, ahead of Elford's Cortina GT, was, once again, the limit of success for the big car on the RAC.

Wrapping up their report on the event, *Autosport* said:

> The rally concluded with a splendid party and cabaret at the Talk of the Town. Prizes were awarded by Wilfred Andrews, chairman of the RAC – a procedure which took a lot of time, and certainly cut down the dancing, etc.'

The Mini Revolution

Doubtless there was a fair bit of 'etcetera' going on in Monte Carlo the following January when Makinen won the Monte in a Cooper-S. The celebrations took on an added poignancy when it was discovered how luck had been on Timo's side during the final night. Peter Browning, assisting the BMC effort, takes up the story:

'Timo set fastest time on five of the six special stages on that last night. On the one stage where he was not fastest, he lost time, and very nearly the rally, when the contact breaker spring in the distributor snapped. Timo and his co-driver, Paul Easter, diagnosed the problem immediately, and as Paul went round to the back of the car and got another set of points, Timo lifted the bonnet and set to work.

'Don't forget, this was in the dark, by the side of the road. Snow, wind; he's leading the rally and it's the last stage. Panic! He undid the screw with his thumb-nail and they changed the points. He then set the gap by putting his other thumbnail in it and screwing it up with his finger. And he did all this in just four minutes! I mean, it would take a mechanic all of that in a well-lit garage.

'So he didn't lose the lead because he had already built up something like a ten-minute advantage. But the joke was, when he got into the car the following day to go and collect first prize from Princess Grace of Monaco, the damned thing wouldn't start. During those frantic few minutes the previous evening, Timo had dropped the fibre insulating washer which holds the spring off the base plate. Somehow, the spring had stayed in place for the rest of the mountain circuit but, when the engine had cooled down, it had slipped and shorted to earth. You couldn't do that sort of thing if you tried. Rallies are not often won by such luck.'

It was also a classic example of the incredible Finnish determination to finish, even if it means driving a wreck which scarcely resembles the vehicle they started out with. Meanwhile, the advertising departments in Fleet Street had flourished once more and this was grist to the mill for BMC. A 'Special Tuning Department' had been formed in 1964 and, for around £425 on top of the price of your new Mini, you could have a car 'similar to the Monte-winning Mini-Cooper S'.

And, of course, no self-respecting rally driver could be seen without a Paddy Hopkirk 'Scandinavian-styled Rally Coat' in rich blue with a red lining; yours for a £9 17s 6d (£9.85). Paddy Hopkirk gloves, sir? For 'safe, sensitive, non-slip grip', you paid a mere £1 17s 6d. All available, of course, through Paddy Hopkirk (G.B.) Limited, in Peterborough.

The Ulsterman was rightly cashing in on his fame and, although he did not win an international rally outright in 1965, Hopkirk did claim a coveted *Coupe d'Argent* on the Alpine Rally, a silver cup awarded for three non-consecutive unpenalised runs.

Rauno Aaltonen had been in the running for the Alpine's *Coupe d'Or* (for three consecutive unpenalised runs) in 1965 but, as Hopkirk recounted in his column in *Autosport*, the Finn was to suffer bitter disappointment:

> It wasn't so much through navigational error as just plain misfortune. Our notes said in a particular village to turn right and a policeman directed us left; this was another way through the village but it meant we were off notes. It was all a bit confusing and Rauno's navigator, Tony Ambrose, wrong slotted and they were two minutes late. Fortunately, Henry (Liddon, Hopkirk's navigator) had recced this village (he'd had a *good* look at it) and this was why we didn't go wrong here as well.
>
> I have seen two crews lose gold *coupes* now. The look on their faces was heart-breaking. I only hope I'm never up for one: the thought of losing it would worry me sick.

The Alpine – or *Coupe des Alpes* as it was now known – was as popular as ever, representing the dwindling number of true road events in Europe. The Liege was about to suffer a terrible indignity, the organisers converting it into an 84-hour thrash over the combined north and south circuits of the Nürburgring race circuit in West Germany. The revised endurance event was won by a Ford Mustang driven by Henri Greder and Johnny Rives, the latter to become the highly-respected Grand Prix correspondent for France's sporting paper *L'Equipe*.

But the prestige and stature of the RAC Rally continued to grow. Indeed, the entry in 1965 was, unlike the Monte, oversubscribed as a vast number of foreign crews showed a willingness to tackle over 400 miles spread across 57 special stages.

Jack Kemsley was tightening the loopholes which had been exploited by the likes of Stuart Turner. The previous year, the canny BMC team manager had sent a so-called photographer's car through most stages shortly before the start, thus gaining a useful insight. For 1965, all practising and note-taking was banned. And in a further move designed to simplify the rally for the growing number of spectators, the positions were calculated on a basis of elapsed time: in other words, Driver A would be leading Driver B by, say, 43 seconds. Previously, spectators would be told that A had lost 1,600 points and B was down to 1,643 points – about as easy to understand as the voting system for the United States Primary elections.

With the growing number of support vehicles following the event, 'Service Areas' had been designated near many of the control points, thereby avoiding the nuisance factor of service crews setting up shop in the middle of tiny villages.

In the event, Turner had no need for shrewd reconnoitring since BMC cars more or less led from start to finish. Victory went to Aaltonen's Cooper-S although the moral winner was considered to be Makinen in the Healey 3000. Despite the Finn's brilliance, he was ultimately defeated by a car which was no match for the more nimble Mini on snow and ice and he lost the lead – and the last chance of an RAC victory for the big Healey – on the final night. Climbing a slippery hill in Wales, the Healey spun its wheels helplessly as the insolent little Cooper S motored by. It was as simple as that.

Aaltonen had given a British team the European Championship for the first time. But, looking at the results, it was not surprising to find eight of the top ten positions filled by Scandinavian drivers, which made fifth place for the Triumph 2000 of Roy Fidler extremely praise-worthy. Saabs were third and fourth, but now no match for the dazzling little Mini-Cooper S. And this success was causing frustration and not a little bitterness in the previously tranquil bastions of motoring competition abroad. If the Mini could defeat the rules, no matter how they were framed, then the Mini would be 'framed' by beating it around the head-lamps with flexible regulations.

The cathedral-like Armstrong-Siddeley Special of Hon. Cyril Siddeley deals with the stop and restart test in the murky conditions at the finish in 1933.

Snow and ice make the going difficult as a Talbot passes through the Welsh mountains en route to Hastings in 1937.

**T. D. Wynn-Weston's Rover Special,
winner of Class 1 in 1933, attempts the
acceleration test on the prom at Hastings.**

**A Hillman is scrutineered before the start of a
1000-mile run to Eastbourne in 1935.**

A typical RAC Rally scene of the Thirties. A Lagonda V-12 sets off on one of the speed tests which decided the outcome of the 1938 event.

An orderly finish at Blackpool after chaos on the snow-bound roads in Wales in 1958.
Pat Moss, at the wheel of a Morris Minor 1000, aims for fourth place and
the Ladies' prize.

It may not look much but the rough track about to be tackled by the Sunbeam Rapier in
1960 marked a turning point for the RAC Rally. Monument Hill measured two miles and
became the first special stage as the emphasis switched from public to private roads.

W. D. Bleakly was rewarded with fourth place in 1956. He hurls the 2.4 Jaguar around a pylon at Blackpool.

The changing face of the RAC Rally is captured by Erik Carlsson and John Brown urging the little Saab 96 along a forest track on their way to victory in 1961.

The 'Big Healey', perhaps the most exciting rally car of the Sixties, almost won in 1965, Timo Makinen having victory snatched from his grasp by the Mini-Cooper S of Rauno Aaltonen. It was the closest the Austin Healey 3000 would come to winning the RAC Rally.

BMC Mini Coopers dominated most of the 1966 RAC Rally
but a Lotus-Cortina finished first.
Tony Fall hustles his 1.-3 Cooper S through Pantperthog
in Wales on his way to fifth place.

The Mini Revolution. BMC were
quick to cash in on their success
in the 1964 Monte Carlo Rally.
Paddy Hopkirk and Henry
Liddon overshadow Bruce
Forsyth and his guests during
the closing scene of the televised
'Sunday Night at the London
Palladium'.

**Timo Makinen and Henry Liddon finished fifth in 1971,
the Ford Escort RS1600 hampered by the appalling conditions which
brought the RAC Rally to its knees.**

In the 1969 RAC Rally, Ford was the only British car to be represented by a manufacturer. Roger Clark and Jim Porter power the Escort Twin-Cam into sixth place.

4

INTO THE FUTURE

Skulduggery!

IF WORD ASSOCIATION is to have any relevance in rallying, then the mention of 1966 should induce the reaction 'Protests'! Take it a stage further and breathe the words 'Monte Carlo Rally' and the immediate response – after much muttering about the 'damned French' – should be 'The Year of the Lights!'.

In 1966, the organisers of the Monte managed to exclude four British cars – three works Minis and a factory Lotus-Cortina – and allegations of cheating were brought against six other competitors. But it was the Mini-Coopers and the Ford who were in the first four places. And, by chance, the fifth-place car happened to be a Citroen.

In fact, the Minis were excluded, not so much as a means of achieving a French victory – after all, Monaco is not part of France, as any Monegasque will tell you at length, given a couple of hours or so – but simply because the organisers did not want those irritating little cars to walk all over the event by means which they saw as being foul rather than fair.

Initially, the culprit was seen to be a loosely-worded rule-book – or to be more precise, a loosely-translated rule-book – although the organisers were out to banish the Minis come what may since they believed BMC had swapped cars at a critical point during the event. But first, a brief explanation concerning the rules.

A revision to the regulations split the cars into various categories, which included, 'Group 1' (standard touring cars) and 'Group 2' (tuned and modified touring cars). The Group 1 cars, for the purposes of competition, were allowed very few modifications indeed and, in the hope of attracting the private entrants, the rally organisers had loaded the dice in their favour by handicapping Group 2 cars by 18 per cent. So far, so good.

Naturally, BMC and Ford could see little point in having one hand tied behind their backs, so to speak, and the Minis and Lotus-Cortinas were entered in Group 1 guise. So much for the chances of a 'privateer' winning; but there was nothing illegal whatsoever.

However, the regulations governing Group 1 were complex and critical. They were also late in being compiled, and subject to a last-minute change. Indeed, many competitors were en route to the event when the change was published in English. And there were certain clauses pertaining to the number and type of auxiliary lights permitted on the cars.

Timo Makinen and Paul Easter simply destroyed the opposition in their Cooper S. They were followed into Monte Carlo by the similar cars of Aaltonen and Hopkirk, with Roger Clark taking an excellent fourth place in his Lotus-Cortina.

Then the trouble began. All four were alleged to have iodine vapour headlights linked to an illegal dipping arrangement. The uproar in Britain was immediate. *Autosport* spearheaded the column inches of indignation pouring from British presses:

> Everyone who was present at Monte Carlo felt disgusted that what formerly was the world's premier winter road event has degenerated into a series of squabbles. The organisers, in excluding certain cars for allegedly having illegal lighting equipment, may have been within their rights, but the fact that this appeared to be applied only after a sweeping British victory seemed imminent savours of chicanery and skulduggery.

Indeed, at the time many observers had been perplexed by the almost maniacal approach shown by the organisers as they tore the Minis apart nut from bolt. They found nothing amiss. Except, of course, the alleged infringement with the lights.

It was to transpire much later that the performance of the Minis on the Mont Ventoux hillclimb had caused disbelief in the cloistered quarters of the rally HQ. These impudent cars had been almost a minute quicker than the works Porsche of Gunther Klass. *Alors!*

Stuart Turner: 'They thought we'd changed cars for that hillclimb, swopped to a Group 2 machine or whatever. And when they took them apart, of course, all they found was a Group 1 car.

'In fact, what happened was I had been there with Donald Morley, having a look at the climb – something like 10 miles up a bloody great mountain – and there were two or three bends with a light fall of snow on them. So, we took the carpets out of the Austin A110 we had and swept the road. Then we went down to the bottom, put Paddy and the rest of them on racing tyres – and they shot up the hill. Of course they were quick! They were quick because the other drivers had studded tyres and snow tyres. There was no rule which said you couldn't sweep snow off the road!'

There was also no rule which said the stewards of the rally could not exclude several cars if they saw fit. And neither was there anything to prevent the organisers from withholding the Finishers' Plaques from the teams in question. It was both petty and spiteful. It was also totally without foundation. The advertising departments in Fleet Street were to be unexpectedly quiet that weekend in January 1966.

Not Cricket

As the Monte Carlo Rally retained its unique and slightly anachronistic standards, the European rally scene in general was expanding and changing. The Geneva Rally included special stages in a forest and even the Alpine Rally now contained one or two unsurfaced roads. There was a mixture of tarmac and dirt roads in the Polish, Czech and Hungarian rallies while the Italian Rally of the Flowers was a special stage event on dirt roads linked by a road section, mainly of tarmac. Paddy Hopkirk, as usual, summed it up succinctly in his column:

> Although this is called the Rally of the Flowers, it's by no means for cissies. The tougher stages of the route are really tough. It's not so much the loose surfaces as the rough roads with hard rocks embedded in them and they're muddy in places, but not like those Scandinavian or forest type roads. It's very difficult to set the car up for corners, you just hammer over the rocks with the sump guard battering the centre of the road a bit lower.

Victory, then, was well-deserved. Or, at least, it should have been for Vic Elford. Unfortunately, his Lotus-Cortina was thrown out of final scrutineering when the number of teeth on one of the gears did not correspond to the paperwork. It was eventually proved to be nothing more than a typist's error. But the Briton and his co-driver, John Davenport, were out.

In his column, Hopkirk expressed sympathy with Elford. A few weeks later, the Ulsterman was to have first-hand knowledge of the frustrations. As Paddy received the congratulations of his colleagues for a well-worked victory in the Acropolis Rally, officials tacked a grubby notice to the bulletin board. The language was Greek but the message was clear; Hopkirk had been penalised.

The whys and wherefores of the alleged infringement (for receiving service inside a control area) are not important since the official concerned had accepted Hopkirk's argument at the time. The issue became unpleasant when it was discovered that a protest had been submitted by Ford – a British team.

This most certainly was not cricket. But it did mean a victory for the Lotus-Cortina of Bengt Soderstrom, who had no part in the protest. Neither, for that matter, did any member of the Ford team in Greece. Instructions had been delivered by 'phone from behind a desk in England. True, the protest was quickly withdrawn. But it was too late; the attention of the Greek officials had been drawn to the matter. The summer of 1966 suddenly seemed long, hot and arduous. Professionalism had taken a strong hold.

An Homeric Struggle

With the reduction of the Liege–Sofia–Liege Rally to a motor racing marathon on the Nürburgring, the Acropolis had become the toughest rally in Europe. Just one look at the special stages justified that title. Conditions on the minor Greek roads had to be seen to be believed.

And even the so-called main roads were treacherous; when they were wet, it was like driving on ice and when they were dry, the glare from the sun was unrelenting.

The Acropolis had been part of the European championship since 1956, when it was won by fast sports cars. Then the 'rough neck' cars such as Carlsson's Saab and Trana's Volvo found their metier in the testing conditions. The going would improve slightly over the years but, in the meantime, the Acropolis called for 1,850 miles of driving in hot, dusty conditions. It was indeed an Homeric struggle and was considered by many to be tougher than the RAC Rally, a tribute which said much about the growing reputation of the British event, although there was a point during 1966 when it seemed it would not take place.

'RAC Rally in Jeopardy' shouted the headline on the May 12 issue of *Auto News*. The paper went on to say that the introduction of a payroll tax was causing concern in the RAC Headquarters in Pall Mall. These fears were quickly allayed when it was pointed out that the majority of people involved with the organisation were volunteers and the increased taxation would have no bearing in this instance.

But the story had substance. There were indeed fears over the future of the rally although it had nothing to do with the Chancellor; or at least, not directly. The Forestry Commission had asked for compensation to cover the cost of damage to their roads, a figure which, the previous year, had reached £4,000. The RAC, while enjoying support from Lombard, now needed to find additional funds and, at the time, they were looking to industry. Mention was also made of a charge of so much per car per mile.

That was one of the many problems taxing Jack Kemsley as he completed plans for the 1966 event. Heeding the previous year's complaints about driving through London, the start and finish were located at the Excelsior Hotel, near Heathrow airport. The route was much the same as before and the scratch system of penalties was included once more; in other words, the car which covered the 55 stages in the shortest time would be the winner.

Entries came from eight European countries. There were five works cars from BMC, four each from Ford and Saab, and Rootes prepared four 1000cc Hillman Imps. Triumph, although supporting private entrants, no longer had a works team but, significantly, the 1966 RAC Rally marked the first appearance of Lancia, a marque whose name would figure strongly on the RAC results sheets during the years to come.

There were two additional points of interest. The Rally was sponsored by *The Sun* newspaper thanks to the enthusiasm of their energetic motoring correspondent, Barrie Gill. And two Grand Prix drivers, Jim Clark and Graham Hill, were to take part. Clark, after instruction from his namesake Roger, would drive a Lotus-Cortina while Hill, with advice from Paddy Hopkirk, would handle a Cooper S.

1966 marked the first appearance of Lancia.

Sheer hard work.
Jack Kemsley (far left)
and Graham Hill.
Sheer genius.
Jim Clark (below left)
with Brian Melia.

Hill never really got to grips with the requirements of a front-wheel drive car on the loose, but Clark, who was the more natural driver of the two, was sensational. True, he had the benefit of rear-wheel drive, which was more akin to the set-up on his Lotus Grand Prix car, but he set fastest time on three stages and had worked his way up to sixth place when he suffered a puncture. Then he hit a bank when he lost control on a downhill bend on the Loch Achray stage in Scotland and he finally went out after a further incident in the Scottish borders. But his enthusiasm was such that he immediately borrowed a car and followed the rally all the way back to London.

'The impression you got', says Stuart Turner, 'was that Graham gritted his teeth and didn't really enjoy it. Jimmy, on the other hand, was in the hunt. And when he went out, he kept turning up everywhere and helping at service points. The old mechanics at Boreham still talk about him. You saw them loving Jimmy Clark whereas the Abingdon mechanics would say, "Bloody hell, what's old Graham moaning about now!" But that was Graham; he definitely didn't enjoy his rallying.'

Roger Clark had, in fact, sat with both drivers during various stages of their training and he agrees with Turner's assessment. 'Graham was awkward with it. He wasn't driving easily whereas Jim climbed into the car, did a couple or three laps and then just went. No problem. He was a complete natural.'

Clark did at least have the satisfaction of seeing a Lotus-Cortina win. Soderstrom, the large, jovial Swede took charge during the latter stages after Timo Makinen retired his Cooper S with a broken bearing on the transmission. Judging by the results, the Minis did not fare particularly well but they more or less dominated before dropping out with various mechanical problems.

Pointers to the future? Roger Clark set the fastest time on the first three stages before damaging a radiator on his Lotus-Cortina thanks to an experimental differential seizing solid at the wrong moment; a Swede named Harry Kallstrom finished second in a Mini and Ove Andersson (accompanied by John Davenport) took seventh in a Lancia Fulvia after gearbox troubles had dropped them from a possible second place. Once again, the Scandinavians dominated, this time spreading themselves across the first 12 with only Tony Fall and Pat Moss (now married to Erik Carlsson) intruding in fifth and ninth places. Not surprisingly, the Scandinavians voted the RAC the best rally in Europe for the second year in succession.

There had been complaints about the standard of the Road Book, a book of navigational and time instructions given to each crew, *Motoring News* summing up the grievances as follows:

> No one expected the road book to be 100 per cent accurate on every page, but the number of errors was far too great for a rally of this magnitude and importance. Its presentation and printing, courtesy of Lombank, was excellent but the errors were numerous.

There were a few grumbles when the Twiglees special stage had to be scrubbed after Aaltonen had set off from the start with the timing clock hooked to a door handle!

But, happily, there were no protests at the end of the day and the rally had survived the troubles predicted by *Auto News*. Ironically, the newspaper folded one week after the RAC had finished.

Meanwhile, the Monte Carlo Rally incident had been brought to the fore once more as the appeals were heard – and rejected. This came as no surprise to those present, particularly when, as reports pointed out at the time, they heard members of the Appeal Court address the Monegasques by their christian names throughout most of the hearing. BMC, however, were to have the last laugh. Sales of the Mini had, if anything, been increased by the publicity generated by the 'year of the lights'. Quite what it did for either Citroen or the piece of mind of the organisers has never been satisfactorily recorded.

A Reasonable Mixture

Happily, there were to be no recriminations in Monaco a few months later when the 1967 event reached its conclusion. But that is not to say the event was without controversy. This was, after all, the *Rallye Monte Carlo*.

In a genuine bid to help the private entrant, a rule had been introduced which said competitors would be entitled to a bonus of 12 per cent off their special stage times if they ran with a restricted number of tyres. It was an offer which no self-respecting works team could refuse. Each car was limited to eight tyres for each of the two loops in the mountains above the Principality. The tyres were ceremoniously marked and had to be carried on board, a requirement which forced the Minis to take two on the back seat and two in the boot. By and large, though, the rule caused very little aggravation, save when officials at the control points wanted to check that all eight tyres were present and correct!

At the end of the day, though, the correct choice of tyres would determine the result. BMC, for example, had eight different types to choose from, something which the private entrant could never aspire to. It was no surprise, therefore, to find Porsche, Lancia, BMC and Renault dominating the running, with Vic Elford in charge until the final night. Conditions had been reasonably dry on the first 24-hour mountain circuit but the weather closed in for the second, snow handing the advantage to the front-wheel drive Mini-Cooper S of Rauno Aaltonen and Henry Liddon. The Finn had made clever use of his tyres whereas Elford slithered and spun his way down to third behind the Lancia of Ove Andersson and John Davenport.

It is worth noting that a relatively unknown Finnish driver, Hannu Mikkola, was holding seventh place in a Lancia when, of all things, his road book was stolen. Hannu, though, would return with a more worthwhile and lasting claim to fame.

The rally had been a close-fought event with Andersson finishing just 13 seconds behind Aaltonen. British co-drivers sat in the first three cars but that did little to encourage their fellow-countrymen to visit Monte Carlo, a point which made an impression on Paddy Hopkirk, as he wrote his column:

Vic Elford: a superb all-round talent.

One thing that struck both Ron (Crellin, Hopkirk's co-driver) and I on our arrival was the change in atmosphere this year. I remember the days when you used to arrive and there were lots of people to cheer you in to the finish. The rally seems to have lost something; there was only a ragged little crowd this year. We especially noticed the lack of British press, but of course this is probably because there are so few British competitors. You used to be able to go along to the British Monte Carlo Rally Competitors' Club and get a glass of English beer, but that seems to have gone and everyone went straight to the tyre park up by the station.

Porsche were to receive some compensation by winning the European championship, Elford taking victory in the Lyons–Charbonnieres, the Tulip and the Geneva rallies. But the combination did not totally dominate the year, Lancia and Renault giving the established teams a run for their money. As for BMC, Hopkirk was to return to Greece and wipe out the unpleasantness of the previous year by scoring a brilliant win.

The victory on the Acropolis was also an encouraging boost for Peter Browning as he tried to make himself comfortable in the position vacated by Stuart Turner a few months before. Given the reputation which Turner had justifiably earned, Browning had an unenviable task, as he recalls:

'Following Stuart was very difficult. He had set such a standard that I don't think it would have been possible to improve on the way things were done. I'd like to be able to tell you that I had introduced radical new ideas but, really, Stuart had the whole thing sewn up so tightly it wasn't true.'

Turner would doubtless have approved of the methods used to preserve second place for Hopkirk in the Flowers Rally in Italy later that year, even though the Mini had broken a driveshaft near the end of the final special stage which, in turn, was a mile or so away from the finish in San Remo.

Hopkirk recalled having received 'a minor collision . . . and a couple of extra small shunts from behind' as he rolled downhill in the company of an Austin Princess service vehicle. Browning is rather more explicit:

'Doug Watts (chief mechanic on the service crew) and I were waiting at the service point at the end of stage as Paddy appeared, having already had a helping shove from a bloke in a lorry. There wasn't enough time to change the drive-shaft but we saw from the map that it was more or less downhill all the way to the finish.

'We lined up in the big 4-litre Princess and, fortunately, the bumpers were more or less the same height. Every time he slowed down, and there was nobody looking, we'd give Paddy a big push. We had to stop at a control halfway down and Paddy had to rev the thing and pretend the clutch was slipping as he crawled away.

'There were other dramas at a T-junction but the worst bit was the approach to the *parc fermé*, which was at the exit of a long tunnel. Doug really got the Princess motoring in there – about 60 mph, I suppose – and we backed off at the last minute just as Paddy shot out of the end of the tunnel, lights on, horns blaring, a hand-brake turn around a startled policeman controlling traffic and just enough momentum left to roll to a halt at the control. I think John Davenport, who was co-driving the third-placed Lancia, was the only person to ask how we managed to get that far with a driveshaft disconnected!'

The Flowers had been won by the Renault R8 Gordini of Jean-François Piot but the French were aware that, short of victory on the Monte Carlo Rally, the next best thing would be success on the *Coupe des Alpes*.

The regulations allowed Group 6 cars (in effect, prototypes) and with no handicap in force, these racers were bound to dominate. BMC entered Minis which were 1 cwt lighter, had alloy doors, plastic windows and no trim whatsoever. Racing tyres were used throughout the rally and, under the circumstances, it was not surprising when the more powerful Porsches and the Alpine-Renault sports cars set the pace.

A combination of punctures and unreliablity, however, swept the fancied runners to one side, allowing an unexpected but none the less well-judged win for Hopkirk, thanks mainly to some superb pace-note work by Ron Crellin.

A force to be reckoned with. The works BMC team of Healeys with, from left to right, Timo Makinen, Don Barrow, Rauno Aaltonen, Henry Liddon, Tony Ambrose and Paddy Hopkirk. On the left, ARX 92B, eventually to become Mr. Browning's motor car. . . .

Promise Unfulfilled

Meanwhile, back in Britain, Jack Kemsley and the RAC had been planning small but subtle changes to their rally, and when the entry list was published, there was quality in depth.

Ford entered Lotus-Cortinas for Soderstrom and Roger Clark while Graham Hill, determined to crack this rallying business, was at the wheel of a works-supported car. The recently crowned Formula 1 world champion, New Zealander Denny Hulme, was down to drive a fuel-injected Triumph 2000 with Graham Robson, while BMC had an impressive line-up of Minis (in the faster Group 6 guise) in addition to a trio of the ungainly 1800s. There were, of course, representatives from Lancia and Porsche and, into the bargain, Rauno Aaltonen was entered in a very special Austin Healey 3000, a car in which team manager Peter Browning held rather more than just a professional interest.

'In 1964,' recalls Browning, 'I had bought the Healey which had won the Alpine. I used it in a few minor rallies and sprints, and when the time came to discuss the 1967 RAC Rally, Timo Makinen said he really wanted to try and finally win this event in a Healey.

'I had to point out that we hadn't got any Healeys; they were actually out of production. So he said "What about your car?" I said he must be joking but he was adamant. He said it was a great car; he knew it well because he had driven it on the Spa–Sofia–Liege and it had been rebuilt before I bought it. So I agreed.

'In fact I was very excited about having a go with this car and the funny thing is, I never thought abut the consequences; you know, my car ending the rally wrapped around a tree! I simply thought I would get a new set of tyres, have the dents knocked out and then return it to my garage. I didn't have an agreement with the company or anything like that. That's how it was in those days.'

The car, registration ARX 92B, was completely stripped, strengthened and raised. The engine was the most powerful ever to find its way under the long bonnet of the Healey; this would be the most potent and highly developed example of the genre.

While all this was being done for Makinen, work was also being carried out on a fuel-injected Cooper S for Aaltonen and, as drivers do, each man was eyeing the other car, sizing the opposition. And, almost before Browning had time to register what was happening, Makinen and Aaltonen had swapped cars!

Aaltonen then spent hours pounding round a deserted field as he worked on the brake balance in a bid to make the big car more manageable on the narrow forest tracks. By the time he had finished, it was perfect. This would, indeed, be a rally to savour.

Sensing the occasion, Jack Kemsley and Barrie Gill (of *The Sun*) had won the interest of ATV. The television company laid plans for the most comprehensive coverage yet seen of a British motoring event. Apart from daily reports from around the country, a camera would actually travel in a rally car. It was a massive commitment, one which would bring the RAC Rally into the homes of Britain.

Viewers would be kept in touch as the 150 competitors made their way from the Excelsior Hotel at Heathrow to the West Country, Scotland and Wales before returning to London four days later. To accommodate the media, the route would not venture as far north into Scotland as before and there would be a sprinkling of circuit special stages to cater for the increasing numbers of spectators. Even so, there would be 69 stages in total covering over 400 miles. And, with the admission of cars in the prototype class, the spectacle would knock previous RAC rallies into the shade.

Sadly, it was not to be. An outbreak of Foot and Mouth disease had caused considerable revisions to the route and many headaches for the RAC as the road books and signs were altered to suit. Then, on the night before the start, a top man from the Ministry of Agriculture visited Rally HQ with the news that the disease was showing no signs of abating. A rally passing through the infected regions could accelerate the spread to a wider area. These were the facts. The organisers had to act as they saw fit. There was no option but to cancel.

'It was heart-breaking,' recalls Jack Kemsley. 'Everything was set up and ready to go. ATV had eight outside broadcast units; can you imagine the cost of that? We had a large map set up for them at the HQ and Dickie Davies was going to link the whole thing. They had even managed to persuade the powers that be to allow a rally programme to go out on Sunday evening at a time when there was usually a religous break. The interest in the event was enormous; we had potentially the fastest cars yet seen on the RAC, we had all the top rally drivers, and two world champions from Grand Prix racing. But there was no question about what had to be done.'

John Davenport, scheduled to co-drive Ove Andersson in a Lancia Fulvia, recalls that day – but not much of the night which followed:

'Naturally, the whole thing was very anticlimatic. So we went off to the Danny La Rue show in town to drown our sorrows or whatever. We got back to the airport hotel at something like half past four in the morning. And there was this note posted, saying we had to report to Bagshot at 7.30 am! They had arranged to run a sort of rallycross for the benefit of television. It was just about the last thing we wanted to do!'

When Jack Kemsley gathered the competitors together the previous evening and made his announcement, Peter Browning was probably the only person present who had mixed feelings. He was sad to see the rally cancelled. On the other hand, he could take home the fastest and cleanest Austin Healey 3000 in the world.

It would have been a fitting epitaph for the Big Healey. In fact, a win on the RAC would have been a suitable signing-off point for the BMC Competitions Department as a whole. From now on, the Mini would be in decline. Ford were about to sweep Abingdon aside.

New Clothes for the Twin-Cam

In early January 1968, Moroccans plodding their way by donkey to market in Marrakesch were startled by the hurried passing of a fleet of identical-looking cars. The locals were probably no more ill-at-ease than the occupants of the vehicles. The Moroccans had come face to face with the mighty British Press as the hacks, struggling with the unfamiliar surroundings both inside and outside the cars, thought mainly about the next watering hole and lunch.

The prime object of the exercise – another product of the fertile mind of Walter Hayes, at the time Vice-President, Public Affairs, Ford of Europe – was to acquaint the press with, among other things, a car which would propel Ford back into the competition limelight.

The Anglia had made way for the Escort, and part of the package was the 1558cc Twin-Cam model – the result of simply lifting the lively four-cylinder engine from the Lotus-Cortina and dropping it into the more nimble and compact Escort. The price (including Purchase Tax), a mere £1,080.

The Twin-Cam which Roger Clark used to win the Circuit of Ireland Rally a few months later cost considerably more than that. But whatever the development figure may have been, the outlay was to prove a mere bagatelle when compared to the rewards which this car, and its successors, would reap for Ford.

Clark recalls his first acquaintance with the car: 'From the moment I first sat in the Twin-Cam, it was obvious that it was a very easy car to drive. It was manoeuverable; everything seemed to go naturally with

"If you weren't looking out of the back window, then you were under control." Roger Clark and Jim Porter with the Ford Escort Twin Cam in 1968.

it. It was perfect for rallying. It was a nice size in that it was smaller than the Cortina and that made it a lot quicker in the handling department. It changed direction easier, yet it still had the same running gear, the same power. It was, if you like, a very nimble Cortina. You could throw the Twin-Cam about and we always reckoned if you weren't looking out of the back window then you were under control!'

The Ford Competitions Department had spent the winter of 1967–68 thoroughly testing the Twin-Cam Escort and it was immediately apparent that power and strength were to be its major assets; so much so that very little modification work was required. Indeed, on its first international – the San Remo Rally (formerly the Flowers Rally) – Ove Andersson and John Davenport finished third without a single mechanical failure.

The San Remo was won by the Porsche of Pauli Toivonen, the Finn going on to become European champion that year. Porsche also had won the Monte Carlo Rally, their air-cooled 911 T going from strength to strength and providing victory for Vic Elford which helped compensate him for the disaster of the last-minute turnaround in the weather the previous year.

Indeed, in 1968, Gerard Larrousse was to become the aggrieved party, the Frenchman losing the lead thanks to a new and altogether more dangerous menace. Spectators on the Turini stage, looking for artificially-generated excitement, had thrown snow and gravel onto the road and the hapless Larrousse crashed his little Alpine Renault into retirement as a result. Larrousse had been lying second at the time and the thoughts directed at his fellow-countrymen as he climbed from the wrecked car can be well imagined.

In retrospect, the incident summed up Gerard's season. Cautious yet very fast, Larrousse would not finish in the top three in any of the championship rounds entered by Alpine that year. It was symptomatic, too, of the season as a whole since the 15-round championship was devalued by the fact that not all the teams entered every event. Porsche won eight rounds. Significantly, BMC could manage no better than third in the Monte Carlo and the Tulip rallies.

But Ford won four championship events, including the Tulip, the Acropolis (Roger Clark) and the Austrian Alpine. On the latter, Bengt Soderstrom was pushed all the way by a Lancia Fulvia driven by Hannu Mikkola. In the end, the power deficiency of the 1.3-litre Italian V4 determined the result. But Mikkola had done enough to earn an invitation from Ford to drive an Escort in the 1000 Lakes Rally. The Finn won – and broke the stranglehold previously exercised on his home event by Timo Makinen. It was the beginning of a relationship which would feature strongly in international rallying during the next decade.

In the meantime, Lancia were struggling. Leo Cella had been killed while testing an Alfa Romeo sports racing car and Ove Andersson had switched to Ford. Saab, despite moving up to a V4 engine, were increasingly off the pace. They were, however, to have one last shout, courtesy of the RAC.

In the Shadow of the Marathon

In a masterpiece of bad planning, the 1968 RAC Rally would end three days before the start of the London to Sydney marathon. As the title suggests, the 10,000-mile rally, billed as the 'greatest motoring event of modern times', was an endurance event of epic proportions, 98 competitors taking the road to Paris, Turin, Istanbul, Teheran, Bombay, Perth and the final mind-blowing 3,500-mile trek across Australia to Sydney. The marathon captured the imaginations of spectators and entrants alike. The RAC Rally was bound to suffer as a result.

As it was, the RAC organisers had other troubles. Once again, *The Sun* had committed themselves to sponsoring the rally, but a few weeks before the start the newspaper was bought by Rupert Murdoch, then in the early stages of constructing his publishing empire in Britain, and the news that he had little or no interest in the rally, meant a hasty revision of programmes and other paraphernalia carrying references to *The Sun*.

Take-over bids were not new, as BMC knew, some would say to their cost. The Competitions Department at Abingdon now faced the future under the umbrella of British Leyland and Sir Donald Stokes, notable for his ambivalent attitude towards rallying. The fact that BLMC, as they were now known, would not play any part in the RAC

Rally had nothing to do with the merger, however, since Abingdon's resources were committed to entering five cars for the London–Sydney event.

Ford were not to be officially represented on the RAC for similar reasons. Even so, there would be one Twin-Cam Escort, entered by Clarke and Simpson Ltd. of Sloane Square, London, for Timo Makinen. This came about thanks to the persuasive powers of one of their salesmen, David Sutton, a rallying fan whose name would become indelibly linked with the future success of both Ford and Audi.

Making up for the deficiency at the top of the entry list, Lancia brought five cars, three of them fitted with the uprated 1.6-litre engines and running in an entirely separate prototype class the 'European Club Rally' to give it the correct title. Porsche and Saab entered three cars each and, apart from a quartet of Wartburgs, that was more or less the sum total of works entries. The chances of a private entrant finishing in the top three had never been better.

There may have been just 115 starters but the format was as arduous as ever. No less than 85 special stages were scattered along a route taking competitors from London's Centre Airport Hotel to its most northerly point beyond Glasgow. By the time the overnight halt in Edinburgh had been reached, over half of the field had retired, including an Escort Twin-Cam driven by Chris Sclater. After showing remarkable potential by holding fifth place, Sclater and his co-driver, Martin Holmes, had clutch trouble on their privately-entered car.

As expected, the Porsches, particularly the 911T driven by Bjorn Waldegaard, had set a blistering pace but the German cars, along with the entire squad of Lancias, proved too fragile for the rough going in the forests. Always in contention, Simo Lampinen scarcely had a moment's bother with his slower but stronger Saab and once Makinen had retired the troublesome Escort, the Finn, with his British co-driver John Davenport, cruised home ahead of their team-mates Orrenius and Schroderheim.

Third place for the Escort of Jimmy Bullough and Don Barrow was proof that this had indeed been a 'privateer's' main chance. Apart from the two leading Saabs, none of the factory cars had survived. The entry for the 1968 RAC Rally may have been diluted but the event's reputation had, if anything, been strengthened. In any case, John Davenport disagrees with the view that the entry was below par:

'I always strongly defend the fact that there wasn't a strong entry. Okay, Timo wasn't in a full works entry – but he was in the next best thing with a David Sutton car. Agreed, he was about five or six minutes ahead of us in Scotland when he started to have his problems. We'd had gearbox trouble in Wales but once we had changed that at Betwys-y-Coed, things were much better. Eventually we ran out the winners by about 15 minutes. But let's put it like this: on the start line, the rest of the entry looked good!

'No matter what, it was a very satisfying result for me because it had been a hell of a ding-dong battle until near the end. Then it was plain sailing once the others had dropped out. I had been ill for most of the rally. I'd had a dose of flu before the start and Simo always maintains that I slept round Scotland. It was a case of him waking me up and getting my seat upright for the special stages.'

Now world-wide attention switched to the London to Sydney event much to the delight of the *Daily Express* who had backed the rally and scored a march on their Fleet Street rivals. It goes without saying that hair-raising stories were legion during the 19 days which brought competitors face-to-face with previously unheard of obstacles. Roger Clark and Ove Andersson looked to be on course for victory until their Lotus-Cortina was delayed by mechanical problems but, undoubtedly, the hard luck story of them all concerned Lucien Bianchi as the great Belgian all-rounder seemed set to win after defeating mud and mountains, sand and swamps, wandering kangaroos and wombats.

With barely 100 miles to go, Bianchi's Citroen DS21 was involved in an accident with a non-competing car. Bianchi, asleep in the back at the time while Jean-Claude Ogier headed for Sydney with eleven minutes in hand, finished the rally in hospital as the lone works Rootes entry, a Hillman Hunter driven by Andrew Cowan, Brian Coyle and Colin Malkin, claimed victory. The entire effort cost Rootes a paltry £25,000.

Scruffy Little People

Prior to success in this marathon, the Hillman Hunter had been considered an uninspiring saloon car. After the event, the cognoscenti continued to view the Hunter as nothing more than a commercial traveller's vehicle but, as far as Rootes were concerned, that was immaterial. Sales had gathered pace at a rate which gave manufacturers every reason to remain associated with rallying; or, at least, every reason to capitalise on any success which came their way.

Even so, the sport continued to carry a dirty fingernail, greasy rallyjacket image. On the day that Bjorn Waldegaard won the 1969 Monte in a Porsche, *The Times* carried a letter from Sir Miles Thomas, under the heading 'Why have the Monte Carlo Rally?'

In his letter, Sir Miles denounced the event as 'a lot of scruffy little cars driven noisily by scruffy . . . little people'. He went on to ask: 'cannot international automobilism devise some more sophisticated method of demonstrating the worth of its products?'

It was a strange observation from a man who had been a director of Morris and Wolseley for many years between the wars and who had himself taken part in the very rally he chose to criticise. Stranger still was the fact that Sir Miles had advised Morris on Sales Promotion and yet the benefits of advertising success on the Monte Carlo Rally, so expertly exploited by BMC, appeared to have escaped him. At the time, Sir Miles Thomas was 74.

None the less, the 'scruffy' image did prevail even though the top teams ran their rally efforts with a professional precision which would have left many a commercial enterprise nodding with admiration. Perhaps Sir Miles was piqued by the fact that, in 1969, there had been a total of seven British entries in the Monte and the two works drivers, Tony Fall (Lancia) and Vic Elford (Porsche) had retired.

With snow covering more than half the route – which included, once again, a loop into the Ardeche region with its excellent Burzet stage – the rally itself had been as demanding as ever, but somehow the rather low-key atmosphere was to be typical of the year as a whole. That, however, should not detract from Waldegaard's win, the Swede surprising everyone with his performance in wet as well as dry conditions.

The pages of *Autosport* carried correspondence from enthusiasts demanding to know why motor sport was not receiving fair coverage on the pages of the national daily press. In October, however, rallying was to win front page treatment which, as usually happens, was far more than the occasion deserved.

The TAP Rally in Portugal, although not a round of the European championship, had attracted one or two leading entries, including the Lancia of Tony Fall and Henry Liddon. The Britons arrived at the finish to receive acclaim as winners. Or, at least, they would have done had they been able to find their way through the unruly crowd (a hint of more serious and desperate times to come in Portugal) towards the final control.

Liddon abandoned the Lancia to search for the time clock and, in his absence, Fall's wife, who had been waiting for some time to greet her husband, jumped into the car to escape the jostling crowds. When Liddon returned, the trio edged forward and it seemed to some ill-informed observers that Mrs Fall had been part of the crew!

The upshot was disqualification for Fall and Liddon on rather spurious grounds concerning the exact location of *parc fermé* and this was to be the most serious anomaly in a rally riddled with minor irregularities – a pity, since the organiser, Cesar Torres, was considered to have laid on an otherwise first-class event. But the damage had been done. Mr and Mrs Fall were pictured cuddled together in the Lancia and 'The Thunderer' saw fit to carry front page news of the drama. Not quite grubby people in grubby cars – but the inference did little to improve the image. It was not the last time the Portuguese Rally would make news other than on the sports pages of the national press.

BMC in Decline

The championship itself had consisted of the usual collection of events but, once again, there was no pattern to the programmes of the various manufacturers. In Britain, the Rootes competitions department had more or less faded away for the time being and BMC Competitions were continuing the struggle to find their feet under the continually shifting and highly political regime of the newly-knighted Sir Donald Stokes.

While the opposition may have been relieved to see the irritating little Mini reach the end of its competitive life, there had been bad news in April 1969 when Stuart Turner returned from a short period with Castrol to run the Ford Competitions department. Bearing in mind the influence Turner had brought to bear upon BMC, rivals watched and waited for the inevitable turn round at Boreham. One of Turner's opening shots was to secure the services of Timo Makinen for 1970.

In the meantime, Makinen would drive a Lancia on the RAC Rally, the Finn intent on maintaining his record of having led the event every time he had entered. Timo was to be accompanied by three more 1600cc Fulvia HFs; Ford would rely on Clark, Mikkola and Andersson in the increasingly competitive Twin-Cam.

Incidentally, Escort owners could buy conversion kits, developed jointly by Broadspeed and the Ford Performance Centre at Boreham. There were three stages on offer, the top level including a modified head, a 'hot' camshaft, new exhaust manifolds and revised carburation. This, according to the publicity handout, was worth $98\frac{1}{2}$ bhp and 112 mph. And all for £115 . . .

Perhaps it was no surprise, therefore, to find the RAC entry list containing 63 Escorts and Cortinas. The strength of the once dominant Mini, on the other hand, had shrunk to a 'mere' 34.

With no competition from a London to Sydney marathon this year, the RAC had returned to its former strength, 151 starters setting off from the Centre Airport Hotel to tackle 73 stages. This time, the competitors would head into the Midlands, Yorkshire and Southern Scotland in order to give officials in the North East a chance to play their part without having to take days off work, as had been the case when the rally spent Saturday and Sunday in Wales and the North West. That leg would take just over 48 hours, the overnight halt in Blackpool then preceding a 31-hour run through Wales and the West Country before returning to London.

Jack Kemsley had stuck with the familiar format although a subtle change saw the scrapping of the type of circuit test where drivers completed a number of laps of the track. Silverstone remained on the itinerary but, this time, the stage would include tarmac, grass and, as it would turn out, clawing mud.

It was a first-class entry and, although Porsche were absent in an official capacity, Bjorn Waldegaard had urged his Swedish-prepared entry into a five-minute lead by the time he reached Blackpool. Mikkola had gone off on the Dalby stage in Yorkshire, the Finn badly shaken by an incident which required the removal of two stout trees before the Escort could finally be retrieved. The corner in question found a place in rallying folklore when it was immediately dubbed 'Mikkola's Bend'; an honour which Hannu could probably do without . . .

Snow had made the going very difficult and, ultimately, the tricky conditions were to catch Waldegaard out as he laboured under the mistaken impression that the Lancia of Harry Kallstrom was catching the Porsche hand over fist. In fact, unknown to Waldegaard, he had opened the gap considerably – such were the rather slow means of communications then – and had the Swede been fully appraised of the situation then he might not have lost control and spent 28 valuable minutes trying to regain the road. In a bid to make up for lost time, Waldegaard again left the road in a Welsh forest and slipped to an eventual 12th place.

Kallstrom was home and free – a suitable end to the year for the man who had been crowned European champion the moment his closest rival, Gilbert Staepelaere, of Belgium, withdrew his entry from the RAC Rally. Carl Orrenius once again showed the competitiveness of the V4 Saab by finishing second ahead of Fall's Lancia, while Andersson, fourth, was to be the highest-placed Escort in conditions which did not exactly suit the Twin-Cam.

The needle-match of the rally turned out to be the battle between BLMC and newcomers Datsun for the Team Award. Rauno Aaltonen and Tony Ambrose brought their 1600SSS into eighth place while the best BLMC could manage with the heavy and unwieldy Triumph 2.5 PIs was 11th for Andrew Cowan.

Brian Culcheth gave the works Triumph 2.5 PI its debut in 1969.

In fact, BLMC treated the event as a proving ground for the 1970 World Cup Rally. But, while the Team Award for Datsun would represent the first rays of the Rising Sun from Tokyo, the 1969 RAC Rally was, in many ways, the twilight for the once great Abingdon Competitions Department. It was to be a difficult time for BLMC Team Manager Peter Browning, as he recalls:

'Once we came under the Leyland umbrella, there were all sorts of pressures and policy changes. We were urged to use cars other than the Mini mainly, I think, because Sir Donald Stokes was very pro-Triumph. Then there had been pressure to use the 1800 on the London to Sydney.

'So, while all this was going on, the Mini was put on the shelf, so to speak. Everyone in the Competitions Department thought there was another season of development to come from the Mini. Having said that, the three Triumph 2.5 PIs did very well on the '69 RAC Rally, bearing in mind the conditions. I seem to remember we wanted nice, firm going, with lots of rocks and so on because the Triumph was like the Healey – it could take a hell of a beating. And then it snowed; it was a really slushy and mucky event. And the final irony is that, under the circumstances that year, the Mini could have gone very well indeed!'

5

PUTTING OUR HOUSE IN ORDER

On Safari

DEATH NOTICES for the BLMC Competitions Department were posted in the motoring press in August 1970. Given the clumsy forces working within the motoring conglomerate, the decision was inevitable, even if the timing was unfortunate, since 1970 saw the dawning of a more uniform international championship structure for rallying in general.

For the first time, the international governing body of motor sport outlined two distinct categories; the International Rally Championship for Makes and the European Rally Championship for Drivers. Since the latter boasted 22 events and a complicated scoring system, it was only natural that the championship for manufacturers, made up of eight rounds of reasonable repute and governed by a straight-forward points allocation, should gain prominence.

Seven European events – including the Monte Carlo Rally, the Acropolis and the RAC – were included. Plus the East African Safari, a unique rally which deserved the championship status conferred upon it by the FIA.

In fact, the event had received international recognition in 1957 five years after its inauguration by the Royal East African Automobile Association to mark the coronation of Queen Elizabeth II. The original purpose of the rally, according to the organisers, was to allow the public to judge the merits of the normal production cars which were available from dealers in East Africa. For that reason, the classes were determined by retail prices rather than cubic capacity and the cars themselves were strictly production models rather than the more specialised examples.

While the technical and professional progress enjoyed by rallying meant the organisers would eventually allow the admission of modified cars in order to keep pace with the sport as a whole, one thing which would never change would be the almost unbelievable conditions and the apparently insurmountable natural barriers thrown in the competitors' path.

The call for a 60 mph average on the fast and straight roads was bad enough but crews had to be prepared for mud, rain, pot holes, broken bridges, detours, swollen rivers, wild animals, the traversing of politi-

The Datsun 1600 SSS of Herrmann/Schuller; winners of the 1970 East African Safari Rally.

cally uncertain countries – and even more mud. A grasp of Swahili, or whatever the local dialect happened to be, was necessary to secure a helping hand when marooned in the red 'murram' mud. On the other hand, the silent offer of a fistful of local Shillings could overcome many a language barrier.

In terms of severity, comparisons were made with the Liege–Rome–Liege. The Safari, however, allowed nightstops, thus placing the emphasis on the stamina of the equipment rather than the crew. And this was the factor which would decide the outcome and nurture the legend that only local drivers knew how to deal with the specialised conditions.

The secret was, and still is, not so much being slow and steady, but being fast and steady while choosing the correct moments to reduce pace slightly and save the car. Many is the time a smiling local, cruising with the efficiency and speed of a taxi, has been overhauled by a European exploiting the hell-for-leather, on-the-limit style which has been his creed ever since he first sat in a rally car. A couple of hours later, one foreigner, transmission in pieces, sits by the roadside as the local, still smiling, motors by.

The Safari expert will be capable of reading the road even when he can't see it. A carefully reconnoitred route can disappear in hours thanks to instant and ferocious flooding. The local, up to his door cill in muddy water, will know it is better to keep right here because on the left there is hidden a deep gulley. Slide into that and all the Shillings in the world won't get you out in time to adhere to the tight schedule.

An Absolute Cracker

So, in 1970, the East African Safari was worthy of inclusion in the championship series, as was the ever-professional Monte Carlo Rally. Yes, there were the usual idiosyncrasies emanating from the *Automobile Club de Monaco* – such as seeding Timo Makinen at 130 simply because he did not conform to the totally inappropriate parameters based on his previous two year's results in the European championship – but, there were 222 entries. An indication of times ahead, however, was a mere eight starters from Britain – and those from Dover, no less.

Reasonably dry conditions allowed Porsche, through Bjorn Waldegaard, to score a hat-trick on the Monte once their strongly fancied rivals, Alpine, had more or less fallen by the wayside with their neat little sports-racers. Ford, to their consternation, were outclassed by Porsche and Alpine and these two *marques* would dominate the manufacturers' championship although a Datsun 1600SSS (driven by Edgar Herrmann, a Kenyan) took the honours in the Safari.

Datsun, in fact, entered just two rounds of the championship, their second outing being the RAC Rally. The participation of the Japanese team nicely rounded off a magnificent entry for the final round of the series, an event which *Autosport* promised would be 'the biggest and best ever'. It would also be one of the toughest; 129 of the 196 starters were destined to retire.

Had they known this revealing statistic beforehand, the *Daily Mirror* could have written many a racy headline in their own inimitable style. And the chances are, the motoring world would have smiled benignly since, at the time, the paper was proving to be an exceptional benefactor to the sport. The World Cup Rally, run from London to Mexico, had passed off successfully that summer and particularly for Ford whose Escorts filled four of the first six places. (BLMC, having their final push towards temporary obscurity, also did well with second place, behind Mikkola's Escort, and fourth). The 16,179-mile event had been sponsored by the *Daily Mirror* and, to everyone's surprise, the newspaper publishers were not turning pale at the mention of rallying or the strangely besotted people associated with the sport.

Four hundred stage miles were included in the RAC Rally, which followed the same pattern as 1969, starting and finishing in London with the route running anti-clockwise taking in the North-East and a loop through Scotland before running through the Lake District towards the single overnight halt in Blackpool. That section alone would take 48 hours. The final leg through Wales and the West Country, before heading back to London, would account for a further 36 hours and a final total of some 2,300 miles of motoring.

The list of special stages did not include any motor racing circuits; the only tarmac areas were to be found on the familiar run at Porlock and the introduction of a blast around Great Orme. At first glance, Jack Kemsley appeared to have discovered a host of new forest stages in Wales but, in fact, these were familiar routes renamed by the Forestry Commission in a bid to keep spectators away. Not for the last time would the exact locations remain a secret.

Spectators could, for the first time, dial a special number and listen to a GPO recording as the telephone official grappled with unfamiliar names. The fight for the championship alone was more than a mouthful for the hapless announcer as Porsche (Bjorn Waldegaard, Ake Andersson and Gerard Larrousse in 2.2-litre 911Ss and Claude Haldi in a 914/6) left the Centre Airport Hotel to do battle with Alpine Renault (Jean-Luc Thérier, Jean-Pierre Nicolas, Ove Andersson and Andrew Cowan in 1.6-litre A110s).

The withdrawal by BLMC had left the way clear for Cowan to ease himself into the little French car and, in fact, Ford was the only British car to be represented by a manufacturer (Timo Makinen and Hannu Mikkola in Twin-Cams and Roger Clark in the BDA-engined RS1600). Then came Lancia Fulvia 1600s for Kallstrom, Munari and Lampinen, plus four Saabs, five Opels, two Fiat 124 Spyders, four of the new Datsun 240Zs, a pair of Skodas and a quartet of Wartburgs. Truly a magnificent entry – and the rally would tear it apart.

Harry Kallstrom: winner for Lancia in 1969 and 1970.

Mechanical failure accounted for most of the 129 retirements and the devastation wrought among the works teams was catastrophic. Saab and Ford, despite having led at various stages through Stig Blomqvist and Timo Makinen respectively, were wiped out; Datsun had one car reach the finish; Alpine lost third place and the championship when Thérier broke down on the final stage – which was ultimately cancelled because it was too muddy, Porsche scrambled home in sixth place to take the title. Opel, by contrast, came away with second, third and fourth places ahead of Cowan's Alpine. And just one Lancia, that of Harry Kallstrom and Gunnar Haggbom, reached the finish. But they were first. They were also very lucky. Kallstrom, now a truck driver in Sweden, is probably still dining out on this story.

With Makinen out with a broken driveshaft (a similar problem having afflicted the remaining works Escorts), Kallstrom found himself in the lead at Blackpool after what had been an effortless rally – thus far.

Trouble began when one of Lancia's large service vans broke down at Blackpool and, to compound matters, the team manager's car ground to a halt shortly afterwards. This, of course, was the signal for Kallstrom's Fulvia to vibrate loose a screw in the oil cooler, in the middle of the Pantperthog special stage. The subsequent loss of oil meant a failure of the big-end bearings. And the spare set were in the back of the van at Blackpool.

At about the same time, Lampinen and his co-driver John Davenport (who was able to report all this from bitter experience in his column in *Autosport*) lost second gear on their Fulvia, but a replacement could not be fitted at the next service halt because the spare was – in the back of the van at Blackpool. Lampinen limped into the control at Machynlleth, where the big-end bearings were promptly stripped from his car and given to Kallstrom.

The repairs cost the Swede about 60 minutes but he drove like a leader dispossessed and reached the next control with 30 seconds to spare. Or, at least, his navigator reached the control with the time card and a couple of seconds to spare. The car was a few yards down the road – the result of Kallstrom crashing into a bank to avoid an extremely large lorry.

The service crew rushed to the scene, raised the front of the car on a trolley-jack and spirited the first eight-wheeled Lancia through the control. Then they set about changing the steering box, driveshafts, front suspension and shock absorber mounts. Proof of the quality of their workmanship was top place five times for Kallstrom on eight of the remaining 13 special stages, leaving him two minutes clear of Eriks-son's Kadett at the finish. The *Daily Mirror* must have had a field day with that story.

If the truth be told, the newspaper management also must have whispered a quiet prayer of thanks when Makinen retired from the lead. The Finn's Escort was decked out in the house colours of the *London Evening Standard*, carrying the orange and white stripes like some psychedelic motorised zebra. It may have been a clumsy way of easing commercial sponsorship into the RAC Rally. It certainly caused a few snorts of indignation within the portals of the RAC, as Jack Kemsley recalls:

Opel took the Team Prize in 1970. Ove Eriksson heads for second place with the 1.9-litre Kadett.

'We had realised advertising was something which had to come, simply because of the revenue which could be generated – and I'm not just talking about advertising on cars. But, at the time, the RAC wouldn't even allow advertising to appear in the Road Books. Mustn't sully the RAC's name and all that! It just wasn't on.

'And, with no advertising allowed on the cars, I had been quietly saying to Wilfred Andrews, Chairman of the RAC, "it's got to come; it must come." So, one day, he asked me to bring a car along and let him have a look at it. Ford duly brought a car to Pall Mall. But it was a car which had been on the Safari Rally and, of course, they allowed advertising because, naturally, it provided a fair amount of revenue for the club. So, the Ford was literally smothered in advertising. When Wilfred Andrews looked down at this car sitting in Pall Mall, I thought he was going to fall out the window! But, gradually, the idea was introduced.'

Out of Step with Progress

An analysis of the 1970 RAC Rally showed the majority of retirements to have been caused by mechanical failures, particularly transmissions. It seemed the forest terrain had put the final test to power-trains which had been under stress in any case due to the increasing pace of engine development. Previously unseen weaknesses in the gears and bearings had come to light and it was clear the transmission designers had some catching up to do.

In much the same way, the rally was beginning to fall behind the expected standard of an international event now receiving world-wide recognition. The rally itself was good, if not better than ever, but weak points were beginning to appear in the fabric of the organisation. Competitors were complaining about the lack of information available to them during the course of the event, but these shortcomings were to be of minor importance when compared with the chaos the following year. Appalling weather would not help, but the communications system would prove to be woefully inadequate.

These were changing times. The international rally scene, although as healthy as ever, was undergoing a steady transformation as brash new events, such as the TAP Rally in Portugal, offered entrants attractive deals and the resulting healthy response, in turn, produced sufficient backing to run the event in a professional manner.

The *Coupe des Alpes*, on the other hand, tried to continue on the strength of tradition and almost no financial incentive to attract the private owner. The result was a mere 35 entries which meant the rally fell below the minimum requirement to count as a round of the 1971 championship for manufacturers, an appalling slap in the face for this French fortress of rallying history. The only cheerful piece of news concerning the classic event was a rare *Coupe d'Or* for Jean Vinatier in his Alpine Renault.

In fact, 1971 was quite a year for Alpine. They led the Monte Carlo Rally from start to finish, and just about the only complaint the team from Dieppe must have had was that the winner was the solitary Swede,

Alpine-Renault may have won the championship in 1971 but they could not come to terms with the atrocious conditions prevalent on the RAC Rally that year.

Ove Andersson, entered with five Frenchmen.

While Porsche, Saab, Ford and Lancia rushed off to East Africa and overspent out of all proportion in a bid to win the Safari, Alpine stayed at home and concentrated on spreading their budget across enough events to give them the championship. Meanwhile, a Datsun (driven by that man Herrmann again!) kept the 'Locals Show Foreigners How' story alive on the Safari for another year.

Alpine won the Austrian Alpine and the Acropolis, leaving the championship neatly tied up with one round remaining – the RAC Rally of Great Britain.

You might think that would have detracted from the entry. Not so. Manufacturers tended to try and win individual events above all else and the RAC was considered to be one of the top three rallies in the world. But why?

No one summed up the attraction more succinctly than John Davenport. A highly-respected navigator, Davenport turned his hand with equal skill to the typewriter as he covered the international rally scene for *Autosport*. This was his introduction to the 1971 RAC Rally:

> One cannot claim that the RAC Rally of Great Britain is the longest rally in the world, though at 2,500 miles its route is long enough to daunt even the most experienced rally drivers. One cannot say that it is the fastest rally in the world for, as many thousands of spectators will see, the rally cars spend a lot of time on public roads trying not to attract the attention of the law while on the special stages the set average is a mere 50 mph, though even that is a lot faster than the 50 kph required in countries like Italy.
>
> One cannot say that it is the roughest rally in the world since some of the African rallies leave nothing to be desired in that respect, though again it is rough in comparison with, say, the Monte Carlo. Why then should it attract almost 250 entries, the majority of whom will be paying for their rallying out of their own pocket?
>
> In this respect, the RAC Rally is equalled by no one in that it is by far the most popular event in the world at the moment. Its unique blend of high speed special stages on private property, usually comprising dirt-surfaced roads, with long easy road sections around the British Isles, is attractive to works and private entrant alike. It appeals both to the dogged, determined finishers who are just going out to get round and to the speed merchants who want to prove their driving skill and maybe just enjoy going sideways. In any case it has the reputation of being one of the best organised rallies in Europe as well as having an excellent record in attracting good coverage in the press and on television.

To back up Davenport's final point, the *Daily Mirror* were sponsoring the rally once more and filling their pages with previews, flowing from the expansive hand of Patrick Mennem, their Motoring Correspondent.

Mennem noted that the rally was breaking with a seven-year tradition by switching the start and finish from London to Harrogate. The route went as far North as Grantown-on-Spey, in Scotland, south to Prestwick and through the Lake District before returning to Harrogate for an overnight halt. Then the familiar run through Wales, with a visit to the Scratchwood service area on the M1 for the benefit of southern enthusiasts before heading North to the finish.

A more important innovation was the introduction of 'showbusiness stages' purely for the benefit of the public. Or, to be more precise, the *paying* public. With overheads continuing to rise, a means of generating income while, at the same time, dealing with the increasing numbers of spectators, was neatly provided by taking competitors into the grounds of Harewood House for the very first stage. It was also the scene of the first chink in the organisational armour.

The stage took competitors past the main house and into the drive, at the end of which there was a sharp right leading into a narrow track. Signs, reading '300', '200' and '100' had been placed on the drive to mark the approach of the right-hander. Several drivers quite rightly interpreted these as markers for a flying finish and kept accelerating. It was not until startled spectators ran for cover that the main gates were revealed and the drivers realised their error. It was too late to save many a potentially serious incident, Shekhar Mehta breaking a bone in his wrist when his Datsun struck a post.

At least it kept the members of the public on their toes on an otherwise chilly day. The weather, however, would get much worse and, by the time the rally had reached the north Yorkshire moors, snow was in evidence. It was nothing compared to what was to come in Scotland.

Chaos at Clashindarroch

The Glendevon stage, to the south of Perth, was cancelled because of drifting snow and at this point the organisers should have taken similar decisions elsewhere but, instead, the rally ploughed on northwards. It soon became clear that there were inadequate contingency plans for rerouting in the event of weather which was deteriorating by the minute.

If snow was to be the lasting memory of the 1971 RAC Rally, then it was being recorded for posterity by Barrie Hinchliffe, a young filmmaker who was to establish a first-class reputation with his impressions of the event. Titled 'From Harrogate it Started', the film, apart from employing a bold approach which dispensed with a droning commentary, caught the atmosphere and the frustration perfectly.

One shot, taken from a helicopter, showed several cars at a standstill in the middle of a special stage. At least one of them was trying to drive in the 'wrong' direction. Such was the chaos and lack of coordination, cars were sent into stages with no means of knowing whether the route was clear. When Jean-Luc Thérier's Alpine became hopelessly bogged down three miles into the Clashindarroch stage, a queue of a dozen cars soon formed. By the time word reached the start – thanks only to the aforementioned helicopter – more than 100 cars were collecting in the narrow country road to start the stage, and the road was already blocked with snow at one end. That was one of many incidents which sent the rally into disarray and competitors into a state of confusion.

John Davenport, in his *Autosport* report, described the scene as he saw it from the navigator's seat in Simo Lampinen's Lancia:

> One would have thought that one such happening (the Clashindarroch chaos) was enough but then at the start of the Bin stage, which led straight off a main road, there was a delay while the timing was set up which promptly caused a three-lane traffic jam on the icy main road which even the police couldn't sort out.
>
> Instead of cancelling the stage and getting the competitors out of the way, the jam went merrily on for hours and then when the competitors finally attempted the stage and drove flat out through it, it was to get to the finish and be told that there was no timing. The fact that the start marshal was completely unaware of this gave the whole thing an air of Lewis Carroll or, indeed, the Marx Brothers.

Describing later events, Davenport went on:

> The stage just after Grantown was run and then a long drag followed right down the A9 towards Perth again and the next stages. It also meant a return to the Carroll/Marx combine, for at the entrance to the Trinafour road a marshal gave verbal instructions that the road over to Glenerrochty was blocked and that competitors should go down to Calvine and in from there.
>
> Along this road they met other competitors coming back so it was clear that the stage was not being run but they still had to go and get the marshal's signature. This led to many close moments, and in the case of Billy Coleman's Alpine, a total write-off after it had been hit by Seppo Utrainen's Saab coming the other way.

The official results were, to put it mildly, fluid for quite some time. There was even a case of one competitor, Dave Thompson, having the rear axle seize on his Vauxhall Viva as he reached the final stages of the rally. Luckily, he found a Dealer Team Vauxhall service crew who changed the entire axle, thus allowing Thompson to make it to the finish – where he was told that he had been disqualified for being late in Scotland three days previously!

As ever, though, the professional teams survived no matter what obstacles were thrown at them. Even so, Henry Liddon looked as though he was ready to burst into tears when talking on Hinchliffe's film about how he and Timo Makinen had lost the lead when their Escort RS1600 encountered gear selection problems in North Wales. All three works Fords were carrying the colours of Wills' Embassy cigarettes and all three were destined to have enough problems to keep Mikkola, Makinen and Clark out of the top three.

Mikkola, though, did come away with two hand-made suits for his trouble, this the prize for being the quickest foreign driver to pass through a sewage works – in a manner of speaking. In a clever piece of promotional work, the good burghers of Bradford saw the potential in running a stage through, or perhaps 'around' would be a better word here, the local Esholt sewage works. It was a tricky enough stage, comprising narrow bridges, some top gear work and the careful avoidance of the Organic Manure Store, a stout stone building built like a sh . . . it was big. It was never recorded just what Roger Clark received for being the fastest driver of all to pass through Esholt in one piece.

Whatever the prize, it made little difference to what was turning out to be a miserable rally for the Englishman. He would eventually be classified in 11th place, 25 minutes behind the winning Saab driven by Stig Blomqvist, yet another Swede with dazzling potential. In fact, Scandinavian drivers, with the exception of Sandro Munari in ninth place, filled the top ten positions; hardly surprising in view of the conditions.

During the seemingly interminable delays which had faced the crews, there had been time for Roger Clark and his co-driver Jim Porter to consider the effect on their progress. Porter, though, was just as interested in the cause of the trouble. The snow he could see for himself. Why, then, were the officials in the rally HQ at Harrogate not aware of the conditions? And, if they were, why had an alternative route not been employed sooner?

Clearly, the communications were either non-existent or in need of an overhaul. The business of sending cars into a white oblivion in the hope that they would come out the other end had no place in an international rally. It was a situation which was made plain to Dean Delamont, Director of RAC Motor Sport Division and Clerk of the Course, when harassed competitors returned to Harrogate. Delamont knew immediately what must be done for the following year.

Call the Porter

The programme for the *Daily Mirror RAC International Rally of Great Britain 1972* (price 20p) carried a list of officials on page 5. Clerk of the Course was D. H. Delamont; his Deputy, P. G Cooper. And Assistant Clerk of the Course, a new name certainly on this page of the programme, J. Porter.

Jack Kemsley was now Chairman of the Organising Committee and Jim Porter was not about to step in and demand instant and far-reaching changes. His job at this stage, as he recalls, was to tighten up the administrative details.

'As far as I can remember, there weren't any major changes required concerning the actual design of the rally. The layout and general content was okay but the thing which had bothered me about the 1971 event was that there did not seem to be a strong enough control over what went on. In other words, if there were snow drifts in a Scottish forest, then that stage had to be cut out and the rally taken around the trouble spot. There was not a strong enough mechanism to do that within the organisation.

'We didn't do anything dramatic in 1972. We simply introduced a number of small ideas, like having a much more detailed and much larger HQ control to monitor what was going on. We had cars out on the road, for instance, making sure the roads were open. We had a much faster and more detailed results system so that we knew, within minutes rather than hours, who was actually leading. But there was nothing dramatic; the key was simply making sure everything *worked*.'

The stream-lining of the operation included the physical separation of scrutineering from the rally headquarters. It was no longer necessary for competitors to clutter the foyer of the hotel housing the headquarters since all of the documentation was carried out at York racecourse. Further isolation of the rally nerve centre in the Royal Station Hotel provided separate phone lines for the screened-off results room, thereby reducing the chances of interruptions while the rally was in progress.

The feedback of information to the results team was to be accelerated by the collection of competitors' time cards on a more regular basis. Whereas in the past, the cards had been gathered in every five hours or so, Porter introduced a network of points which would provide a feedback to Rally HQ every hour, sometimes twice an hour.

A more compact route also helped, as did the axing of an entire night's motoring. The headquarters was moved to York and the figure of eight pattern was reversed; in other words, Wales was first on the agenda on the Saturday. By dawn on Sunday, competitors would reach the Severn Bridge with the rest of the day taken up mainly with spectator stages at Blenheim, Silverstone, Sutton Park and Donington before returning to York for the night. Yorkshire, Scotland (but no further north than the Firth of Forth) and the Lake District would occupy Monday and Tuesday, the event finishing at York Racecourse in the late afternoon.

The reduction in length to 1,800 miles was not quite the gift horse it seemed. The rally may have been less arduous as a result but the special stage mileage remained as high as usual, thanks to the familiar sprinkling of 72 stages – all sponsored by Unipart. The shorter road distances meant less time to repair damaged cars and the RAC turned the screw a little tighter by forbidding servicing in certain areas adjacent to special stages. And, on top of that, several major components on the cars were marked before the start, the object being to hand out penalties if the parts in question were changed during the rally.

With the revised organisational network primed and ready to go, it remained to be seen whether it actually worked. In the event, not only did it achieve the aims of Dean Delamont, Peter Cooper and Jim Porter, there was also the added pleasure of handling and recording a splendid British victory.

Roger Clark:
on top form in 1972.

Clark Defeats the Scandinavians

The decision was unanimous. The 1972 RAC Rally of Great Britain was a huge success although perhaps the judgement was tinged a little by a brilliant win for Roger Clark and the irony was that the new-found role for Jim Porter he was not sitting alongside his long-time chauffeur. Tony Mason took over Clark's navigator's seat while Jim helped mastermind the show; but Clark's win was not easily foreseen. Casting a prediction in the official programme, Pat Mennem wrote:

> Who will win? Gerry Burgess in a Ford was the last Briton to win the rally, and that was way back in 1959. And if we are honest, the chances of a Briton winning this year are very thin.
> I'd love to see a home-grown driver win our own rally, but the chances are that it is going to be another Scandinavian driver.

It was difficult to fault his logic. The date had been moved to December and, while some argued that this would mean more consistent weather patterns rather than the drizzle and fog of November, the chances of snow were very strong. In which case, most pundits had their money on Stig Blomqvist's Saab for a second win in succession since the Ford Escort had proved to be less than ideal in the difficult conditions encountered in 1971. In 1972, however, there was no snow to speak of and the Escort, now with an aluminium 2-litre fuel-injected engine, was in its element. So was Clark, for that matter.

Having spent the season winning the RAC British championship, he was completely in tune with the forests; not intimate with them, merely in tune. Clark disagrees with the widely held belief that a driver in his position had an unfair advantage when it came to reading the secret forest stages.

'You don't actually *learn* any of the forests. You can remember the odd bend where you nearly went off, but the truth is you can only remember the character of the forest. I didn't do enough rallying through each forest to enable me to get to the stage where I could start remembering it. With each national rally, you would only pass through once, so you weren't familiar enough with the roads to take a crest flat and so on. You couldn't trust yourself to that extent. You needed to go over a stage four or five times to get an advantage.

'In any case, the stages could have changed since your last visit. If the forestry people have been working and taking trees out, the character of the road changes. Lorries cut the corners up, and if there is a boggy section, they can go so far as to divert the road itself which means you are faced with an entirely new piece of special stage. But there's no doubt it gave a psychological advantage in that the other drivers *thought* I knew the forests!'

In the two weeks leading up to the RAC Rally, Clark took a break from the gravel and pine and went to Kenya on holiday. Fully refreshed, he returned to Britain the day before the rally was due to start. He had, as he would later admit, fully unwound, with not a care in the world, ready to jump into a rally car and start driving.

By the time he reached the Severn Bridge, Clark was leading Blomqvist by a minute. He was also on his own now, since team-mates Mikkola and Makinen were out. It was one thing leading but quite another keeping it, bearing in mind the special stages yet to come. However, Clark used the power of the BDA to full effect in the fast Yorkshire stages and increased his lead to three minutes. Then, as he explained in his regular column in *Competition Car*, he began to think about reducing his pace:

I had started off with the intention of taking it reasonably easy although, in my own mind, I knew that on the RAC Rally we'd have to travel quickly from the word go. So psychologically I suppose I did get at it . . .

As the first section drew to a close, I knew there had been a lot of tarmac stages which suited the Escort. From then onward, the rest of the stages (close on 40), from the half-way halt were all in forests. It did strike me that, if we encountered some really rough ones, Blomqvist and the Saabs would start to shine.

We'd geared the car so that at 9,000 rpm in top we'd be pulling about 115 mph. This was to see us in good stead on the fast Yorkshire stages. We started off the second half of the rally going really quickly. In fact, it was the hardest I drove in the whole event because I knew the Yorkshire stages were fast, in daylight and with a lot of straights. So we took advantage of them. But in actual fact, when it did get rough up in Scotland, the Escort proved a damned sight better over the really rough stages than the Saab.

95

> Once in Scotland, I could conserve myself, having pulled out a nice healthy lead over Stig, and prepare for the weather to deteriorate. In fact, Scotland was just wet and windy (thank God) and, when it did get really rough, the Escort's suspension was coping better than the Saab's.
>
> Halfway through the last night, we found ourselves with a $4\frac{1}{2}$-minute lead over Stig with Anders Kullang's Opel a similar distance behind and therefore not really a worry. He had been going extremely well despite an earlier delay. Opels eventually won the team prize, but it's not difficult for them, having quite a reasonable car in the Ascona, which is able to produce consistent results going at a consistent speed. It's easy to go 90 per cent. It's the last five or ten per cent which takes the getting.

The same could be said of the organisation. No effort was spared in 1972 to work at 100 per cent and the new approach produced a fresh confidence which many competitors noticed. In Clocaenog Forest, for example, a faulty time clock at the end of one of the stages was causing more than a little agitation among the leading crews when it delivered times which were 20 seconds adrift from the correct figures. Rally HQ was onto the trouble immediately and the stage was cancelled without further fuss.

It was attention to detail like that which brought the nod of approval from the foreign teams. They probably didn't feel quite so happy, however, about the commanding performance from Roger Clark. It was little consolation to know that Clark and Ford were the only British driver *and* car to finish in the top 10.

In a way, it was appropriate. Ford had already set tradition on its ear seven months earlier when Hannu Mikkola and Gunnar Palm drove an Escort into first place in the East African Safari. This was the result of Stuart Turner's methodical preparation, an extremely strong car, a superb driver, and the fact that, for once, the Safari was more or less bone dry. The Datsun 240Zs (winners of the team prize on the RAC Rally) provided a major threat but when Herrmann ran into trouble and lost the lead, Mikkola was on course to smash the myth and prove that a well-drilled team and thorough preparation could overcome local know-how.

Ford were delighted with their 'double'. It didn't matter a great deal that they were fourth in the international championship for makes, since a well-orchestrated advertising campaign announcing a Safari victory could do more for car sales than mention of a title which was still meaningless to the celebrated gentleman on the Clapham omnibus.

Even so, Fiat and Lancia put a great deal of store by the title and the in-house battle (they were both owned by the same consortium) saw victory in the FIA series go to the Lancia Fulvia, a car which was thought to have passed its best.

Lancia got off on the right foot by winning, at last, the Monte Carlo Rally, Sandro Munari taking a well-deserved victory once the Alpine-

Renaults had either broken down or run into trouble in a snow storm on the Burzet stage. There was mechanical mayhem of the highest order in the Moroccan Rally, a tough but well-organised round of the championship, and when Simo Lampinen emerged as the first of just six finishers, Lancia – soon to have backing from Marlboro cigarettes – were well on their way to the manufacturer's title. The European drivers' championship, by the way, was still running in a lengthy and confused state, 24 events counting in a series from which Raffaele Pinto emerged as the man with most points. It was therefore concluded that he must be the winner.

This devaluation of the driver's role in rallying did nothing for the image of the sport and moves were afoot to switch the emphasis away from the manufacturers and place the public spotlight on the human aspect.

More Misery in Monaco

But, of course, it was a waste of time. The governing body of motor sport, the FIA, were deaf to such logic and the championship structure continued into 1973 along the same lines as before. The upshot was that only Alpine and Fiat took a serious run at the manufacturers' championship and, in the event, the French team dominated by winning six of the first 10 rallies in the 13-round series. And they kicked off with an emotional victory for Jean-Claude Andruet in the Monte. It was a brilliant win. The same could not be said of the rally itself.

Things had been running too smoothly for too long. People were actually saying what a fine, thoroughly professional hassle-free rally it was. In 1973, the French police and the blasé organisers changed all that. The rally was totally chaotic.

In truth, part of the problem was increasing concern over the tough average speeds required on public roads. On the approach to the stage at Le Corobin, the police were out in force with their radar traps, so much so that the special stage was allowed to look after itself with the inevitable disarray as spectators parked at their convenience and generally did what they pleased.

Traffic offences were noted, but not in the manner prescribed in the regulations and so crews reached Monte Carlo to be told they had broken the law at such-and-such a place and were therefore penalised. Some were actually disqualified. In most cases, it was the first the competitors knew of it.

There was worse to come at Burzet. Here, a combination of an accident and falling snow blocked the road for a considerable time but rather than cancel it, the organisers merely decided to summarily dismiss from the rally those who had not yet tackled the stage. This applied to 144 competitors in all, and they were not best pleased. They did their cause little good by blocking the route elsewhere although the result of their efforts was to throw the rally into total confusion. The resulting publicity was both poor and disproportionate but the organisers only had themselves to blame. It did not detract, however, from a clean sweep by Alpine.

The Dieppe company (30 per cent of which had recently been acquired by Renault) also dominated the TAP Rally, which was now a worth-while addition to the championship. The switch to a March date, however, caught teams by surprise as the rough roads, made worse by the ravages of winter, decimated the entry.

This sort of treatment was to be expected on the East African Safari Rally and Alpine gave that one a miss, leaving the way clear for a tremendous tussle between Ford (reputed to have spent £65,000 on their five-car attack) and Datsun. Clark and Makinen led for Ford but their retirements allowed Mikkola (Ford) and Aaltonen (Datsun) to come forward. They had such a battle that both drivers left the road a mere 100 miles from the finish.

Shekhar Mehta was first to reach Nairobi but, because the left-front wing and headlight were missing from his Datsun 240Z, he was docked one minute, leaving him on exactly the same score as Harry Kallstrom's Datsun 180B. Victory was awarded to Mehta since he had gone the furthest without penalty. He also earned a message of congratulations from Idi Amin, the President of Uganda noting: 'The Safari this year was not a true East African event, since it took place only in Kenya and Tanzania because of the imperialists' sabotage tactics and although you are now a refugee in Nairobi after the milking of Uganda's economy for the last 70 years, your success goes to show the determination of Ugandans.'

Mehta, aged 27 at the time, probably wished he had come second after all.

Politics were to have a hand in the RAC Rally as well. With Europe in the increasing grip of the so-called Energy Crisis, there was the expectancy, right up to the last minute, that the rally would be cancelled. There had been a call by the government for a 10 per cent reduction in the consumption of petrol. Jim Porter was heavily involved in the RAC's response to the emergency.

'The energy crisis came up once we had organised the route in its final version. With the rest of the country committed to reducing consumption, we took the straightforward approach of simply cutting the route by 10 per cent. Fortunately, it was easy to do because, for once, we had planned a loop to the north of Glasgow. So, we simply chopped that out and everyone more or less went to bed for the night when they stopped at the rest halt outside Glasgow. It seemed to be an acceptable compromise all round.'

Even so, Dean Delamont, then the RAC's Director of Motor Sport, was threatened by an elderly lady with an umbrella when he arrived at the rally headquarters in York!

The normally reliable Opels were beaten by the tough conditions on the 1973 **RAC Rally.**

The route, although revised, was still tough enough to maintain the rally's reputation. Once again, there was a rough figure of eight format with the lower loop, lasting almost 36 hours, taking in the Midlands and Wales. Then the usual run to Scotland followed by Cumberland and Westmoreland before returning to York 34 hours later for the second overnight halt. As an innovation, there would be a final dash to the Yorkshire forests in time for a return to York for the finish at lunchtime the following day.

Timo Makinen, his works Ford supported by the Milk Marketing Board, took a familiar position at the front from a very early stage. He had done this sort of thing before – almost every year, in fact – and the question remained whether he could maintain his advantage.

Makinen was harried all the way by the BMW 2002 of Bjorn Waldegaard, the Scandinavians swapping places for a long time until on the final loop into Yorkshire, Waldegaard left the road in the Pickering Forest. By then, however, Bjorn was more interested in keeping Roger Clark at bay. The Briton, suffering throughout the rally with a heavy cold, began to feel better towards the end and was making massive inroads on the surprisingly swift and reliable BMW when Waldegaard disappeared into the trees.

As the Swede set about the difficult task of retrieving his car, he was joined by an Escort driven by a Finn whose name was on everyone's lips – partly because it was reasonably easy to pronounce. From the first two special stages of the rally (at Braham and Clipstone), where he set second fastest time behind Clark, spectators were consulting their programmes and asking 'Who's this bloke Markku Alen in the Escort?'

This bloke Alen, in fact, got it all wrong in the Sutton Park stage later that day and flew off the road. He rejoined in 177th place and his climb through the field was one of the highlights of the rally, if not the decade.

Alen was not alone in being caught out by this deceiving, right-hand bend. No less a personage than Hannu Mikkola broke a bone in his right hand while trying to prevent his Escort from rolling. Russell Brookes was, you might say, a trifle more fortunate in that he didn't break any bones – but he did allow his works-loaned Escort to roll into retirement.

John Davenport had been sitting alongside Mikkola. He remembers it well:

'I recall spending the first day of the RAC Rally that year sitting in some hospital in Walsall trying to make Hannu understand that he couldn't have a private room at the drop of a hat.

'The corner in question was an almost flat right, uphill. But because you had the horizon coinciding with where the bend actually turned, and because there was a little bit of a dip in the bank, it looked as if it was an absolute straight over the top of the crest job.

'You would be doing, I suppose, about 80 mph, and at the last minute the realisation would dawn that you were about to make a mistake. And, of course, because there is always a little bit of margin left, Hannu tried to turn and he had the lock on when he actually hit the bit of bank or whatever it was and the kick-back through the steering caught his wrist.'

Alen, then, was lucky to emerge reasonably unscathed and it was the same story at Pickering, Waldegaard even offering a helping hand to see the Finn on his way to third place behind Clark.

It had been a difficult rally for Datsun, or to be more precise, their UK team manager Mike Greasley. The win for the Japanese company on the Safari rally had led them to believe anything was possible; the RAC Rally should be a piece of cake. Greasley and his drivers, Tony Fall, Chris Sclater and Harry Kallstrom knew better but it was difficult to get the message across. At one point on the RAC event, a fibreglass sump guard on Kallstrom's car had worn out and needed replacing. The chief engineer from Datsun refused point blank to change it. The

Oriental influence. The Datsun drivers had a struggle to defeat the elements and the computerised logic of the Japanese manufacturer.

computer, apparently, said it should last the distance and that was all there was to it. Greasley blew a fuse:

'I remember, in the middle of Scotland somewhere, grabbing this gentleman by the throat. Time was ticking away and we were arguing about whether we could change the sump guard or not! Then someone pointed out that he was a karate expert! I decided that perhaps the sump guard didn't need changing after all . . .'

The Datsun drivers also had the greatest difficulty in convincing the engineers that the brake bias ought to be towards the rear of the car. The Japanese insisted that the braking should major on the front wheels on this heavy rear-wheel drive car. During the RAC, all three cars had atrocious difficulties with their rear brakes, a problem which would send Sclater into retirement. It eventually took a trip to Tokyo by Greasley and Sclater, and the extensive use of a blackboard, to explain how the driving technique necessary for loose surface work required locking rear brakes to unsettle the car. The word oversteer, apparently, was something of a novelty to the Japanese.

All of this was a fundamental prerequisite of rallying which would have been second nature to Timo Makinen. His win on the RAC, at the expense of the very best from the world of international rallying, was seen as a suitable way to end what had been considered a truly excellent event. Jim Porter's remedial work behind the scenes had continued apace and the timing and results were working at a hitherto unknown level of competence. The House of the RAC Rally was back in order.

As a final, clever piece of PR, bearing in mind the mumbling about rallying wasting valuable fuel, Ford arranged for Timo Makinen and Henry Liddon to motor from York to London in a standard Escort 1100 at the recommended temporary speed limit of 50 mph. They averaged 47 mpg and 47 mph. How they kept awake for a journey which took four hours and 31 minutes, we'll never know.

6

SUPERCARS AND SPONSORS

Built to Win

THE WINTER of 1973–74 was a torrid time. Fears over the oil crisis grew longer as the days grew shorter and motor clubs spent the dark days playing an ingenious system of table-top rallying inspired, almost inevitably, by Ford. Meanwhile, any rally pundit who reckoned he was worth his salt grasped the mighty pen and filled the columns of the specialist press with his views on how the world should be put right.

There was very little optimism. The Monte Carlo Rally was cancelled. After the shambles of the previous year, the Monte was destined not to be a round of the championship in any case but it was thought the name would have carried the event no matter what. The Swedish Rally went by the board as well, but the TAP Rally kicked the championship back to life, Fiat, having wisely snapped up Markku Alen, taking the first three places.

In fact, the championship for manufacturers (the drivers were still more or less ignored on an international basis) would be fought out between Fiat and Lancia, with the latter taking the title thanks, in part, to the appearance of a car which would point the way to the future of rallying. On the San Remo in October, the Lancia Stratos made its international debut – and won.

It was a sensational car by any standards, which was hardly surprising since it had been designed and built specifically for competition. The wedge shape had about it an undeniable Italian flair; the howling Ferrari V6, an unmistakable racing pedigree. Enough examples (400) had been built to conform with the regulations and yet, by so doing, Lancia had revised the parameters of rallying. Some saw the policy of deliberately producing an out-and-out racer – a 'homologation special' – in bulk simply as a sinister move. For anyone with racing blood in their veins, it was the most exciting thing to have happened for many a year.

My personal impressions of the Lancia Stratos are memories of a Hillman Minx, and the incredible sing-song whining from the Lancia's close-cut gears. When sitting in the passenger seat of the left-hand drive Stratos, the whistling symphony came from somewhere behind your left shoulder.

**The Lancia Stratos:
memories of the
Hillman Minx.**

I experienced it for myself as I sat beside Billy Coleman on the day he took a Stratos down the terrifying Esgair Dafydd stage in Wales, and it is just about the only thing I can remember clearly after a high-speed dash which filled me with a curious mixture of sheer joy and rank terror. This was during practise for a televised Rally Sprint, where top drivers rushed up and down the side of a mountain (and that is no exaggeration) against the clock.

Coleman had been selected to drive a privately-owned Stratos. He hadn't sat in the car for some time. And when he did, he couldn't find his driving shoes. Or, to be precise, his left driving shoe. The one on the right foot, a grubby green gymshoe as I recall, allowed heeling and toeing but he was still keen to know what had happened to the other shoe as we set off to explore the unknown. I had the distinct impression he hadn't seen the stage before either. He kept saying 'Jayzus', or some-such expletive, and I'm not sure whether that referred to the road or the car.

You had a strong impression of sitting *in* the Stratos, thanks mainly to the high-sided door panels, with windows tapering back towards the roof, the huddled central seating for driver and passenger and the curving windscreen which seemed to envelope them both. The interior was matt black and dusty. To the novice such as I, it looked decidedly second-hand. When the harness was pulled tight and the door slammed shut by the mechanic, you were *in*, brother. And here's this idiot worrying about his left shoe.

I soon forgot about that. And so did Coleman. If ever a car kept the driver busy then this was it. The V6, barking crisply through the funny little perspex panel behind your head, rocketed up and down

103

the rev range. And, for some strange reason, I fleetingly remembered a ride in my uncle's Hillman Minx many years before.

Uncle's speedometer had broken and the red needle was free to do as it wished. Maybe it was working normally, I don't know, but every time uncle hit a bump – which was frequently, given the standard of his driving and the local roads – the needle would fly round the dial, then swing back, crash onto the stop and bounce round to 70 mph again.

It may seem odd to draw an analogy between a Hillman Minx and a Stratos, but the Lancia's rev-counter appeared to be performing just as wildly as uncle's speedo, so much so that Coleman was a blurr as his right hand constantly snatched the gearlever. And he had to find time to do that as the car danced nervously over a loose forest road which had, for most of its length, a drop to oblivion on one side – Billy's side. But it didn't make much difference to me. Nor, it seemed, did it make much difference to Billy.

I recalled an article by Peter Newton, one of the best descriptive writers in rallying, relating how he had been captivated by a few laps of Bagshot in a Stratos driven by the supremely talented and sadly missed Grand Prix driver, Tom Pryce.

I also remembered watching another Grand Prix star, Patrick Depailler, handle a Stratos for the first time during a Rally Sprint event at Donington. Part of the deal was that the regular driver, Andy Dawson, would sit alongside the little Frenchman during practice and pass on tips.

When the run had finished Depailler, who always felt that the driving limit was there to be explored, lit another untipped Gauloise and described the Stratos as very exciting, but *very* difficult. Dawson had been most impressed by Depailler's swift reactions for, it seemed, that's what was required if the potential of this thoroughbred was to be exploited fully. This was no saloon car with stiffened suspension. When the tail broke away, it threatened to spin like a top.

Coleman didn't have an expert sitting alongside. Not that he needed one. As we plunged downhill at over 100 mph, we could see for ourselves what Dawson had meant. It had to be admitted that this particular Stratos had led a busy life but, even so, the steering wheel appeared to be on fire. It flew every whichway in response to Coleman's constant flurry of corrections, these the product of incredible reflexes which, in terms of raw, natural ability, summed up the man. Throughout, Coleman sat slightly hunched forward, as though all this was catching him by surprise. Which, as I was to discover at the bottom of the hill, it was.

'Jayzus it's quick,' he said in that lovely lilting Cork accent. 'I didn't get lookin' at the rev counter,' he added, pointing to the largest dial on the rather grubby and untidy instrument panel stretched before him. 'What were we pulling in t'ird?' He may as well have asked a mugging victim whether he had caught his assailant's name.

To my surprise, I found I had the power of speech and mumbled an apology. It didn't matter. Billy was calmly rummaging around in the door pocket looking for that other shoe. Driving the Stratos was all in his day's work. I was lost in total admiration.

John Davenport had a rather similar experience in 1974, although on a more professional footing, it should be said. He had accepted the offer of a ride with Markku Alen on the Welsh Rally, a brave move when the young Finn's antics on the previous year's RAC Rally were taken into account. They would share a works Ford Escort and it was arranged that they should get to know each other a bit better at Eppynt. They ran into difficulties straight away. Davenport takes up the story:

'We were issued with an Escort Mexico and told to go and have a look around Epynt because, obviously, this would form a large portion of the Welsh Rally. It was during the day and we had driven past the red flags and all the rest of it when we were stopped by the Army. We were about to be thrown into clink, or whatever the Army's equivalent of jail is, when the guy took a look around the car, then suddenly stepped back, saluted and said, "No trouble sir. Thank you, sir. Please carry on!"

'I had a closer look at the car when we got out later on. It was the car Prince Michael of Kent had driven and it still had the badge of the Royal Hussars on the side! No wonder the bloke started jumping to attention!

'But the rally itself was a terrific experience because, at the time, Markku had a completely raw talent; it seemed to brim over. He had one or two close moments on the forest stages but he was so super at correcting them – in fact, afterwards it was possible to consider that maybe he meant to do that anyway! I think, too, it looked much worse from the outside than it did from within. I remember at one stage wav-

Sandro Munari gave the Lancia Stratos a sensational debut on the 1974 Lombard RAC Rally.

Naked runner. Bjorn Waldegaard ran without the tail section on his Stratos for a time during the 1975 event.

ing at a spectating Stuart Turner. He looked very pale! But we won the rally. Markku was superb.'

Superlatives did not spring to mind as competitors made their way home from North America in October 1974. The championship now embraced the Rideau Lakes Rally in Canada and the Press on Regardless in the United States. The former (won by Munari's Stratos) was as efficient as the latter was shambolic.

Alen led the US event from start to finish but both the Fiat and the Lancia teams were penalised for their service crews allegedly speeding. This was the unfortunate final act in a rally where a sad lack of public relations work with the local community had led to the sheriff of Dickenson County, in Michigan, trying to close down the rally single-handed. Protests flew thick and fast and the upshot was a one-point lead in the championship for Lancia as the teams moved to York for the RAC Rally, now to be known as the Lombard RAC Rally.

The Lombard Connection

The timetable and the 2,215-mile route were much the same as 1973. 190 starters left York at 9 o'clock on the Saturday morning, the aim being to return for a night's sleep at 7 pm on Sunday with an 8 am re-start on Monday for the run north. By 7 pm on Tuesday, the survivors had returned to York knowing that the Wednesday morning loop through the fast Yorkshire stages could easily upset the leader board. They almost did.

Timo Makinen had started out with a two-and-a-half-minute lead over Stig Blomqvist. The fact that Blomqvist was there at all was a tribute to his tenacious driving since he had lost four minutes when he rolled his Saab on the Myherin stage in Wales. There were to be further excursions in the icy conditions as Stig made up for the deficiency in horsepower but, when Makinen stopped to have the clutch on his Colibri-sponsored Escort changed first thing on Wednesday morning, Blomqvist put his head down.

Makinen had been under pressure almost from the moment he had taken the lead on Sunday. Apart from anything else, he was the sole Ford representative at the front thanks to Mikkola losing the lead in the Dovey Forest when wheel studs sheared on his Escort. Clark, lying sixth, had dropped to 32nd when he made a rare mistake, and took time to get motoring again. There was nothing, however, which seemed capable of stopping the Stratos of Sandro Munari. Nothing, that is, except team orders and a hurried British dinner.

Munari and the Stratos may have been appreciated by vast crowds, particularly in the forests of North Wales, but their progress was unexpected. It was one thing to win the San Remo and then deliver all that power on the smooth forest tracks in Canada; the RAC Rally, it was predicted, would soon bring this fragile racer to its expensive knees.

Sure enough, Munari had set to work on the tarmac spectator stages. At the Esholt sewage works, he was seven seconds faster than Mikkola. It was much the same on the prom at New Brighton (a new fixture), where the wedge-shaped device was fastest yet again. Going into Wales, Munari was tying with Mikkola for the lead. This would sort the strong from the weak.

But no. In the first stage in the Clocaenog Forest, Munari was second fastest, four seconds slower than Blomqvist and six faster than Mikkola. Then, joint fastest with Blomqvist on Clocaenog 2 and fastest on Clocaenog 4 by seven seconds. To rub it in, Munari was quickest again on the two stages in Penmachno. And the Stratos was running like a clock.

By the time the Welsh loop had been completed, team tactics came into play. Cesare Fiorio had decided that Munari should back off and aim for a finish. They had made their point; the championship was more important now. This was just as well, perhaps, since Munari bolted down a meal on his return to York and felt off colour for the rest of the rally, so much so, that a doctor was rushed from service point to service point to check his condition. Nevertheless, Munari and Piero Sodano finished third, setting joint fastest time on the last stage for good measure. Lancia, barring the cruelest of luck in the final round, the *Tour de Corse*, were assured of the championship.

Despite being the fastest driver through the Dalby Forest, Stig Blomqvist had to settle for second place behind the brown Escort with its cream signwriting. It was an excellent win, the second in succession for Makinen and Henry Liddon, and it was in keeping with what was regarded as a successful liaison between the RAC and Lombard.

Since John Davenport had been able to get on with his journalistic duties sooner than expected, thanks to Hannu Mikkola's early retirement, he was able to watch the organisation at work from a different angle. He summed up the event in *Autosport*:

> It is an organisational marathon calling into its organisation thousands of dedicated and interested people who do everything from marshal on a hilltop in Wales to compute the results in York. As well as the workers from the RAC, there are those connected with the sponsors, Lombard North Central, who did an excellent job of promoting the rally, those from Centrefile who helped to compute the results, those from the City of York and its motor club who did so much to make the start and finish a roaring success. And, most important of all, the spark of genius that ignited all this and came from somewhere between Jim Porter and Jack Kemsley. All these people were rewarded with a rally that ran virtually without problems and gave a clear, unequivocal result.'

The Lombard RAC Rally of Great Britain had successfully entered a new phase. Sponsorship would ensure its survival; cars like the Lancia Stratos would provide ingredients of an equally high quality. In the meantime, we were not yet done with the Escort. Not by any means.

Different Body; Same Results

It seemed they were trying to confuse poor Billy. In April 1975, Ford entered two of their Mark 2 Escorts in the Granite City Rally for Roger Clark and Billy Coleman. This was the first competition appearance of the latest bodyshell, complete with flared wheel arches and aerodynamic spoilers. The floor pan and the running gear were identical to the original Escort. The only difference was in the weight and its distribution. That, and the rearrangement of the minor controls inside. After a few miles of this top quality national rally, Coleman wistfully told co-driver John Davenport that if he didn't get the hang of the indicators soon, no one would know which way he was going on the special stages!

There was no problem with the car, however, as Clark and Coleman finished first and third respectively and it seemed Ford had just the tool to defend themselves against the might of Fiat, Alpine and Lancia on the international scene. Overall, though, Ford had reduced their programme to the extent of missing the Monte Carlo and the Safari rallies in the cause of what was seen as cautious economy.

Ford, it turned out, were not alone in giving the Monte a miss. The Monegasques planned the longest route seen for many a year in response to what they thought were the wishes of the private entrants. Whoever conducted the survey was wide of the mark, as a mere 96 starters (only two of them British) were to prove and it was clear that nobody was in favour of motoring around Europe for four days before getting down to the rally proper. And when the event did get under way, Sandro Munari, soon to become the sole representative of Lancia, stamped his authority on the rally to take a brilliant win, his second in succession.

The championship structure, with the emphasis on the constructors rather than the drivers, remained the same. Lancia carried off the title and, although Maurizio Verini earned enough points to become the European champion, Munari was generally considered to be the top driver. His all-round ability was confirmed when he nursed the Stratos (at one point without rear bodywork) into second place on the Safari Rally. A greater contrast in events could not be found.

The Safari, run entirely in Kenya due to political problems in Tanzania and Uganda, was won by the Peugeot 505 of Ove Andersson; but by leading several times before dropping to third place with gearbox trouble, Bjorn Waldegaard underlined the value of intense development work on the Stratos. With drivers of such standing, backed by a capable and enthusiastic team (many of the suspension modifications had been carried out by the former Ferrari Grand Prix driver, Michael Parkes), it was not surprising that they should win four events and finish second once.

It should be said, however, that Lancia were aided in part by Fiat not making full use of their driving potential; namely, Hannu Mikkola and Markku Alen. Mikkola took a Fiat Abarth 124 Spyder into second place on the Monte but he drove the uncomplicated Peugeot 504 to victory in the extremely rough Moroccan Rally and, by the time the Lombard RAC Rally came round, he was already working with Toyota, for whom he would drive in 1976.

As for Alen, he was not impressed by Fiat's decision to miss the British round of the championship and the Finn insisted that they send a car. Otherwise, he said, he would be open to offers. Such was Markku's enthusiasm for the RAC Rally, but it was an ardour which would cool with the passing of time and the accumulation of experience. In the meantime, Alen had increased his bargaining power by winning the Portuguese Rally in the same year that another promising young driver, Walter Rohrl, had also scored his maiden championship victory, the lanky German claiming the Acropolis Rally at the wheel of an Opel Ascona.

Alen's entry in the RAC Rally – driving an Abarth 124 Spyder of course – formed a major item in the pre-event publicity, of which there was an abundance thanks to Lombard's efforts and the setting up of a more professional press and public relations exercise. *The Observer* Business News devoted a full page to discussing the financial and commercial aspects of the rally and the Sunday paper summarised their investigation as follows:

> Whether all the cash that is poured in is more or less cost effective than any other means of promotion nobody can really tell. But it certainly adds up to a mammoth publicity exercise by dozens of companies – and they can't all be money frittering fools. Not in 1975.

Given, too, the rather depressed state of international rallying in general, 250 starters was a mark of the rally's reputation, as the editorial in *Autosport* confirmed:

> The event is now synonymous with the best rally drivers and cars in the world, and in global terms it ranks perhaps alongside the Safari as *the* coveted and prestigious competition in which a manufacturer can participate.

Manufacturers clearly endorsed that remark with entries from Ford (230 bhp Escorts for Clark, Makinen and another rising Scandinavian star, Ari Vatanen); Saab (175 bhp 96s for Blomqvist and Eklund); Lancia (250 bhp – minimum! – Stratos for Waldegaard and Munari, a Beta Coupe for Lampinen); Fiat (200 bhp Abarth 124 Spyder for Alen); Toyota (a new organisation with 240 bhp Celica GTs for Ove Andersson – who was also running the team – and Mikkola); Opel (220 bhp Kadetts for Rohrl, Aaltonen, Kullang and a British Dealer Opel Team example for Tony Pond); Datsun (Violets for Kallstrom and Klient) and a British Leyland Dolomite Sprint for Brian Culcheth, the official return of the British firm having been announced a few weeks before.

The plan to bring the rally to a much wider audience continued apace with a number of spectator stages included in a loop which would bring competitors back to York for an overnight halt after a mere nine hours of motoring. The second loop, lasting 45 hours, ventured into the south-west for the first time in many years, a special stage at the delightfully-named Cricket St Thomas, near Chard, Somerset, providing the turning point for the run north towards the forests of Wales. The handicap associated with the route spreading south was a heavy pruning of the Scottish stages on the final 24-hour run to the north of York, but even so Jim Porter had included 72 special stages and the route changes meant that many stages which had been run at night in the past would now be tackled in daylight, and vice versa.

As an aid to the quicker cars, the results from the opening stages would be used to compute the re-start order from York. This classifica-tion would end complaints from fast drivers who had been seeded behind slow ones; now their performances in the first and second legs could move them up the order. On the other hand, it remained to be seen what a top seed's reaction might be should a puncture or some such delay find him languishing halfway down the running order at the re-start.

In practice, there was a major reshuffle to the running order at York although this was due to retirements more than anything else. The weather, which remained clear and rather cold, could not be blamed. The breakages appeared to be caused by the pace set by Ford as rivals attempted to keep in touch with Makinen. The Escort may have been basic in concept when compared with the Lancia, but it was well-engineered and thoroughly tested. Clark, on the other hand, was to have an appalling rally due to a variety of mechanical problems, com-pounded by a brush with a pile of logs in the Kielder Forest, and he showed great tenacity by climbing back to take second place, the Cossack-sponsored Escort finishing just over a minute behind Makinen's car carrying the colours of the Allied Polymer Group.

By the time it reached the finish, Makinen's car also carried a consider-able amount of plastic padding and the prayers of the driver and his navigator, Henry Liddon. They had been plagued by a leaking sump during most of the final leg but the temporary repairs held out. In any case, Makinen couldn't afford to hang about since he had spent the entire rally being harried by either Waldegaard or the remarkable Blomqvist. Indeed, at the second overnight halt, the Saab – having been modified by a seemingly inevitable roll in a forest, this time on the Clipstone stage – was just two minutes behind Makinen but Stig's remarkable run was eventually cut short by a broken crankshaft on the Whinlatter stage near Bassenthwaite Lake.

Looking at the special stage times, it is difficult to understand why Waldegaard did not win by a country mile. The Stratos was fastest on more than 40 stages but, most of the time, Waldegaard was making up for a costly drive-shaft failure at Clipstone and, in the end, he was ruled out for having exceeded the time limit as a result of repairs to the transmission. It was a huge anticlimax for the Swede as he reached the finish with the rear of the Alitalia sponsored car tied on with wire and string – the result of a hairy moment in Kielder.

Indeed, the second leg of the rally had got off to a bad start in Sutton Park when the Stratos ground to a halt after ford water penetrated the electrics. Pentti Airikkala and John Davenport had been delayed in their Vauxhall Magnum Coupe for similar reasons and Davenport recalls the efforts made to dry out the engine:

'Before we left York, I had bought a copy of the *Sunday Times*, not because I intended to read it in the middle of the special stages you understand, but because, being an inquisitive journalist, I wanted to know what was happening in the world and I intended to browse through it in a quiet moment. When the car spluttered to a halt, we had to use my paper to try and dry the engine out and I can tell you that the *Sunday Times* did not use paper with a high rate of absorption!'

Ari Vatanen discovered that British trees could eat rally cars whole when he left the road while driving flat out in fifth gear on the Clipstone stage. He was lying sixth at the time and the accident cut short not only his rally but also a valuable source of information for Independent Radio News who were backing the Escort in return for live coverage of the event from Vatanen's co-driver, Peter Bryant.

Ford, however, were well represented, the semi-private Escort of Tony Fowkes and Bryan Harris taking an excellent third place after a superb battle with the similar car of Russell Brookes, destined to be one of no less than 146 retirements.

The organisers were not without their problems either, an unnamed gent conveniently rolled a Course Car on the Sutton Park stage, and Cesare Fiorio, apart from fighting Waldegaard's exclusion, had discussions with the Stewards over Munari completing one lap too many at Oliver's Mount. The arguments were to be become more or less irrelevant when Munari, having worked his way back to fifth, went off on a notorious right-hand bend in Dovey.

Apart from giving Timo Makinen and Henry Liddon a hat-trick, the 1975 Lombard RAC rally was not considered to be a classic. It did, however, allow the RAC an opportunity to show a continuing improvement in their organisational skills, which John Davenport noted in his *Autosport* report when he concluded:

Certainly, the organisers of the RAC Rally, from Dean Delamont, Jack Kemsley, Jim Porter, Neil Eason-Gibson and Sue Winwood down to the humblest marshal in the wettest and darkest forest can pat themselves on the back for running an excellent rally. Considering the difficulties of running such a big event nationwide and of standardising procedures, it went off remarkably well. The only difficult thing is to find a way of making it even better for 1976 for it sets such high standards already.

7

THE PRICE OF FAME

Going West

JOHN DAVENPORT was right; the 1975 Lombard RAC Rally did prove to be a difficult act to follow, although this had little to do with a move from York to Bath.

Initially, there had been a marked reluctance to leave York after four successful and enjoyable years. Relationships had been forged; the city seemed to be at one with rallying and the demands of the sport's gregarious if rather motley crew. Gerry Phillips, writing in *Motor Sport*, summed up the association between the two:

> The rally circus and its multi-national entourage of many tastes, languages and customs took to York like bards to the Gorsedd. (Mr Phillips is Welsh!). It seemed that traffic jams would fray the tempers of those finding themselves held up during the simple journeys from hotel to garage, but it wasn't like that at all. There was hardly any inconvenience, there were hotels to suit all tastes, there was an ideal place in the race course for scrutiny/start/finish and the townsfolk seemed eager to do everything possible to make the visitors' stay as pleasant as it could be. Indeed, the rally people were more than just the tourists to which the city is accustomed, and after four years at York there are many friendships which will survive the test of time. Garage owners went out of their way to provide whatever facility the visitors wanted, whilst hoteliers just about gave open houses, altering their routines and schedules to meet the irregular requirements of visitors.

York was also notable for the introduction of a 'Help' service, provided by the local motor club. This was precisely what it said, the local enthusiasts taking it upon themselves to provide not just information but free taxi services for competitors and officials, a reception centre for messages and the procuring of unusual items at all hours of the day and night.

Bath Motor Club carried on the good work in 1976 and their efforts helped to ease the switch from Yorkshire to Somerset. Certainly, there were to be few complaints about the venue and this was due in part to the preparatory work carried out by John Davenport and Joe Hawkins, a local member of the CID who also happened to be a rally enthusiast.

Pentti Airikkala and
Mike Greasley: in tune
with the British forests
throughout 1976.

Hawkins took four weeks holiday to help smooth the way by opening doors which otherwise might have remained firmly barred. Pockets of hostility were spotted and eliminated by Hawkins and the cooperation of the police was almost guaranteed when it was arranged for Hannu Mikkola to take one of the local Chief Superintendents around the Bagshot in a works Toyota. The officer, by all accounts, came away a changed man and fully in favour of rallying . . .

John Davenport's involvement came about through a change of vocation which saw him leave the navigator's seat for a cumfy chair in the offices of the RAC Motor Sport Division in London's Belgrave Square. He was not allowed to sit still for long. Having lived not far from Bath, Davenport was immediately given responsibility for looking after the rally from the moment competitors arrived until they left the city. And, to add to the logistical problems, there would be a night-halt in Bath between the two 36-hour legs, the first running north to the Scottish border, the second looping through the West Country before criss-crossing Wales and returning to Bath after 1,900 miles of motoring.

There were reservations about the route itself since there would be a 'mere' 370 stage miles spread across 75 stages and linked by lengthy road sections. Doubts were creeping in over the absence of elements which had given the rally its reputation as one of the most gruelling events on the calendar.

It did not affect the entry, 200 starters leaving Bath on the Saturday morning. Spectators stages dominated the run towards Yorkshire and, by the rest halt at York, a privately-entered Ford Escort, crewed by Pentti Airikkala and Mike Greasley, was leading.

As they entered the Dalby forest, Roger Clark and Stuart Pegg in the Cossack-sponsored works Escort, had begun to move forward to challenge the Finn, but in the difficult terrain of the Kielder Forest Airikkala rattled off a string of fast times. When they reached Kirkbride, Airikkala led Clark by just under two minutes, an advantage which had been extended further by the time they returned to Bath. Greasley, having partnered Airikkala during the British championship, was neither surprised nor unduly worried about the pace of his driver:

'He was as safe as houses and yet he destroyed the opposition from Day One. Pentti was in top form since he had been driving in the British forests all season and, really, we couldn't believe how easy it was.'

Searching for a story, the press latched on to the fact that Airikkala was seen running Dunlop tyres on various stages even though he was supposed to be using Avon products. This was the period when Dunlop were developing their 'A2' tyre which, in simple terms, was based on a compound used in motor racing. The relatively smooth tread of the Dunlop tyre confounded all predictions by providing excellent grip on the rough forest stages, yet it was not prone to frequent punctures.

Dunlop's new product had been introduced at the previous year's RAC Rally and played a major part in helping Makinen score his hat-trick. If Airikkala was to win this rally, then he felt he had no option but to use the Dunlop tyres even though his car carried heavy identification with another brand. There was much muttering among the Avon hierarchy. Greasley's only recollection, seen through the mists of diplomacy and time, is that 'once it got dark, I'd say we were definitely on Dunlops!'

Airikkala was to have problems of a more serious nature following the re-start. As he tackled the stages in the West Country, a misfire at high revs led to a long halt where the electrics and various components were changed, but to no avail. Worse still, confusion over a route change and the location of the check-in at Weston-Super-Mare meant Greasley was something like five seconds over the maximum time allowed when he rushed into the control.

With the strong possibility of exclusion hanging over their heads, an appeal was lodged immediately and Airikkala kept motoring. By the time he reached Llandudno on a miserably wet and windy Tuesday morning, the Escort was officially declared over the permitted time limit but, believing the appeal, based on very solid ground, would be upheld, Airikkala continued.

Bearing in mind the possible embarrassment over the precise brand of tyre which had been used and the inevitable uncertainty over the appeal had they finished first, perhaps it was fortuitous that clutch trouble should intervene, the Escort refusing to leave the line at the start of a stage. The subsequent service work meant they were unquestionably over the time limit no matter what.

'We were drunk before we got back to Bath,' jokes Greasley. 'We'd had tremendous support from everyone, particularly from other competitors. I remember, when the clutch trouble started and we couldn't even climb a hill on the way out of Machynlleth, Barry Lee tucked his car in behind ours and gave us a push.

'Of course it was disappointing, particularly as we were to learn unofficially that we had excellent ground for appeal. But, all things considered, perhaps that clutch trouble was a merciful relief. If we had been first back to Bath then the whatsit would really have hit the fan . . .'

The retirement/exclusion of the David Sutton-prepared car left the way clear for the works Escort of Roger Clark to take a most popular victory. Unlike the previous year, Clark had no major problems with the car. While it was clear he could not catch Airikkala, Clark was kept busy fending off the remarkable Stig Blomqvist in the new Saab 99 EMS. On the final morning, Blomqvist had reduced the gap to a mere 18 seconds after coping with high winds, rain and patches of ice in the Clocaenog and Penmachno forests.

Then, two punctures in one stage (which was followed almost immediately by yet another stage) put paid to his efforts and he concentrated on defending his position from Bjorn Waldegaard who, to the consternation of Lancia, was keeping Sandro Munari out of third place.

Lancia were miffed since, shortly before the rally, they had scratched Waldegaard's entry, the result of a fit of Italian pique over the Swede's decision to move to Ford for 1977. When they learned of the hurried withdrawal of the Stratos, Ford and Waldegaard made contact and the Swede expressed his interest in a drive on the RAC. Although it meant the hasty preparation of a car, Ford were more than happy to oblige.

It was indeed fortunate that the Ford bow had been strengthened by another entry because Ari Vatanen, the recently crowned British champion, developed engine trouble which led to his retirement in Yorkshire. That might have been almost acceptable had Ford not already lost Makinen, executing an uncharacteristic roll at Speech House on the second stage. The shock to the rear axle, which prompted the eventual failure of the differential, was almost as profound as the jolt to system of the previously unchallenged master of the event.

The unexpected departure of the number one seed had taken some of the pressure off Airikkala, but by the time he reached York the Finn was aware of a surprising performance by Tony Pond and his TR7.

A British season, hamstrung by mechanical shortcomings, did not place the Leyland car among the favourites to earn a high placing but, by York, Pond was in third place, seven seconds behind Airikkala. His challenge and the patriotic response from the massive crowds thronging the forests ended in Kielder when the red, white and blue car hit a large rock and dropped Pond and co-driver Dave Richards from contention.

A Hint of Trouble to Come

Kielder, with its boulder-strewn surfaces, came in for criticism and the generally poor condition of the forest complex was exacerbated by the rally turning south without using the more suitable tracks in the forests of southern Scotland. This was dictated by the need to return to Bath and, in general, the organisers were taken to task for the excessive road mileage linking what were considered to be short stages.

Chris Lord, firing a particularly heavy broadside from the columns of the specialist press, condemned the poor organisation. The 1976 Group One champion had this to say during an interview:

> The rally, even more than any other, should be run for competitors. In my book, there are sponsors, organisers, spectators and competitors in the rally business. On the RAC Rally, competitors were last on the list of priorities. In fact we [competitors] seemed to be running the event for everyone else. Rallying certainly needs 'Mickey Mouse' [spectator] stages to fill the coffers, but any contact between organisers and competitors was purely coincidental. At one point we were asked to do 350 road miles for a return of 14 miles of stages. Only the RAC Rally could get away with this state of affairs. We received long-winded, nondescript mumblings as a response to constructive criticism – I'd like to see them leave their gin and tonics and second-hand opinions back at the plush hotels and come out for a looksee.

Lord's typically outspoken comments may have ruffled a few well-preened feathers; some of his points may have been verging on the offensive but the main thrust of his argument could not be denied. Other competitors had voiced similar misgivings and the RAC took note.

Perhaps not unnaturally however, Clark had few complaints or, if he did, they have mellowed with the passing years.

'There may have been problems with the route, I can't remember for sure. I mean, anything can be improved if you look hard enough. As far as I was concerned, this was the rally which had been set by the organisers and you got on with it. Maybe the road mileage was a bit long here and there but it was probably better to have that than have some stupid "Mickey Mouse" stages dropped in the middle just to fill the time in.

'I do remember that it was a busy old rally. The '72 event had been a straight fight between Stig and myself and that was one hell of a good race. In '76, it was a bit messy up at the front; three or four of us all jockeying for position.

'The plus point about rallying for Ford at the time was that I would have one mechanic allocated to me for the whole year. Obviously, you bring others in when you are busy, but a chap called Norman Masters

Roger Clark and Stuart Pegg in 1976: 'a busy old rally'.

used to build my car full time. Therefore I knew exactly how the car was going to be. He knew exactly what I wanted. I could even get to the start of a rally and he would have set the lights exactly as I needed them; seat belts how I needed them and so on. It was a terrific combination. Throughout the years I was with Ford, I never had a problem which could be put down to hands and fingers . . .'

Complaints aside, Clark's result made the rally seem a resounding success and, fortunately, the move to Bath was otherwise perceived as a good one.

The media had been enticed by the blandishments of Lombard and their slick press and public relations team, led by the abrasive, but highly efficient, Nick Brittan. The rally received excellent coverage in print and on radio and television, but such welcome exposure was to backfire on the organisers when a car left the road in the Speech House stage and ploughed into ill-advised spectators who had taken it upon themselves to stand across an escape road which was located just after a blind brow.

During the following weeks correspondence columns were filled with the views of spectators and officials alike, each blaming the other. Whatever the reason for the incident, the competitor, Heinz-Walter Schewe, could not be held responsible. The fact that there were no fatal injuries was seen as an important warning of what was to come if the rally continued to produce such a rapid growth in popularity. The dramatic treatment of the German champion's Porsche Carrera ploughing into the crowd as a foretaste of how Fleet Street would react when faced with a story which could literally stop rallying in its tracks. The bonhomie and old pals' act would go straight out the window. This would be front page news and would be treated accordingly.

The national dailies, however, continued to pay scant regard to international rallying once it departed from Britain. True, there had been a line or two of coverage for the Monte, although attempts by the organisers to cut costs for the 'privateer' by introducing a 'one tyre' formula merely served to confuse. Certainly, it helped Lancia who opted (and this had to be done before the event started) for a Pirelli P7 tyre which, as it turned out, proved ideal for the conditions and allowed the Italians to dominate. Roger Clark finished an excellent fifth and, when asked if it was possible to defeat the Stratos one-two-three, was heard to remark: 'Take their wheels off – it's the only way.'

Certainly, Lancia were only defeated on outright endurance events or those run entirely on snow and ice and they carried off the manufacturer's title yet again with Sandro Munari being generally regarded as the unofficial champion. Lancia, in fact, were only bothered by Opel and this was largely through the consistent results achieved by private entries rather than a concentrated team effort.

At the end of the year, though, everyone was trounced by Ford on the Lombard RAC Rally. It may have been the only win in the world championship for the British team, but they chose one of the most prestigious events on which to exercise their authoratative team-work and back-up. In the year ahead, however, Ford were to discover that technical and driving brilliance alone would be no match against a Fiat steamroller powered by sackfuls of lire.

Little and Large

Ari Vatanen gave panel-beating a new dimension in 1977. His first experience of the international season left a trail of cars wrecked by a mixture of exhuberance and inexperience. It did not make a positive contribution to the Boreham effort but, on the other hand, Ford did not exactly help themselves at a time when they should have pushed Fiat aside as the Italians got to grips with their latest car, the 131 Abarth Mirafiori.

Strangely enough, Ford's limited resources and Fiat's sledgehammer approach made for superb competition throughout a year when the FIA's preoccupation with the manufacturers continued to diminish the importance of the drivers and, as a result, rallying as a whole. And for good measure, the championship scoring system could only be contemplated by those possessing a degree in mathematics and a deep understanding of French logic.

Although the 131 was not particularly nimble on loose surfaces, Fiat won five events. Ford, though, had the upper hand, particularly when a relatively unknown driver, Kyosti Hämäläinen, took a brilliant win on the 1000 Lakes in Finland. This victory in Hämäläinen's home country was perhaps not surprising when his dedication to the task became known. The 32-year-old was not averse to heading off, perhaps three times a week, to put three or four hours of driving under his belt as he learnt the highly specialised and very fast terrain which made up most of the rally. Furthermore, the Finn had no need of pace notes and his extraordinary affinity with the loose surfaces meant his works Escort led half of the rally.

It was a splendid win for Ford but they let the momentum tail away rather than gather speed. In the face of a massive entry by Fiat, Ford sent just two cars to Canada for the *Criterium de Quebec*. Roger Clark was beaten into second place by an inspired Simo Lampinen (one of five Fiat drivers), but more significant perhaps was the first win outside Finland for a bespectacled young driver who, eight years later, would dominate the championship. His name was Timo Salonen.

Quite what name the mechanics at Boreham chose to call poor Vatanen when he crashed on the San Remo Rally has not been recorded. This was another disastrous weekend for Ford (despite superhuman efforts by Waldegaard), Fiat then adding further to their points advantage by taking victory in New Zealand as Australasia joined the championship structure.

Fiat: champions in 1977.

Bjorn's Triple Crown

By the time the Lombard RAC Rally came around in November, Fiat had won the championship. The driver of the year, however, was considered to be Bjorn Waldegaard, thanks to wins on both the Acropolis and Safari rallies. He was about to add yet another classic to his portfolio of victories.

It was clear that the RAC had taken note of criticisms. The route incorporated several detail changes, most of which were for the benefit of the competitors. In the light of the accident in the Forest of Dean the previous year, however, the spectators had not been forgotten either. The first day would be spent almost entirely on stages where the enthusiasts could be controlled more readily and, to cut down the peak-viewing period as it were, the rally would start on Sunday rather than Saturday. Jim Porter:

'When I first became involved in 1972, they had just started to use stately homes and public parks on a limited scale. It soon became obvious that the thing to do was to start the rally on a Sunday and fill the day with spectator stages. Okay, we had the inevitable complaints from drivers about these so-called "Mickey Mouse" stages – but, in return, we got upwards of 100,000 paying spectators. And, if the drivers stopped to think for a minute, it did their sponsors as much good as it did the rally itself.'

As a means of accommodating these stages while catering for spectators in the southern half of England, the rally started from Wembley and then moved north to make York the rally headquarters for the remaining four days. It was then that the competitors' real work would begin and it would become apparent that this was an altogether tighter and tougher event.

The ten stages on Sunday may have measured a mere 35 miles but there followed the promise of 12 miles in Dovey, 19 miles through Hafren and 45 miles on the Brechfa West stage before returning to York on the Tuesday night. Wednesday and Thursday had such joys as the 16 miles of Grizedale 2, in the Lake District, as competitors made their way towards southern Scotland. Then, the final agony of more than 60 miles spread across three stages in the Kielder Forest followed by familiar territory in Yorkshire. In all, there would be 460 miles contained within 68 special stages, 32 of which would be run in daylight.

The Sunday stages may have been tedious for the competitors but, of course, there was the media coverage to think about (always intense on the first day) plus the fact that the results from the first three stages would determine the re-start order from York the following morning. (The cut-off point, after just 11 miles of tarmac motoring, was necessary simply to allow time to notify competitors when they arrived in York later that evening.)

This, in fact, was part of a modified timing system which was generally well-received. It also assisted with the compiling of results which, for the first time, were being handled by an NCR computer located in the rally headquarters and dedicated exclusively to the event.

On Sunday Evening, the NCR machine revealed that Hannu Mikkola's Toyota was leading Pentti Airikkala's Chevette by four seconds. Lurking a further four seconds behind the Vauxhall, however, was Bjorn Waldegaard in his British Airways-sponsored Ford Escort. Over a minute behind, and lying in seventh place, the Fiat 131 of Markku Alen but, during the stages in north Wales, Alen set consistently fast times to follow Waldegaard to the top of the leader board. Really into his stride now, Alen recorded the fastest time to shave 20 seconds off Waldegaard on the nine-mile Pantperthog stage and, at the end of it, they were separated by 38 seconds. It was as close as anyone would get to the Swede during the 1,633-mile rally after a broken oil pipe in the middle of the Hafren stage led to Alen's eventual retirement.

This left Waldegaard with some breathing space but he almost lost the lot by spinning on a downhill right-hander near the end of the 11-mile Cwmhenog stage. Bjorn was not alone in his embarrassment and at least he had come to no harm. The same icy, adverse-camber corner was to catch out several drivers, notably Timo Makinen and Ari Vatanen as they rolled their respective Fiat and Escort cars out of places in the top six.

Waldegaard's only serious problem turned out to be a nut which seized on the stud during a wheel change in Kielder. This was eventually cured, but not before Bjorn had been forced to complete a stage with only three nuts holding a rear wheel in place. It provided a tense moment or two for the service crew, not to mention Waldegaard and his co-driver Hans Thorszelius, since Hannu Mikkola was no more than a couple of minutes behind in his Celica GT.

Bjorn Waldegaard led Ford's domination of the top six places in 1977.

Driving at the top of his form – and perhaps buoyed by the agreement he had signed to drive for Ford in 1978 – the Finn set the fastest time on all three stages in Kielder, taking no less than a minute off Waldegaard.

At the end of the rally, however, Waldegaard had set the fastest time on 25 stages to win by over two minutes. The Scandinavians had been untouchable although, had it not been for a series of mechanical disasters on the first two days, Russell Brookes might have been able to reduce the margin of eight minutes between himself and Mikkola. As it was, Brookes was second in the 'Fastest on Stage' league, the Escort being quickest through 15 stages.

As ever, Brookes's performance was seen by one or two Europeans as the obvious benefit of a local driver's knowledge in an event where pace notes and reconnaissance were forbidden. There may have been a grain of truth in that but Bjorn Waldegaard, who had not competed on a single mile of Forestry Commission land since the previous year's RAC Rally, shattered the argument by leading from the minute the rally entered the forests of Snowdonia. On the first stage at Beddgelert, to the west of Blaenau Ffestiniog, he was 21 seconds faster than anyone else. He never looked back. And Ford, with five of the first six places, never looked better.

8

THE ESCORT'S FINAL FLOURISH

Ford Go Private

THE SEQUENCE RAN: Harrogate, York, London, York, Bath – then Birmingham. There was mild disbelief when Britain's second-largest city was revealed as the headquarters for the 1978 Lombard RAC Rally. The Midlands in November did not conjure attractive images and Birmingham was not exactly noted for its Roman influences but, in the event, the city and in particular, the Holiday Inn, fitted the bill admirably.

The only complaints seemed to focus on the failure to provide a compact social life. When the crews and service personnel returned to base for the two night halts, they went to ground among the concrete flyovers. Mind you, the tight schedules meant few people felt inclined to live it up by the time they returned from the depths of Northumbria and Yorkshire.

The first day, Sunday, was the usual cocktail of spectator stages; Bewdley, Weston Park, Trentham Gardens, Alton Towers, Sutton Park, Stow Mill (better known as Bardon Quarry) and Donington. Then, two 36-hour loops. The first encompassed Yorkshire, Kielder, the Scottish borders and the Lake District; the second took in Wales before finishing at Birmingham's National Exhibition Centre on Thursday afternoon.

Bearing in mind Ford's record on the RAC Rally, it was not surprising to find the specialist press tipping Boreham to carry off their seventh win in succession. But there were mitigating factors.

First, Ford had not enjoyed a good year in the world series even though Bjorn Waldegaard and Hannu Mikkola kicked off with a splendid one-two in Sweden. Fiat, now combining their forces with Lancia, set the pace throughout by scoring a total of six wins and, indeed, they seemed to be the only team with a serious development programme.

Second, Ford were in the grip of a strike. Due to a closed shop agreement, the mechanics at Boreham had heeded a strike call by the AUEW (Associated Union of Engineering Workers) five weeks before the start of the rally and it soon became clear that Ford would be forced to forget about the cars which were under preparation and look elsewhere. It turned out to be a mammoth task for Peter Ashcroft and Charles Reynolds at Boreham.

Markku Alen and the
Stratos: beaten yet again
in 1978.

The works drivers were released from their contracts in order that they could drive for Ford dealers who would prepare cars and provide service. Waldegaard would drive an Escort prepared by Thomas Motors of Blackpool; Mikkola's car would be worked on by David Sutton who, as a matter of course, was dealing with Vatanen's Marlboro-backed Escort, and Haynes of Maidstone made up yet another dealer team with two cars for Clark and John Taylor. Ford management personnel, who were not on strike, would have the task of overseeing the operation, which also included an Escort for Russell Brookes. It was an ideal plan – in theory. But it had been hurriedly put together. Could everyone cope?

If anything, the Ford effort turned out to be overrun, with too many pairs of willing hands coming to the aid of the party. It was a 'Dealer Team' in the true sense of the word and navigators spoke of rolling to a halt in a service area and before they had opened the door, the car had been raised, back and front, and work was under way. Indeed, at one stage strict lines of demarcation had to be drawn lest this over-enthusiasm saw a car leave service without fuel or new tyres; each willing helper believing the job had been completed by someone else. And, as the rally progressed, there were rumours of service vans nipping in and out of Boreham under cover of darkness.

Ford were up against Lancia, who provided Alen and Munari with a Stratos each, and Fiat, with a 131 Abarth for Rohrl. Alen, who was seen as the unofficial world champion, had asked for a Stratos since he genuinely believed he could beat the Fords on their home ground. The 131 Abarth was okay if the driver had pace notes and could keep the power fully applied, but the Stratos had winning potential even though it was more difficult to drive.

There was quite a stir during scrutineering at British Car Auctions when the Fiat was wheeled in with the co-driver's seat mounted in the back. In an attempt to improve rear-wheel traction, the seat had been positioned in the right-hand rear corner (the car was left-hand drive of course) during testing but if was found that this upset the handling. By placing the seat in the centre and pointing it slightly to the right to accommodate Rohrl's co-driver, Christian Giestdorfer, an improvement in stage times was expected. Giestdorfer, meanwhile, was not advised to take a heavy breakfast . . .

Fiat's logic could not be questioned on the first day when heavy rain made the going very slippery. Indeed, after Weston Park, the rally was led by the Ford Escort of the young British driver Graham Elsmore but, by the time the competitors had returned to Birmingham, Alen led Rohrl by 17 seconds, with Waldegaard, followed closely by Mikkola, a further 50 seconds adrift. Ford were not unduly worried. The serious business was not due to start until around 5 pm on Monday as the cars entered Wykeham, Staindale and Dalby in Yorkshire.

Mikkola was quickest through Wykeham; Alen and Mikkola were joint fastest at Staindale; Mikkola was fastest by 10 seconds at Dalby 1; Alen had the advantage at Dalby 2 but Mikkola was 14 seconds clear of the Stratos at Dalby 3. The battle was well and truly joined.

Slowly but surely, Mikkola whittled down Alen's advantage. By the time they reached Kielder in the early hours of Tuesday morning, the Lancia driver's lead was less than a minute. The Kielder complex consisted of five stages; Mikkola was fastest on all five. On the first, measuring 15 miles, he took 64 seconds off Alen and the Escort was 67 seconds faster over the next 19 miles. By the time they reached the service area near the village of Byrness, the damage had been done. Alen was a beaten man and he knew it.

Any hopes of a revival by Alen were to be shattered in the Twiglees stage, near Lockerbie, when the Stratos rolled to a halt with a broken gearbox. This left Mikkola with a lead of over seven minutes from Waldegaard, who was comfortably ahead of Rohrl and Giestdorfer, the poor navigator feeling as though he was attached to the end of an automotive pendulum.

With the pressure removed from the leaders, attention switched to Tony Pond as the Englishman enjoyed an energetic last fling with BL cars. Having announced his imminent departure to Chrysler, Pond was hurling the heavy TR7, now with a lusty V8 engine, through the stages to record a succession of top six times. This was to make up for a mechanical disaster at Trentham Gardens on Sunday when a broken handbrake caliper had jammed the right-rear wheel solid. Despite the best efforts of navigator Fred Gallagher, the car refused to move and, when it finally broke free and shot off (without Gallagher!), the time spent on subsequent repairs cost them dearly.

Pond, however, was not to be in the limelight on Wednesday as competitors began the final run towards Wales. On the very first stage at Burwarton, a fortuitously-placed television camera caught Russell

Brookes clipping a gatepost. Viewers were then treated to Andy Dawson going one better as he hit the post a mighty thump with the rear of his Datsun Violet. Then, for the finale, Roger Clark did a proper job, the Esso-sponsored Escort performing a neat roll before landing on its roof. In mid-flight, Neil Wilson's road book had sailed through the window. The co-driver would have no further need of it. Clark remembers the incident well!

'The stage basically ran through fields on a farm road and these were farm gates. We came over a crest, into an easy right and then the gate was on a very easy left, with a little kick out actually at the gate itself.

'I changed down and the circlip, which held the clutch slave cylinder to the bell-housing, broke and came off. The clutch went to the floor, I missed a gear and the gate post was bent over quite nicely to form a super launching ramp. Up we went!

'The car wasn't badly damaged – it had just flattened its top – and it was quite driveable. But, with no clutch and a very high bottom gear, we couldn't get the damned thing started. We tried all sorts, but without a clutch it's very difficult to bump-start a car. You're knackered . . .'

Walter Rohrl, driving with what would turn out to be a broken wrist after hitting a rock on the Dalby stage, was overhauled by Pond, who now had Brookes and third place in his sights. Pond set the fastest time on the first two stages in the Clocaenog Forest but, as the night wore on, a leaking head gasket meant that he and Gallagher were merely hoping for a result since they had no time in hand for servicing. At the finish, they were over four minutes behind the consistent Brookes, who had been either first or second fastest on no less than twelve stages since leaving Birmingham on the Wednesday morning. And this after Brookes had suffered an eye injury before the start of the event.

As for Mikkola, he maintained the seven-minute advantage over Waldegaard to give the Eaton's Yale-supported Fords a handsome victory. The Swede had set fastest time on 21 of the 76 stages. Mikkola, on the other hand, had dominated 30 of them as he set a pace which no one could match. It was his first victory on the RAC Rally and, after such a faultless performance, it was clear that he now had the measure of the event.

Finding his way around the British forests for the first time, a 22-year-old Finn showed exceptional promise by finishing ninth in a Chrysler Sunbeam. We would hear more about Henri Toivonen, perhaps sooner than expected.

First and Last

'The RAC Rally is the most important rally for me to win. I have been training, keeping fit, getting myself ready to win the rally. Ford have won this rally seven times in a row and I would like to end that. The whole team thinks this. Ford has won too many times and we would like to kill that.' – Markku Alen, speaking after the 1978 Lombard RAC Rally.

Alen felt much the same way 12 months later. A measure of his obsession with the RAC Rally was the persuasion of the Lancia/Fiat management to dust down their sole-surviving Stratos in order that Alen would have the best possible chance of winning in the forests of Britain.

Lancia, in fact, were hard-pressed to find enough parts to make the car serviceable. That is not to say they had severed all connections with this splendid machine, but a re-structuring of the competition programme for 1979 saw a drastic reduction in the factory effort by both Lancia and Fiat on an international basis. The Stratos did win the Monte Carlo, San Remo and Corsican rallies, but in private hands. Fiat enjoyed just one victory – the 1000 Lakes, with the 131 Abarth – and all in all the rally effort from Turin was a shadow of its former self.

All of which played into the hands of Ford. For the first time in 12 years of rallying with the Escort, Ford carried off the manufacturer's title. And then, in September 1979, they decided to withdraw from the international scene at the end of the year.

This was an appropriate summary of a period of uncertainty in rallying. New regulations would come into force in 1982 and, in the meantime, development began to grind to a standstill. Indeed, the only innovation in 1979 was the first win for a turbocharged car when Stig Blomqvist urged his heavy front-wheel drive Saab 99 Turbo to victory in the Swedish Rally.

In the face of this reduction in momentum on a world-wide scale, it was typical that the Monte Carlo Rally should emerge from a period in the doldrums. With an entry of 270 cars there was clearly nothing wrong with an event which boasted its usual mixed bag of starting points scattered across Europe, with an assembly point at Vals-les-Bains in the Ardeche.

For most of the rally, the Fords of Bjorn Waldegaard and Hannu Mikkola dominated. Then Hannu was penalised for a traffic offence. Even so, Waldegaard had six minutes in hand at the start of the last night. At the end of it, he was six seconds behind the Stratos of Bernard Darniche, the Ford driver very unhappy about losing time when he had to free the underside of the car of rocks which had apparently been placed in the road.

Waldegaard's progress throughout the remainder of the season was steady rather than spectacular, although a fine victory on the excruciatingly tight Acropolis Rally helped the tall Swede lead the Drivers' World Championship (a long-awaited innovation) by the time the Lombard RAC Rally came round in November.

Ford, in a final flourish, entered seven cars, the 1998cc BDA engines now pushing out 260 bhp. Using the power to good effect on the 450 miles of special stages, Hannu Mikkola and Bjorn Waldegaard were expected to spearhead the Boreham attack although, as ever, it would

Hannu Mikkola gave
Ford their eighth—and
final—victory with the
Escort in 1979.

be necessary to keep an eye on Ari Vatanen even though the blond
Finn had not enjoyed a happy season.

While helping lift Mikkola's car after an accident during practice for
the Portuguese Rally, Vatanen had injured his back. It was serious
enough to keep him lying flat for some weeks but the recuperation,
plus timely backing from Rothmans, meant he was able to finish third
in New Zealand and Canada and second in the 1000 Lakes. Indeed,
until engine trouble had intervened, Vatanen had been leading in Finland and the RAC Rally would provide the opportunity to exploit his
largely unspent talent.

Jim Porter had gone to his usual meticulous lengths to provide a
challenge which the 175 starters (selected from 230 entrants) would
enjoy. By moving the rally headquarters to the beautiful city of Chester,
Porter had eased one or two problems by placing the focal point of
the rally closer to the important stages in Wales and the north-east of
England. This meant a more compact route, comprising two 36-hour
loops with the night-halt in Chester. The event, measuring 1,700 miles,
was no shorter than before but it would take one day less to complete.

This was in keeping with a trend which had been evident ever since
Porter became involved with the organisation. Whereas Jack Kemsley
had favoured rough special stages and more than one night in succession
out of bed for the competitors, Porter was gradually switching the
emphasis from surviving to driving.

'It was easy in theory but difficult to put into practice,' recalls Jim.
'I think it probably started from the basis that the event will be popular
if you make it popular with the competitors. And you will go a long
way towards making it popular with the competitors if you use roads
which they enjoy using. You don't find too many people who enjoy

127

really rough roads – particularly if they are paying their own bills!

'So, yes, there was a conscious decision to cut out the really rough roads. That wasn't always possible, of course, because you could find a really super stage with, maybe, half a mile of mucky stuff in the middle that you simply couldn't avoid. But, the general rule was, the smoother the better.'

The inclusion of spectator stages continued, of course, Sunday's work taking in 4.5 miles of tarmac roads in the Knowsley Safari Park, near Liverpool, followed by Trentham Gardens and the now-familiar parks, gardens and Donington race track in the Midlands.

The difference this year would be an immediate transfer to the forests of Yorkshire and Northumbria. By daybreak on Monday, the cars would be thrashing through the Castle O'er and Twiglees stages before taking a rest halt in Carlisle and finishing the first loop with the usual forest runs in north-west England. The various delights of the Welsh forests would be left until Wednesday night and the early hours of Thursday.

Markku Alen made it clear from the start that Lancia's efforts would not be in vain. By the time the crews had reached the rest halt at 'Flamingo Land', near Pickering, Alen led Mikkola by 16 seconds. With the stages in Yorkshire and the border region to follow, it was a carbon copy of the previous year. This time, however, the issue would be decided before they reached Kielder.

At Wykeham, on the fringe of the North Yorkshire moors, Alen increased his lead by three seconds. Then Mikkola went to work as they moved north-east to Langdale, where he pulled back 11 seconds. They set joint fastest time at Staindale and there was only one second difference between the times over the eight miles which made up the first stage in the Dalby Forest. On Dalby 2, Mikkola took the lead with a time which was 13 seconds faster at the end of 11 miles of hard motoring. Then, deep into the third Dalby stage, Alen left the road.

A broken rear brake pipe caused the front wheels to lock and several precious minutes were lost regaining the road. Any hopes Alen may have had of destroying the Ford run of success were lost.

Rubbing salt into the wound, Mikkola was fastest at Cropton, Kilburn and Boltby. By the time he reached the Hamsterley Forest at 1.30 on Monday morning, Mikkola was leading Waldegaard by more than a minute. When they emerged at the end of the 16-mile stage, Mikkola had again set the fastest time and Waldegaard was several minutes behind. The Swede had suffered the first of the many punctures which would wreck his chances and, to make matters worse, the jack would not work properly.

All of which allowed Tony Pond to move his Talbot Sunbeam Lotus into second place. This had been predicted since the nimble little car, homologated the previous April with the 2.2-litre Lotus Elite engine, had proved its worth by finishing fourth on the San Remo Rally, and

Up to their axles in mud. Mike Stuart's crew attack his Ford Escort during a service halt in 1981.

The power and, in short order, the glory of the Peugeot 205 T16.

In the frame. Tony Pond captured the imagination
of the British public in November
1985 by taking the Austin Rover MG Metro 6R4
into an excellent third place
at the end of an intensely competitive
Lombard RAC Rally.

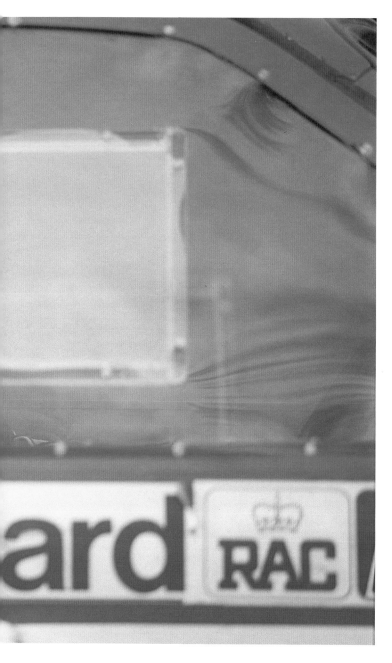

131

**Henri Toivonen and Paul White gave Talbot a welcome boost in 1980 by defeating
Hannu Mikkola in a straight fight between Sunbeam Talbot and Ford.**

**The Lake District special stages (right) have rewritten the story
of the RAC Rally on many occasions.**

Markku Alen/Ilkka Kivimäki
and the Lancia Delta S4;
perhaps the most
exciting combination
in the Supercar era but
one which was destined
not to win
the Lombard RAC Rally.

The Audi Quattro and the Lancia Rally 037;
only the beginning of a technically
absorbing but short-lived breed of Supercar.

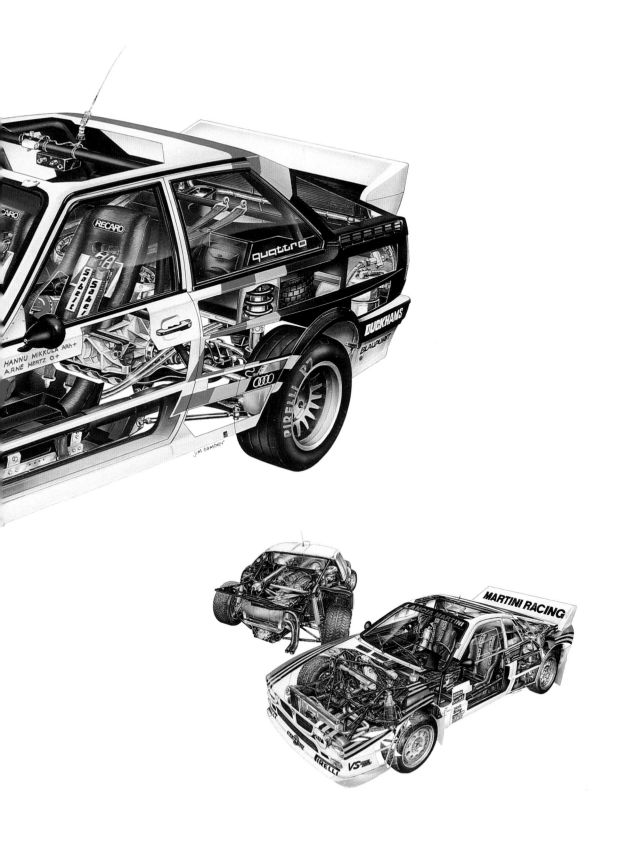

Rallying contrast. The appeal of the sport at international level is summed up by the sno

138

narrow bends of the Monte Carlo Rally and the dust and narrow bridges of the Safari.

Shekhar and Yvonne Mehta finished eighth in 1984,
their two-wheel drive Nissan 240RS
outclassed by the four-wheel drive battle for the lead
some 45 minutes ahead of the
Kenyian couple at the end of the British event.

Salonen and Alen, the double act which emerged
as the front runners of a ferocious battle during the
1986 Lombard RAC Rally. Salonen's cool professionalism
gave Peugeot their second win in three years; second place was not
enough to give the Lancia driver either the world
title or the British victory he wanted so much.

Victory on the Lombard RAC Rally; worth as much, if not more, than a win on either the Monte Carlo or the Safari Rally.

Pond's speed was never in doubt. It was simply a question of reaching the finish without something going wrong with car or, for that matter, the driver.

The car gave trouble first. Once into the massive Kielder complex, the drivers would be busy for two and a half hours as they covered 86 miles spread over six stages. Almost immediately Pond had clutch trouble, and fastest time by Ari Vatanen on the third stage gave the Escort second place. Kielder had, as usual, caused havoc and Alen, rarely among the top six fastest, summed up the dark, forbidding forest as a 'maximum bad place'.

Mikkola's Escort, meanwhile, was running perfectly and he held a five minute lead over Vatanen when they arrived in Chester for the night halt. The Escort of Russell Brookes was third, with Pond less than a minute behind.

Working their way through the Radnor forest in the late afternoon on Tuesday, drivers found black ice beginning to form on the fast, smooth Welsh stage. It was to be the undoing of one or two fine performances and, regrettably, it saw the end of a superb battle between Brookes and Pond. A mixture of a lethal surface and a deceptive arrow saw Brookes slide off the road. A few minutes later, Pond did likewise. The difference was Brookes recovered whereas Pond, having traded times with the Escort, was travelling a shade faster and his trip into the ditch ended in silence, save for the cursing of driver and navigator as they released themselves from the wreck.

If the icy conditions were proving difficult for the Group 4 cars, the less powerful Group 2 machines were more at home, an advantage which Timo Salonen used to the full in his Datsun 160J. He was fastest at Glasfynydd, second to Alen on Esgair Dafydd and quickest over the 13 miles of Nant-yr-hwch. This unrelenting effort had pulled Salonen into third place and Brookes was aware of this menacing presence. Brookes's reply soon put the Finn in his place.

Covering the 23 miles of the Hafren stage, Brookes set the fastest time to average nearly 50 mph – at night. The 37 seconds gained on Salonen destroyed the Datsun driver's earlier work and, to a degree, his morale.

As the crews made their way towards North Wales, Mikkola led Vatanen by eight minutes. It was a considerable gap – but it was to become 10 minutes longer, not through any fault of Vatanen, but through the shuffling of paperwork. Vatanen's co-driver, Dave Richards, had checked into the control at Machynlleth too early, and this was the penalty which was awarded some time later.

The effect was a fall from second to fifth place for the Rothmans car. But all was not lost since Alen, who had driven superbly, was only 40 seconds ahead of Vatanen. Unfortunately, the news was not imparted to the Lancia driver.

There were three stages through the Clocaenog Forest remaining.

Vatanen was fastest on them all. By the end, he was fourth, 30 seconds ahead of Alen. The Finn was fit to be tied when he learned what had happened.

Sailing serenely ahead of this furious action, Hannu Mikkola rolled into Chester with more than 10 minutes in hand over Brookes who, in turn, was two minutes ahead of the remarkable Salonen. Mikkola looked fresh, as did his car, the Escort having suffered just one puncture and no serious mechanical problems to speak of. He had set fastest time on 24 of the 59 stages. It was a dignified exit for the Ford Escort and a suitable ending to a trouble-free event.

Rupert Saunders, writing in *Autosport*, summed up the rally:

> For the teams, particularly Ford, the Lombard RAC Rally was a great success. For the spectators, the Lombard RAC Rally was a great treat. The weather was good, very cold but dry, the stars kept running until the end, and the crowds were bigger than ever. What more could the biggest rally in the world want? What better epitaph will ever be found for the Ford Escort?'

The increasing popularity of the Lombard RAC Rally, evident at scrutineering in Chester in 1979.

9
THE START OF
SOMETHING BIG

Sunbeams Everywhere

FOR THE 1980 Lombard RAC Rally, Talbot Sunbeam had at their disposal a Public Relations man. To save possible embarrassment, we will call him Mr. Smithers.

Mr. Smithers arrived at the rally headquarters in Bath with a spring in his step and a lady by his side. This would be a pleasant weekend. The Beaufort Hotel, situated by the river, was a hospitable establishment; a jolly nice place to spend a few days in November.

Work? Well, yes, there would be a little of that. Keep an eye on the progress of the three Talbots, report back to head office, field the odd query from members of the press, be a thoroughly pleasant and sociable sort of chap. Nothing too taxing.

The pressmen, you see, would be kept busy with the Fords of Hannu Mikkola and Ari Vatanen. They would be more interested in Bjorn Waldegaard in the Toyota . . . and okay, Fiat may have given the event a miss, but there was always the mighty BL entry to hold the media's attention. Frankly, Talbot were a nice, hard working bunch and, yes, they've got a very promising driver in young Henri Toivonen. They can never be discounted, of course, but . . . it should be an enjoyable few days.

Certainly, the blue-and-white Talbots hardly merited a second glance as they were wheeled through the cramped scrutineering bay in The Pavilion in Bath's North Parade Road. It was accepted that Toivonen had massive potential but his press-on style would surely lead to trouble at some point during the 467 miles of special stages. In support, Guy Frequelin would be quick, but the Frenchman's open dislike of secret stages was indicative of a lack-lustre performance. Of course, Russell Brookes was now driving a Talbot but, even so, the recent merger with Peugeot was generally perceived as a disruptive influence on Talbot's competition plans.

BL Cars, on the other hand, received warm applause when the TR7s appeared. With Tony Pond on the driving strength, the Triumphs were seen as the standard bearers of a possible British victory and, what's more, Pond was backed up by Roger Clark (who had been driving a TR7 in the British championship), Per Eklund and John Buffum. The

A disastrous start to the 1980 Lombard RAC Rally for the Triumph TR7 of Tony Pond and Fred Gallagher.

David Sutton Cars Ltd handled the Ford Escorts in 1980, Hannu Mikkola finishing second while the Rothmans car of Ari Vatanen crashed.

V8 had over 300 bhp available and the entire red, white and blue package had gelled into a competitive force – albeit a difficult one, as Clark recalls:

'With that big V8 stuck up front, it was nose heavy. It was a very uncomfortable car, a clumsy car if you like. It was either all understeer or all oversteer. You couldn't balance it out nicely because, basically, it was an unbalanced car anyway. Also, I like to sit upright, as high as possible because those extra couple of inches can make all the difference when it comes to peering over crests and round corners. In the TR7, you sat very low, which was not good for forest racing. But, generally, it wasn't as quick or as nice to drive as the Escort.'

Ford may have withdrawn their factory team, but David Sutton Cars had allowed Vatanen and Mikkola to show that they remained among the fastest drivers in the world as they exercised the Escort to the limit. Indeed, Vatanen had scored his first world championship victory on the Acropolis Rally although this superb highlight of a private team's year was offset by incidents such as the one in the Portugal, where both Rothmans cars went off at the same corner and landed on top of one another. But that was in the past although, for the RAC Rally, Sutton had turned back the pages of history by adding Timo Makinen to the driving strength, an arrangement which probably increased Mikkola's desire to equal his fellow countryman's hat trick of wins on the RAC.

There was a great deal of interest shown in the Opel Ascona 400. Here was a car which, on its first outing, had finished in the top ten on the Monte Carlo Rally and then gone on to win in Sweden. It was a car designed with rally success specifically in mind and there was no reason to doubt that it would not work on the forest tracks, particularly when driven by Anders Kullang, an experienced Swede.

There were more than 20 different manufacturers represented one way or another although, regrettably, Mercedes-Benz was not among them. At the beginning of the season, it had been predicted that the German team would dominate the endurance events on the calendar. This assumption was based largely on an impressive occupation of the first four places on the Bandama Rally in the Ivory Coast at the end of 1979 but, when the 450SLCs failed to blitz the opposition on the Safari Rally – when the engineering was found to be, whisper it, fallible – the impetus was lost. And so too was a technically interesting and promotable addition to the international scene.

Fiat, by contrast, had started off the year in a more relaxed frame of mind. It was not until Rohrl won the Monte and the Portuguese rounds that the Italians decided to take a run at the championship. Rohrl scored two more wins (the Codasur, in Argentina, a successful addition to the calendar, and the San Remo) and, by finishing second on the *Tour de Corse*, he not only secured the driver's title but he also ensured that Fiat would not feel the need to travel to Britain.

But, with 150 starters drawn from an oversubscribed entry, the Lombard RAC Rally was not lacking in either quality or depth. Mr. Smithers was right; it would be an interesting and enjoyable few days.

It was hardly a pleasant start, however, as drivers set off from Great Pultney Street under heavy grey clouds and a chilly wind. By selecting Bath, Jim Porter had reduced the flexibility of the routes available if he wished to return competitors to base for the overnight halt. But, by choosing Windermere, in the Lake District, for a stop-over, Porter neatly solved the problem. He could take in the traditional forests of Wales and the north without asking the crews to hike all the way down the motorway simply to have a night's rest.

On the other hand, a benefit of setting out from Bath was the handy location of the popular spectator stages. Longleat was close at hand and the drive north east to Blenheim Palace would lead on to Silverstone and Donington, two venues which offered easy and controlled spectating. Then, it was a short dash along the M1 before taking in Blidworth and Clipstone, two forest stages which were not mentioned on the route maps made available to the public.

North again to Braham Park, near Leeds, before the event became really serious as the forests on the Yorkshire moors beckoned. Then a change. Instead of continuing along the east coast, drivers would head west to take in stages in the northern end of the Lake District before passing through Carlisle on the way to the Scottish border. By the time they had finished with the Eskdalemuir and Craik Forests to the west of Hawick, the spectre of Kielder would not be a pleasant one since darkness would be falling on the second day, Monday. After that, the 12-hour stop in Windermere would be more than welcome.

The re-start on Tuesday morning launched competitors into three more stages in the Lake District as an appetiser for a night spent thrashing through the forests of Wales with the final tests taking place in the Forest of Dean. By then, Mr. Smithers would be packing, ready to make a speedy exit once the final report had been filed.

Jokes about Longleat were legion. The five miles of tarmac were something to be done with as quickly as possible, in every sense of the expression. It was wet, muddy and very slippery. A bit of a nuisance, really.

Ari Vatanen was the first to spin off. The Escort backed into the fencing surrounding the lion pen (the lions, it should be pointed out, had been moved elsewhere!), causing considerable damage to the boot, not to mention the fencing. Others lost control at the same point and disappeared through the opening kindly provided by Vatanen, but Tony Pond went through the gap quicker than most. Fred Gallagher had a front-row view of the impending accident:

'Tony was being regarded as a favourite to win the rally and I suppose we were a bit psyched up. I remember the stage was very, very slippery and as we went down the hill towards the corner, Tony started to brake but not much seemed to be happening. I think the plan was to bounce off the fencing. We didn't realise that someone had had the same idea a few minutes before!'

Once on the wet grass, the TR7 gathered momentum and did not slow down until firm contact was made with a feeding trough. Since lions tend to throw their weight around when food is at hand, the trough was constructed of railway sleepers and iron girders. One such caught the Triumph on the roof-line and smashed the windscreen as the nose of the car slithered underneath. Pond and Gallagher were unhurt. The same could not be said for the car. By the time the battered TR7 reached the end of the first stage, three minutes had been lost.

While the headline writers in Fleet Street rubbed their hands with glee, the chastened Pond immediately set about hauling himself back into contention. Meanwhile, British honour was being upheld by, if you will excuse the expression, two 'young lions' as Tony Brise and Malcolm Wilson set the early pace in their Escorts.

For more than a year Wilson had been heralded as the man to watch and not even appalling leg injuries, sustained on the Scottish Rally earlier in the year as he hustled the Scandinavian stars, affected his obvious talent. Unfortunately, a blown engine later at Silverstone dashed his RAC hopes, and Brise also suffered an early retirement when the electrics gave trouble.

For a day which was dismissed by rally experts as being commercial and of no consequence, there were a lot of important incidents taking place and worse was to come as the late afternoon approached. Mikkola made a mistake 200 yards into the Blidworth stage and left the road briefly but, at Bramham, a Polonez driven by John Lyons swerved to avoid a spectator who had slipped down a bank and fallen onto the road. It was a terrible irony that Lyons should then lose control and slam into three spectators who were watching on the other side of the road. One was seriously injured but eventually recovered.

Tony Pond and
Fred Gallagher:
Lyon's Quick Brew?

Pond . . . lions . . . accident . . . Lyons. Fleet Street couldn't believe its luck.

As the rally headed into the Yorkshire forests, Anders Kullang's name appeared consistently among the fastest times. Vatanen and Pond, making up for lost ground, were also among the quickest, but Pond received another set back when he left the road in Calderdale and lost a further 15 minutes.

Into Dalby now and, averaging 58 mph over 26 miles, Hannu Mikkola set the fastest time. But, Waldegaard and Kullang were just one second slower. By the time they reached Carlisle, Mikkola had gone off yet again and slipped to eighth, whereas Kullang and Waldegaard were fighting tooth-and-nail for the lead.

It was about now that Henri Toivonen began to make an impression. Fastest at Wykeham and on the 17-mile dash through Hamsterley, he had moved into third place, a position which would be maintained thanks to the fastest time through Castle O'er, Redesdale, Chirdon Head and Wark.

At Windermere, Toivonen was still third, 81 seconds behind Waldegaard who, in turn, was a mere 13 seconds adrift of Kullang. Mikkola was fourth, but Russell Brookes and Guy Frequelin had urged their Talbots into fifth and sixth places. None of this was lost on Mr. Smithers as he hurriedly telexed the good news; may as well make the most of this windfall.

The first stage the following morning would take the surviving cars through the 6.1 miles of Grizedale South, followed by 16.3 miles of Grizedale North. These stages were not considered to be of great strategic importance; more a warm-up for the 30 hours or so that lay ahead. In the event, Grizedale North would change the complexion of the entire rally.

Kullang suffered not one but two punctures, and by the time he had limped into the Opel service area in Coniston 17 minutes had been lost. That should have given Waldegaard the lead; but an oil filter had worked loose and the Toyota Celica GT had run its bearings and had to be towed out of the stage.

Henri Toivonen now led, Hannu Mikkola was two minutes behind and Russell Brookes and Guy Frequelin were third and fourth. Mr. Smithers blinked in amazement and reached for another cigarette. There was already talk of the senior management paying a visit to the rally. But this, surely, could not last? Mikkola would simply devour the inexperienced Toivonen in the Welsh forests . . . wouldn't he? Smithers anxiously checked his supply of Talbot press kits. Several people had already asked Toivonen's age. This could be serious.

Moving into Wales, Kullang continued to set the fastest times – but Toivonen was consistently faster than Mikkola. As the rally moved south, Mikkola had two punctures, Brookes suffered three and, rather than attack the Escort as he had hoped, the Englishman found himself defending his position from an attack by Frequelin. True, clutch and gearbox problems did not help Brookes but Frequelin produced one of the most astonishing performances of the rally when he came down Esgair Dafydd – at night, in fog – ten seconds faster than the next man, who happened to be Henri Toivonen. And when Brookes spun on the same stage, Frequelin was third.

As dawn broke on a wet, miserable morning, Mikkola confessed that he had little hope of catching his fellow-countryman. Toivonen had not cracked; Mr. Smithers was valliantly trying to do likewise.

There was near-panic in the Press Room. Smithers had long since dispatched his girlfriend. Bleary-eyed through the lack of sleep (although perhaps not for the reasons Smithers had originally hoped) the Talbot man pounded furiously at the telex while coping manfully with a stream of enquiries which would have engulfed a PR person with a weaker disposition.

As the leaders passed through the Forest of Dean, Smithers's phone rang constantly; men in smart suits arrived to demand the latest information; Frenchmen waved their arms (whether in anger or excitement Smithers neither knew nor cared); the stack of Toivonen profiles disappeared yet again and rally officials demanded to know what plans had been laid for interviewing the winning team.

As it happened, Talbot had previously booked the Georgian Pump Rooms in Bath for an informal gathering after the event. Now, of course, it would be a victory celebration. And what a victory. The entire assembly stood as one and applauded Henri Toivonen who, at 24, had become the youngest winner of the RAC Rally. It was a victory which

Henri Toivonen, at 24, became the youngest-ever driver to win the Lombard RAC Rally.

was shared by Henri's navigator, Paul White, and Des O'Dell, the team manager, who had lived through the past 24 hours in a state of nervous tension.

First, third and fourth places were a wonderful tonic for Talbot. And it had not been an easy victory by any means. This had been an exceptionally tough event even by the standards of the RAC Rally, with the leaders under continual pressure.

As for Mr. Smithers, he performed brilliantly under the circumstances but it had to be admitted he was a shadow of his former self as he crept quietly out of the hotel after a pleasant few days, all expenses paid. He was never seen again.

Enter the Quattro

In March 1980, Audi had unveiled the Quattro at the Geneva Motor Show. Turbocharged and featuring four-wheel drive, it was bristling with innovation. A change to the rules in 1979 meant four-wheel drive was permissible in international rallying, but even when Hannu Mikkola used the Quattro as a course car in the 1980 Algarve Rally and set fastest time on 24 of the 30 special stages there were many who doubted such sophisticated machinery would be suitable for the heat and variety generated by a full season. Reliability and servicing would be the car's Achilles' heel from an engineering standpoint; inflexible handling would make it impossible for the driver to take the Quattro to the limit.

In fact, the Audi Quattro would rewrite the performance parameters and totally change the face of world championship rallying.

Talbot broke the Ford domination in 1980. Henri Toivonen and Paul White power through Cumbria.

10

HE WHO HESITATES IS LAST

Audi get a grip

Michele Mouton: more than a touch of glamour.

IN ONE RESPECT, 1981 was not a classic year. In another, it provided a major turning point. With the rules calling for a change in thinking for 1982, most teams understandably lacked commitment to the job in hand in 1981. There was, however, one exception.

Audi knew precisely which way they wanted to go, and while the season may have been peppered with teething problems, there were occasions when Hannu Mikkola was able to prove the devastating efficiency of the Quattro. Better still, particularly for those watching rather than competing against this increasing threat, the second Audi Quattro was driven by the attractive Michele Mouton.

Mikkola, for instance, had built up a five-minute lead in the snow which dominated the opening phase of the Monte Carlo Rally. When the conditions became dry, the Quattro lost ground and Mikkola subsequently crashed. The belief that the Audi would only work when the going was slippery was strengthened by a win for the Finn in the Swedish Rally. Indeed, some observers attached more importance to the fact that this was the first time in 30 years that a Swedish driver had not won at home!

Mikkola led in Portugal until side-lined by engine trouble, a similar problem ending the *Tour de Corse* for both drivers. If they thought that was bad, there was worse to come on the Acropolis.

Walter Treser, the Audi team manager, was burned when petrol ignited during a service halt and the poor man's recovery must have received a considerable setback when the organisers chose to disqualify the Quattros on a technical point. Secondary headlights had been removed and this allowed air to pass through – quite by chance, of course – to an oil cooler and a radiator. After that, the only way for the team was up.

Michele Mouton became the first woman to win a world championship event when she gave Audi a fine victory on the San Remo Rally. And, since snow was the last thing to be found in such hot and dusty conditions, the San Remo can be regarded as a major turning point in more ways than one.

The same applies to the Corsican rally, mentioned earlier. By moving the event from October to April, the drivers encountered warm and dry weather for a change. And although the *Tours de Corse* organisers could no longer hope to decide the championship, their event was to play a major part in shaping its outcome.

Until this point, the Talbot team had not been taking the championship seriously; but when Guy Frequelin finished second, Talbot changed their tune, since they now led both the manufacturers' and the drivers' divisions. Significantly, Tony Pond had finished a brilliant third in Corsica and the points would help Datsun keep Talbot on their toes until the last round, the Lombard RAC Rally.

Similarly, the drivers' championship stumbled to a climax in Britain, thanks to Ari Vatanen being declared the winner in Greece and scoring well-deserved sets of maximum points in Finland and Brazil (the latter a new addition to the world series).

Vatanen's success was made notable by the fact that he was driving a Rothmans-backed Ford Escort, a car which was becoming somewhat long in the tooth, certainly when compared with the four-wheel drive Teutonic wonder car which, when it worked, left Ari far behind despite his unrelenting commitment. Even so, as the chill of November approached, Vatanen was in with a chance of the championship, and as far as Audi were concerned, the Lombard RAC Rally would provide them with the stiffest test yet.

Advantage Audi – by 10 Minutes

The clued-up towns and cities in Britain had realised the benefit to be had from staging the Lombard RAC Rally. Not only did it bring prestige, it also brought foreign visitors at a time when Britain was hardly at its best. The shops, gearing up for Christmas, welcomed the boost to trade and, in 1981, Marks & Spencer's store in Chester would temporarily run out of sweaters!

It is easy to understand, therefore, why Jim Porter no longer had to search high and low for a suitable venue; the towns and cities were beating a path to his door in Belgrave Square.

'By 1981, we could more or less take our pick,' recalls Jim. 'But it had taken a long time before we had what you might call a rush of towns. York was the first one to come along and offer their services, so to speak.

'The places I used – York, Bath and Chester – are all tourist towns, with Birmingham being the exception. But they are places where a foreigner can bring his wife and she can enjoy herself shopping. They've got good hotels and restaurants and the event was not lost in an industrial conglomerate where there were lots of other attractions taking place.

'On the other hand, we were approached by towns with plenty of money but, unfortunately, they had a poor selection of hotels, pretty miserable surroundings and even worse reputations. But you can't blame them for asking.'

Chester's main attraction to Jim Porter, however, was its location. It was a relatively easy matter to devise the now familiar route: Chester to the Border region, taking in the forests in the north-east and the north-west before returning $38\frac{1}{2}$ hours later to Chester. The final 30-hour section would be devoted largely to Wales, leaving the difficult Penmachno and Clocaenog forests to the last. A total of 65 special stages, making up 464 competitive miles on the 1,700-mile route.

By sending the competitors north in a clockwise fashion, Jim Porter had ensured that, for once, spectators in the north-east would have a chance to see the cars in daylight. It also meant that the Grizedale Forest in the Lake District would be tackled at night. Grizedale had been the turning point of the previous year's event. It was to have a fair say in the shaping of the 1981 Lombard RAC Rally as well.

In the comparatively short space of time it had taken competitors to complete the Sunday spectator stages and head north, the rally had become something of a bore, thanks to Hannu Mikkola and the indecently unspectacular Quattro. He had pulled out a lead of 40 seconds in just five stages, and at that rate of going he promised to kill the event stone dead before the night was out.

Then he fell off the road on the dreaded Grizedale North stage. In rain and fog, Mikkola had arrived too quickly at a 90-degree bend, the Quattro rolling into the mud. Spectators helped Mikkola and Arne Hertz right the car and suddenly we had a graphic demonstration of yet another advantage offered by the four-wheel drive Audi. Mikkola simply drove out of the mire, the entire incident cost him just 57 seconds.

It also cost Mikkola first place and, to the delight of the partisan crowd braving the elements on this extremely miserable Sunday night, Tony Pond's Vauxhall Chevette took charge. That, at least, made up for the disappointment of seeing Russell Brookes fall victim to the same stage at Grizedale.

This time, however, the Talbot-Sunbeam driver had greater difficulty regaining the road, a struggle which was to prove a waste of time since a broken driveshaft would force the Englishman's retirement. Elsewhere along the 16-mile stage, Henri Toivonen left the road in his Talbot and Jean Ragnotti, driving a mid-engined Renault 5 turbo, spun. Suddenly, the rally had come alive.

Mikkola soon put a stop to that. By setting the fastest time on 13 stages he romped back into the lead, and on his return to Chester the Audi held a ten-minute advantage. The Quattro had been almost a minute faster than anyone else over the 29-mile Dalby stage, the longest on the rally. It was here that Pond retired with broken transmission, leaving Vatanen to consolidate second place and, more important, the championship.

As for Talbot, they had been heartened by Stig Blomqvist's fourth place at Chester since the British team only needed to finish seventh or higher to beat Datsun. In the event, Blomqvist would turn in an immaculate performance, the Swede claiming third place after a torrid night in Wales as drivers faced rain, snow, wind and fog. Mikkola said he had never known weather like it and, under the circumstances, he had the perfect car for the occasion.

The conditions proved too much for Michele Mouton as she fought back the effect of a heavy cold while defending third place. Mlle. Mouton startled the menfolk by setting the fastest time on that notorious Grizedale stage, but on the final morning the Beddgelert stage proved her undoing, the Audi ending the rally at the bottom of a 50 ft embankment.

Mikkola scarcely figured in the top six times over the final stages, such was the cushion afforded by a winning margin of 11 minutes over the new world champion, Ari Vatanen, in the David Sutton Escort. The disparity in performance between the two said all you needed to know about the exciting new era which was about to unfold.

Which Way to Run?

In 1982, the restructuring of the regulations would see the fastest cars in Group 4 make way for Group B, a category which called for manufacturers to build a minimum of 200 examples within a 12-month period. That relatively simple requirement, coupled with a generous allowance in the modifications which could be carried out, paved the way for a new breed of Supercar.

These devices would be built specifically for rallying, and old favourites, such as the Ford Escort RS and the Talbot Sunbeam-Lotus, would be rendered obsolete overnight. The manufacturers, however, were not in accord over which avenue of development to follow.

Ford were already committed to a turbocharged rear-wheel drive RS1700T, a major constriction here being the need to have a car which was based on a model in the company catalogue, in this case, the Escort Mk 3. Opel were already working on the rear-wheel drive Ascona and the Manta 400 derivative would be something of a compromise.

Even Lancia, with their striking mid-engined 037 Rally, would not have the benefit of four-wheel drive. Mind you, that remarkable fountain of motor sport gossip and speculation, the Italian magazine *Autosprint*, had suggested that Lancia were already working on a turbocharged version of the Delta and there was the thought that this car would have four-wheel drive. Lancia dismissed the rumours which, at the time, were no more than that. As we would see, however, *Autosprint* had been remarkably prescient in their guesswork.

But, for those who wished to take note of solid, indisputable facts, the 1981 Lombard RAC Rally had provided proof positive that turbocharging and four-wheel drive worked – on snow and loose surfaces, at least. And the significant point was that the Quattro had been designed as a road car in the first place, even though Audi would ask to have it approved for Group B.

If the Quattro set such incredible standards of traction and power what, then, could a manufacturer achieve if he set out to design a machine with the sole intention of rallying it? The mind boggled.

The lesson was not lost on Jean Todt, Guy Frequelin's co-driver on the Lombard RAC. Todt returned to Paris and convinced Peugeot-Talbot Sport that they should not consider anything but a four-wheel drive turbocharged package. Thus, the Peugeot 206 Turbo 16 was conceived.

Meanwhile, at Williams Grand Prix Engineering, at Didcot, Oxfordshire, Patrick Head was applying knowledge gained in the aerodynamics and construction of Formula 1 cars to rallying. The Williams designer had been visited by John Davenport, of BL Cars, with a view to using the Williams know-how in the building of a Group B car, based on the Metro. Various ideas were kicked around, but the increasing success of the Quattro in 1981 led to the inevitable conclusion that four-wheel drive was essential and this, coupled with a win on the Monte Carlo Rally for a mid-engined Renault 5 Turbo, spawned the development of the Metro 6R4.

The Supercar revolution was under way. Some Supercars would be more super than others; some would be sensational. But the bottom line would be a tragic end to a remarkable era which was just dawning.

The turbocharged four-wheel drive Audi Quattro: lifting rallying onto a new level.

11

A NEW BREED

No Substitute for Experience

HOW COULD Audi fail? Making predictions for 1982 was an easy business in the light of what had taken place during the preceding 12 months. And, when the Monte Carlo Rally kicked off the new season, only a fool would have discounted the chances of a win for either Hannu Mikkola or Michele Mouton. In the event, Audi's humbling defeat by Opel would prompt urgent revisions to the form book.

It is true to say that exceptionally dry conditions on the Monte played into the hands of Walter Rohrl but the German drove brilliantly as he edged his Ascona ahead of Mikkola and eventually forced the Audi driver to spin at the height of their tense battle on the final night. Mouton had crashed on one of the occasional patches of ice which had caught several drivers and, in retrospect, this was a bad omen for Audi.

Rohrl's success was a tremendous boost for the Opel team, now enjoying substantial support from Rothmans and heavily committed to winning both the drivers' and manufacturers' championships. Opel, making use of a one year period of grace for Group 4 cars, knew they would never have a better opportunity since Audi were still finding their feet.

The calendar originally contained 13 rounds but the Falklands War forced the cancellation of the *Codasur* in Argentina. Opel were alone in competing on the remaining 12, such was their determination and such was the extent of their backing.

Walter Rohrl: a thorough professional with a thorough dislike of the RAC Rally, won the San Remo Rally for Fiat in 1980.

At times, taking part in just one event during a season seemed more than Audi could cope with. Whereas Opel, under the guidance of Tony Fall and serviced by an experienced team of mechanics, performed with the speed and efficiency required by the tight schedules, Audi were in disarray. Roland Gumpert, the Audi technical director, had problems in man management. And as for dealing with the one lady on the team, the poor chap had no chance.

Mlle. Mouton may have pouted and then exploded in that wonderful French way but it did not detract from her driving. If anything, it may have contributed to performances which were notable for a tireless resolve to finish first.

For Mikkola, however, 1982 was a year which he would rather forget. He slid off the road while leading in Sweden; a problem with the pace notes saw the Mikkola/Hertz combination out of contention in Portugal

159

while silly mechanical problems intervened in Greece. And, to cap it all, a mechanic wrote off Hannu's car just before the start of the *Tour de Corse*. In between finishing second in the Monte Carlo Rally in January and winning the 1000 Lakes at the end of August (only after Stig Blomqvist had been ordered to slow down in a third Quattro), Mikkola did not score a single point.

Mouton, on the other hand, was something of a sensation. When she had won the San Remo the previous year, the chauvinistic response attributed victory to the car rather than the driver. In 1982, Michele made the critics eat humble pie by winning in Portugal, Greece and Brazil. No one else managed three victories during the season, but Mouton's aggression was finally beaten by Rohrl's consistency as he gathered points in a cool manner which, as the season wore on, reflected his attitude towards the Rothmans Opel team. Even so, the proud German did not take kindly to being beaten by a woman and the fact that his undeniable best in the rear-wheel drive Ascona was no match for the Quattro did nothing to patch up the widening chasm between driver and team.

Frequently, Walter would casually dismiss requests to attend sponsor's functions. They could no longer rely on him when it came to playing a key part in the expensive promotions which formed Rothmans' *raison d'etre* for being involved in rallying in the first place. It all came to a head at the Lombard RAC Rally in November.

Honour and Disgrace

Rohrl, scoring just his second win of the season, had wrapped up the drivers championship on the Ivory Coast Rally at the beginning of November. For most of the event, however, it seemed that the championship would be decided in Britain as Mouton led during the closing stages, despite this being her first attempt on an rally notable for appalling conditions.

Then she rolled the Quattro onto its roof, leaving just the manufacturers championship to be sorted out on the RAC Rally. With Audi leading Opel by two points, the Asconas would be hard-pressed to overhaul the Quattros in the forests. But then, with 450 miles of special stages, reliability and a cool head would be just as important as traction – ideal circumstances for Walter Rohrl to exercise the talent which had earned him the championship in the first place.

Except that he disliked the event – and didn't mind who knew it. Rohrl was not in favour of rallying through the forests without pace notes and his general lack of enthusiasm was not lost on the Opel management. The final straw was Rohrl's absence from a major party hosted by Rothmans on the Friday evening in York.

The following morning, Opel sacked him. Rohrl would be driving for Lancia in 1983 in any case, but enough was enough. With less than

24 hours to go before the start of the Rally, Jochi Kleint and Gunter Wanger flew from Germany to replace Rohrl and Geistdorfer.

That piece of news fairly set the press room humming, and Audi must have been relieved to hear it. Opel had already secured the services of Ari Vatanen to bolster their efforts, but rain on the Saturday evening, with the promise of more to come, did not fill the team with hope.

In all, it was a miserable start, compounded by the hostile attitude displayed by the York traffic wardens as they appeared to dispense parking tickets as though operating on piecework. It did little to foster a warm relationship with the foreign crews, and the unpleasant effects of such energetic scribbling detracted from a rally organisation which promised to be slicker and more professional than ever.

Jim Porter had recruited Phil Short to play a major part in planning the route. Short, an experienced navigator of some standing (about 6ft 4ins, actually!), took competitors into Monmouth and South Wales by visiting spectator stages in the Midlands. Among them was Clumber Park, near Worksop, the first time National Trust property had been incorporated in the route.

By the time the five 'Mickey Mouse' stages had been dealt with, Mikkola, by setting fastest time on four of them, held an easy lead but the Audi team were in for a minor shock as Mikkola headed into the Forest of Dean.

Fastest through Speech House, Serridge and Swallow Vallets, Markku Alen pulled back 35 seconds on Mikkola and assumed the lead as he went to work in the striking Lancia 037 Rally. The Group B car had made a troubled debut on the *Tour de Corse* in May and, although it had not figured in the results of subsequent events, the car's potential became clearer when Alen led briefly in the San Remo. Since then, the Italians had won a British national event and spent many hours carrying out tyre tests in the Welsh forests. Now, although Markku had his head down, such a comparatively fragile racer seemed destined to retire on the rough RAC roads.

If that was to be the case, it was taking quite some time for the Martini-backed car to fall apart. Alen held onto his lead until the 17th stage at Esgair Dafydd, where Mikkola finally overhauled the Lancia and left Alen to deal with Vatanen.

Mikkola had been somewhat surprised by Alen's pace but the Lancia was unable to respond to Mikkola's attack, thanks to a minor problem with the distributor. By the time it had been fixed, Vatanen was second, the former world champion beginning to feel more comfortable with the Ascona after seven years spent flinging Ford Escorts around the world. Ari had been fastest through Pantperthog, to the north of Machynlleth, and he consolidated his position with fastest times through the Penmachno stages.

Then he flew off the road in the Clocaenog Forest and the terminal damage to the engine (caused by a punctured radiator) left Opel with just two cars, since Klient had spun into retirement some time before. One of the Mantas, however, was driven by Henri Toivonen and he took over where Vatanen had left off. By the time they reached York, Mikkola was nearly four minutes ahead of Toivonen but Alen, his Lancia working properly once more, was a mere 34 seconds in arrears and closing.

In terms of the championship however, Audi were in good shape. Apart from Mikkola reeling off the fastest time on half of the 36 stages held so far, the German champion, Harald Demuth, was holding fourth place in the Quattro which Stig Blomqvist had used to win the San Remo Rally. This car was now entered for Audi Sport UK by David Sutton and Demuth was nearly two minutes ahead of Michele Mouton in fifth place. All five were raring to go at 9 o'clock on Tuesday morning as they headed towards Hamsterley, Kielder, the Borders and the Lake District.

Mikkola gained more than a minute on Toivonen through the 18-mile Hamsterley stage but Demuth was to make an even greater impression here as he set joint second-fastest time and moved into second place overall. Kielder, though, would decide matters once and for all.

If the weather conditions had been wet and miserable in Wales, they were appalling in Northumbria on Tuesday evening. Competitors spoke of having to change down a gear simply to get through the clawing mud and, of course, the four-wheel drive Quattros were at an advantage straight-away.

Mikkola emerged from the five-stage complex with a lead of six minutes and the bad news for Opel was that a third car, that of Jimmy McRae, had fallen by the wayside with a broken driveshaft. Indeed, this was yet another blow to British hopes, Tony Pond having backed his Vauxhall Chevette HSR out of the rally on the first leg. Russell Brookes, though, was still in the hunt in another Chevette and, as ever, the Englishman's consistency would pay off to give him an eventual sixth place despite changing gearboxes as frequently as other drivers changed tyres.

In the meantime, Toivonen was shouldering the Opel team's responsibility by holding second place even though he was being hotly pursued by Mouton, the French lady showing tremendous courage by setting fastest time through two stages. Alen was now fifth, behind Demuth.

As dawn broke on Wednesday, bringing with it a halt in the seemingly incessant rain, Mouton had cut back Toivonen's advantage by setting fastest time at Elibank, Castle O'er and Twiglees. It was a remarkable performance, which brought the Audi to within 32 seconds of the Opel as they returned to York for a second time. Normally this would have been the end of the story, but Phil Short added a nasty finale to the event.

Leaving the walled city at midnight on Wednesday, the survivors faced another 70 miles of competitive motoring during a ten-hour dash

Hannu Mikkola led an Audi one-two in 1982.

through Yorkshire. It would provide a superb climax to the battle for second place.

Mouton set the fastest time on the first four stages, reducing the margin to a mere eight seconds. Toivonen was the faster, by one second, at Cropton, but Mouton edged ever closer by taking the fastest time on the next stage. When Toivonen gained two seconds with fastest time on Calderdale, it was clear that the 26.5-mile Dalby stage could settle the issue.

The Audi would have the advantage in terms of traction out of the muddy, ninety-degree corners. On the other hand, Toivonen, and in particular his co-driver Fred Gallagher, knew the stage well. As if to counter this, Arne Hertz was seen advising Michele's partner, Fabrizia Pons, of some of the most tricky points on this very fast stage.

At the end of just over 25 minutes of flat-out motoring, Mouton was eight seconds faster – and only one second ahead of Toivonen over-all. That left three stages, one of which would almost write off several cars and, at the end of the day, contribute nothing to this nailbiting finish.

Trouble arose at the end of the Langdale stage, where a bend located between the flying finish and the stop line caught out, among others, Toivonen and Mouton. The Opel went off the road and was hit by the Toyota of Bjorn Waldegaard as the Swede became a victim of the same poor piece of organisation. Toivonen's car was eventually recovered but worse was to follow.

Henri had covered the stage 11 seconds faster than Mouton, but since they, along with 14 other crews, had completed the stage under the bogey time, all 16 were credited with the bogey time. Toivonen's work had been for nothing.

Now there were two stages remaining, the final one at Oliver's Mount consisting of 4.5 miles of tarmac which undoubtedly would benefit the Opel. Mouton, therefore, added another ten seconds by setting fastest time through the penultimate stage at Wykeham. Could Toivonen recover 11 seconds on the motor-cycle track?

Henri, who was keen on motor racing in any case, put the Ascona

163

on its ear and beat Mouton. But it was not enough. The Frenchwoman, having set the fastest time on 16 stages, finished the rally nine seconds ahead to give Audi a resounding one-two at the end of a difficult year.

The trouble was, everyone had expected the German team to dominate the results in this manner. The reality of the season had been a long, hard struggle from beginning to end. Now Lancia were into their stride, with Alen coming home fourth and expressing delight about the reliability of the 037 Rally. Audi may have won the manufacturers championship, but they had expected to make much more hay while the sun shone.

Nowhere to Hide

Lancia were giving Audi a hard time. Sensing the mounting threat, Audi rushed through their latest version of the Quattro, the A2, and, instead of matters improving, they got worse. Much worse.

The A2 made its debut in Corsica in May 1983. Prior to that, Mikkola had won in Sweden and Portugal and dominated the Safari before problems late in the event denied Audi what looked like being a remarkable result.

Then the A2 arrived. The internal dimensions of the five-cylinder engine had been reduced fractionally to qualify the car for a lower capacity class which, in turn, permitted a lower weight limit. Even so, the Quattro produced some 360 bhp, and with eight finishes from 11 starts for the team thus far, they were feeling more confident than of late.

Both cars retired in Corsica, Mikkola puncturing a rear tyre and wrecking the suspension as a result of hitting a rock. In view of what was to follow in subsequent events, Mouton's failure was highly significant; her car caught fire.

The *Tour de Corse* was dominated by the Lanica 037, Markku Alen scoring the first world championship victory in two years. On the Acropolis Rally, it was Rohrl's turn to win, with Alen taking second place, thus moving Lancia ahead in the manufacturers championship.

For Audi, another disaster. Mikkola had been leading during the closing stages when, of all things, a hinge pin failed, leaving the boot assembly of the Quattro trailing through a rocky stage. This might not have been quite so critical had the oil coolers on the Audi not been mounted beneath the rear spoiler. Mouton had crashed on the first stage and Blomqvist had to contend with various problems (among them a fire caused by a loose filler cap) before finishing third. Audi were supposed to dominate this gravel event. Now they were falling apart in every way.

In New Zealand, Audi instigated a major row when they entered a third car after the closing date. That management fiasco resulted in Stig Blomqvist travelling to Auckland for nothing. Mikkola, too, had an early flight home thanks to an engine fire and Mouton suffered an engine failure while leading, leaving Lancia and Rohrl to collect maximum points. Mikkola could see the drivers championship slipping from his grasp.

Wins in Argentina (back on the schedule at the expense of Brazil) and Finland revived his hopes, only to have them dashed terribly on the San Remo Rally in early October. Audi had won the event for the previous two years but, if anything, the A2 was slower. Mouton had a misfire, Blomqvist committed a rare error and crashed on the final night – and Mikkola's car caught fire. The finger was pointed at excessive turbocharger temperatures; the result was an inferno which consumed the Quattro, leaving a charred shell and an engine-block which had melted in the heat. Alen, meanwhile, led home a one-two-three, thus giving Lancia the manufacturers championship.

By finishing second on the Ivory Coast, Mikkola more or less assured himself of the drivers championship and that at least eased the fact that Audi had been beaten in Africa by an incredible performance from Bjorn Waldegaard in the rear-wheel drive Toyota Celica Turbo, easily the best of the 'conventional' cars in 1983.

Stig Takes his Turn

Throughout Mikkola's championship campaign, Stig Blomqvist had played a supporting role. His speed and commitment had been masked by team orders, as well as accidents in Portugal and San Remo, but it was clear he was a potential winner, given his head. The final round of the championship in 1983, the Lombard RAC Rally, would provide him with the perfect platform to demonstrate his potential.

Besides having spent the year winning the British Open championship in the British forests, Stig was perfectly in tune with the requirements of what would be one of the longest and toughest rounds of the world series. Regrettably, Blomqvist's almost total domination of the rally would also make it one of the least exciting in recent times.

Having won the manufacturers' championship, Lancia upset the British enthusiasts by ignoring the RAC Rally. Not even Markku Alen could persuade them to send one car in the faint hope that he could take the driver's title from Mikkola. In fact, it was not until Alen confirmed that he would not be present that Mikkola could finally accept that the championship was his.

Lancia had not only exhausted their budget, they had gone into the red in their battle with Audi. They had not set out with the avowed intention of defeating the Germans and yet the irony was they had come away with the glory while Audi soldiered on with their plan to contest every round and, in the final event, perhaps draw some consolation from a frustrating year.

With the main opposition on the RAC coming from the Rothmans Opel team (now working with the Manta 400) and Toyota, the battle

Henri Toivonen/Fred Gallagher (Opel Manta 400) retired with head gasket failure in 1983 Lombard RAC Rally.

for supremacy would almost certainly be an in-house one with Mikkola and Mouton in factory cars ranged against the British-built David Sutton Quattro for Blomqvist. As the sole member of Sutton's compact, and, dare it be said, more efficient team, Stig would run this rally as he saw fit. Which is to say, flat-out from the start.

In fact, the taciturn Swede would be champing at the bit for the best part of two days. During that period, the rally would cover just 42 competitive miles, spread over no less than 11 stages. It was a case of spectator stages taken to ridiculous extremes.

The route had been devised by John Brown, a former winner of the event while navigating for Erik Carlsson in 1961. The rally would start on Saturday, a day earlier than usual, taking in Longleat (twice), Ashton Court near Bristol, Castle Combe and Colerne; a total of 19 stage-miles.

Re-starting from Bath at 7 am on Sunday, competitors faced another day of spectator-orientated motoring as they moved towards Leeds but, in case anyone thought John Brown had gone soft in the head, his intentions for the rally soon became clear the minute the cars entered the forests for the first time.

At 8 pm on Sunday evening, Hannu Mikkola, the Number One seed, would set off through Dalby on a stage representing 40.5 miles of fast motoring. Hard on its heels, almost 10 miles through Wykeham, followed by 12 miles spread over two stages in Langdale before a rest halt of two hours in Middlesbrough.

Into their stride now, the crews would rush into the early hours of Monday morning with 20 miles of Hamsterley Forest to set them up for the inevitable run through Kielder. A short break at Hawick would bring some relief after Falstone and Rooken before sending the crews south for a night's sleep, but not before they had experienced the delights and difficulties of more than 70 miles of mixed stages.

A fairly leisurely start on Tuesday morning would be the prelude to one of the toughest final legs yet devised for the modern era of the Lombard RAC. The forests of North Wales would be familiar. So, too, would many of the stages used in the south but, by sending competitors through Cymer, Resolfen, Afan and Margam twice, John Brown had managed to pack in about 25 per cent of the event's stage mileage during the final 12 hours. When Stig Blomqvist set off from Bath on the first day, he clearly meant to have the result settled long before reaching South Wales.

Blomqvist had shown Mikkola the way through three of the first five stages and, when they left Bath for the second time, he extended his lead further through Bewdley, Weston Park and Trentham Gardens. Mikkola, though, was only a few seconds behind after claiming the fastest time though Sutton Park and Oulton Park. A night-long duel seemed likely, but Mikkola cancelled any such hopes when he had a spectacular incident while negotiating the 4.19 miles set out through the Knowsley Safari Park, near Liverpool.

Cutting a corner too closely, the left-front wheel of the Quattro hit something solid. A broken strut caused the wheel to jam under the car until, finally, it broke free and Mikkola was forced to stop. With Arne Hertz sitting on the tail of the car in an attempt to relieve the front corner of some weight, Mikkola limped out of the stage. He had lost six minutes and dropped to 28th place. Now Blomqvist was reasonably safe, for the time being. With a stage measuring 40 miles coming up, anything could happen. And it did.

Blomqvist had reasoned that Dalby could set the pattern for the entire rally. Forget the fiddly bits that had occupied the previous 36 hours; a fast time and, perhaps more important, a trouble free run could provide a useful margin which rivals would have great difficulty in clawing back.

The cars started at one minute intervals as usual, but such was the length of the stage and the equally impressive pace of the Audi that Blomqvist soon found himself catching the Opel Manta of Henri Toivonen. And the Finn was not exactly holding back since he was disputing second place with Waldegaard's energetically driven Toyota.

Blomqvist and Toivonen understood each other's predicament and, as soon as the opportunity arose, Henri let the Audi through. But it had taken a couple of minutes to find a suitable passing place without asking Toivonen to back off too much. During that time Blomqvist's bank of six spot lights had been covered with mud flicked up by the Opel. It was a setback which only became apparent the minute Stig moved ahead. It was like following a car through fog. You think he's being excessively cautious. So you overtake, only to discover you can't see a thing.

Blomqvist persevered, his task made difficult by the fact that the mud had been baked solid by the heat of the lenses. Toivonen, of course, was glued to his tail and the Finn and his co-driver Fred Gallagher, were able to witness Blomqvist arrive at a corner too quickly, pitch the car sideways – and smash the left-rear corner into a tree.

'It was incredible,' recalls Gallagher. 'Stig disappeared down a ditch on one side, shot back onto the road and almost disappeared into the ditch on the other side. And, all the time, there were bits flying off the car in all directions. At the next corner, he went wide again and we drew alongside. It was like a drag race, but the four-wheel drive took a grip in the mud and Stig was away. He completely covered our car with mud!'

Luckily, the damage to the Audi was not as severe as it might have been. Even the tyre did not puncture. Had it been otherwise, then the outcome of the rally might have been a different story entirely.

But that is idle speculation. The simple fact is that in spite of such a remarkable drama Stig Blomqvist still managed to complete the stage no less than 80 seconds faster than anyone else! After such a performance, no one could possibly deny Blomqvist victory.

The damage was gradually patched up as the rally went on, the David Sutton team moving through Northern England and Southern Scotland like some high-speed mobile body repair shop. By the time Blomqvist had checked into Windermere, the half-way point, he had eight minutes in hand over Mikkola. The rest were nowhere. Or to be more precise, they had retired and were on their way home.

Waldegaard's forceful drive had ended when he left the road in the Lake District, the Toyota holding second place after Toivonen had stopped with head gasket failure and before the hard-charging Mikkola engulfed him. All of which left Jimmy McRae and Russell Brookes to produce a fine cut-and-thrust battle for third place. Their pace was such that both drivers made mistakes, but Brookes' excursion down a 30-foot bank in mid-Wales was serious enough to end the Vauxhall driver's hopes of keeping the Opel Manta out of third place.

In the end, the nasty loop through the forests to the north of Swansea would have no effect on the result. Blomqvist, just to rub in his superiority, was fastest over the final stage, giving him a grand total of 36 out of the 57 stages which actually counted (two being cancelled). The gap between the leaders at the finish was almost ten minutes, with Mikkola nearly 12 minutes ahead of McRae.

The rally, run in unseasonally dry conditions, had been watched by vast crowds throughout the five days. The margin of victory may not have been a suitable advertisement for the sport, but it was a fitting tribute to Blomqvist and the benefits of four-wheel drive.

The latter point had not been lost on Stuart Turner the previous February when he became Ford's Director of European Motor Sport. His first act was to bury the RS1700T project. Plans for a mid-engined four-wheel drive RS200 were soon under way.

A dominant performance from Stig Blomqvist in the David Sutton Quattro in 1983.

Meanwhile, eight months later, down in the Dordogne, something stirred. Jean-Pierre Nicolas gave the Peugeot 205 Turbo 16 its competiton debut in a French national rally. This purpose-built rally car had been unveiled in Paris in February and the French were pleased with progress.

As for Lancia, they were quick to realise the limited potential of their 037, despite the promise shown during 1983. Project 038 would be under way in early 1984, and when it finally reached the light of day as the Lancia Delta S4 the following December, FISA would begin to have some inkling of the monster that was evolving from the apparently innocuous Group B regulations.

12

A STUNNING SPECTACLE

Peugeot, on Cue

JEAN TODT said he would have the Peugeot 205 Turbo T16 ready to rally by 1984 and he was as good as his word. Given the Frenchman's vast experience, that was expected. What was not expected was the instant competitiveness of a totally new car, 'straight out of the box', so to speak. Not only did it lead first time out, the Peugeot very nearly won!

Todt brought two of the mid-engined 205s to Corsica. It was a tough arena in which to make an international debut since the twisting tarmac roads were tailor-made for the sleek Lancia Rally. But then Todt did not expect to win straightaway. He did, however, expect to find out more about the strengths and weaknesses of the little car, which was one of the reasons why he had signed Ari Vatanen. The Finn would soon explore the limits of the 205 T16 and, hopefully, give some indication of the potential the French were looking for.

From the moment Vatanen completed the first 24-mile stage a mere 35 seconds slower than the Lancia of Attilio Bettega – and this despite brake problems – Peugeot knew the signs were good. On the next stage, measuring 15 miles, he was quickest and Peugeot knew the signs were more than promising.

On the eighth stage, a 31-miler, Bettega went off the road. Vatanen claimed the fastest time – and took the lead. Setting the fastest time on five more stages, Vatanen resisted a strong attack from Alen's Lancia.

Then, in heavy rain and the blue darkness of early morning, Vatanen was caught out by mud and water cascading across the braking point to a corner. The Peugeot shot over the edge of the road and tumbled down a rock face. Fortunately it did not reach the sea but became wedged between two rocks. Vatanen and his co-driver, Terry Harryman, managed to scramble free moments before the car caught fire and burned to a cinder.

It was a sorry end to a rally which could easily have belonged to Peugeot. None the less, once they had established that the crew were safe, the Peugeot management were happy enough with the car's performance. In any case, there was more than adequate consolation to be gained from Jean-Pierre Nicolas finishing fourth behind the Lancias

Ari Vatanen and Terry
Harryman continued to
show the potential of the
Peugeot 205 T16 in Greece.

of Markku Alen and Massimo Biasion and the Renault 5 Turbo of Jean Ragnotti.

Meanwhile, a sense of forboding was rapidly spreading through the competition departments in Turin and Ingolstat. Lancia and Audi had more or less had things to themselves until now. Walter Rohrl had won the Monte Carlo Rally for the third year running at the wheel of a third different car (Opel Ascona, Lancia Rally and, now, Audi Quattro A2) and Stig Blomqvist, second on the Monte, had moved to the top of the drivers championship by dominating the Swedish Rally. In Portugal, it had been Mikkola's turn to win for Audi and move them 10 points ahead of Lancia in the manufacturers championship. Bjorn Waldegaard excelled himself on the Safari to give Toyota their only win of the season. And then came Corsica, Alen taking the lead of the championship while moving Lancia to within four points of Audi.

It had been a bad weekend for the Germans. Not only could they manage no better than fifth place for Blomqvist, but the performance of the Peugeot had dominated the first appearance of the Audi Quattro Sport. But, then, perhaps they preferred it that way since the comparitively bulky looking Sport entered for Rohrl was plagued with overheating problems and finally blew up. This stubby car with the reduced wheelbase featured an engine which was worth more than 450 bhp! The straight-line performance was, as the American ad-men say, 'truly awesome'. The handling, though, was truly awful, certainly by the more precise standards of the Peugeot.

But, on with the motley – Blomqvist and Mikkola marched home first and second on the Acropolis to tilt the championships in favour of Audi and the silent Swede. In New Zealand, Blomqvist went even further ahead by leading from half-distance (with the older A2 Quattro, as in Greece), a result which did Alen's championship hopes little good even though he finished second. The momentum really seemed to be in favour of Blomqvist and Audi when they scooped first place in Argentina, with Mikkola adding further to their tally by finishing second. It all came to an abrupt end in Finland on August 26 1984 when the Peugeot 205 Turbo 16 won the first of many splendid victories.

The Ari and Terry Show

There was national pride at stake during the Rally of the 1000 Lakes. This was not called the 'Finnish Grand Prix' for nothing and, from the outset, the pace was shattering. Blomqvist held a tenuous lead in the A2 Quattro for the first three stages with Alen's Lancia taking charge for the next nine. By now, Vatanen was into his stride and, by setting the fastest time over the next eight stages in succession, he took a lead which, barring mechanical problems, he never looked like losing. Alen never gave up, although in the end they would be separated by two minutes.

Toivonen's Lancia was third, but more important was fourth place for Blomqvist. This gave the manufacturers championship to Audi – not that you would have known it. Apart from having their noses rubbed in the Finnish dirt by Peugeot and Lancia, both Mikkola and Mouton had crashed their Quattro Sports. The writing was on the wall – and it was in French.

The record books say that Vatanen and Harryman carried off a second win five weeks later on the San Remo Rally. What the fact sheets do not record is the absolutely terrifying conditions the crews had to work under.

Wind, rain, mud and fog made the already difficult stages even more treacherous. Some say the rally should have been stopped. But it was not, and Vatanen was left to defend his lead from an attack by Rohrl. There was no one else in the contest, Alen and Blomqvist, the championship contenders, having retired.

Would Vatanen crack under similar circumstances to the Corsican rally? In the end, it was Rohrl who crashed. But, in truth it was only a matter of luck for on more than one occasion Vatanen had teetered on the brink of disaster.

'These were the worst conditions I can ever remember,' says Harryman, recalling more than 20 years' experience as a co-driver. 'It was horrendous. In fact, I was disgusted that one stage in particular was not cancelled. I think irresponsible is perhaps the wrong word here, but it did show how little the organisers knew about the kind of risks the competitors faced. They think you simply slow down if the conditions are bad. Well, of course, you are forced to slow down to a certain extent, but even so. . . . They were very lucky that there was not a more serious accident. We had a *big* moment and came out of it okay. Walter was not so lucky . . .'

Luck or no luck, the momentum was most certainly with Peugeot. Stig Blomqvist won the Ivory Coast Rally. By so doing, he not only became world champion but he also gave the Audi Quattro Sport its first victory. And, by the confusing and contorted politics which governed Audi, Stig also did himself out of a drive on his favourite rally, the Lombard RAC.

Audi were more interested in developing the Quattro Sport for the forthcoming season although their intentions were perhaps misunderstood when a Quattro Sport was entered for Mouton in order to fulfill the Frenchwoman's contract. As for Mikkola, he would drive an A2 for Audi Sport UK. Blomqvist, the previous year's winner, therefore would be a spectator. It was a strange omission at a time when Audi were squaring up to the rising menace from Peugeot. And since Lancia were staying away for the second year in succession, Audi would be alone in this most public contest.

The entry was not exactly brimming with stars from the international arena. Once you had discussed the Peugeot/Audi battle, it was then a matter of seeing who would pick up the remaining places. With Jimmy McRae and Russell Brookes both driving Opel Manta 400s, there was clearly a personal duel on the cards there. Toyota had Celica Turbos for Bjorn Waldegaard, Per Eklund and rising star Juha Kankunnen, while Timo Salonen, Shekhar Mehta and Terry Kaby would represent Nissan with the 240RS.

John Buffum: a Yank at the wheel.

There was an A2 Quattro for John Buffum, the persistent star of the American scene (and Videovision videos of the Lombard RAC), plus a more elderly Quattro A1 for Malcolm Wilson, the young Briton doing his best to re-establish a career which had been left high and dry by a nasty accident and the shelving of Ford's plans to rally the RS1700T.

Then there was a Rover Vitesse for Tony Pond. This was seen as a major contender for victory in Group A, a category introduced as part of the new rule package at the beginning of 1984 allowing limited modifications to cars of which a minimum of 5000 had to be produced per annum. Pond was backed by the *Daily Mirror* and the paper confidently expected one of Britain's most popular drivers to provide the odd story or two during the course of the next five days.

They would get just one story from Pond. It would be something of a show-stopper and it would come rather sooner than expected.

The rally, based at Chester for the third time, would be made up of the now traditional loops to the north and into Wales. They would be prefaced by the Sunday run through seven spectator stages in the Midlands followed by a night-halt at Chester. In total, there would be 551 miles of competitive driving spread over 56 stages.

Two miles into the first stage, Tony Pond crashed into a tree and destroyed the front left-hand corner of his Rover.

It was an incredible error which showed both the slippery nature of the stage and the fact that this preamble to the main event should not be treated lightly. The incident occurred at Knowsley Safari Park, the stage where Hannu Mikkola had crashed the previous year.

And, lo and behold, the Swedish driver spun his Quattro yet again, although this time there was no damage. Even so, it was a bad start for Audi as Vatanen set the fastest time and eased out a 39-second lead during the rest of the day.

A 5 am start on Monday left competitors in no doubt over the intentions of the organisers. By 8 o'clock, they were pounding through Grizedale and, for once, the Lake District stages would not have a major say in the outcome of the rally. Fastest time on Grizedale North helped Mikkola haul himself into second place, but a string of fast times from Vatanen at Kershope, Castle O'er, Twiglees, Craik, Ogre Hill, Redesdale and Falstone consolidated the Peugeot driver's lead.

But Mikkola was not done yet. The Audi was fastest through Bewshaugh, Wark, Hamsterley and Langdale. The most telling performance, however, came in the long and fast Dalby stage. Here Mikkola, by his own high standards, covered the stage quickly and without error, yet Vatanen was 34 seconds faster. He had survived an on-board fire extinguisher going off in the Lake District and the Peugeot's bonnet flying off near the Scottish border. In spite of all this, Vatanen was leading by four minutes when the cars returned to Chester on Tuesday night.

There was little Mikkola could do except wait and hope for a mistake by Vatanen. The odds, in some way, were in Mikkola's favour. Vatanen now had the difficult task of pacing himself on the way north through Wales without either spinning off because he was going too fast, or losing concentration because he was going too slowly. Even a potentially time-consuming puncture in the Forest of Dean had occurred towards the end of a stage. Everything was going too well.

Ari's worst fears were confirmed at around 10.30 on the final night. It was a wet and miserable evening with pockets of mist and fog lurking in the depths of the forest. Vatanen had covered about a fifth of the 28-mile Morgannwg stage, situated to the north-east of Neath, when he arrived at a corner too quickly, the Peugeot digging into the ruts on the edge of the track and rolling onto its roof. But even at that hour, in such miserable conditions, in the middle of nowhere, spectators materialised from the gloom and helped right the Peugeot.

'It was the second time we had passed through the stage,' says Harryman, 'so, it had been cut up very badly since our first run through. The car went into one of the ruts, came out and then more or less tripped over another. It went over very gently, but finished on its roof.

'Once the spectators arrived, the car was righted very quickly. In fact, had Ari and I known it would be that easy, we would have done it ourselves. There was not much damage but the windscreen was the worst bit. At that point, Per Eklund arrived and we let him go ahead of us. We tried running behind Per but the stones flicked up by his car damaged our lights, so we couldn't follow him.'

All told, it cost about five minutes. Vatanen was now second, 40 seconds behind Mikkola. Ari gained 17 seconds on the next stage and a further two seconds on Lady Megan, to the north of Carmarthen. By the time he reached Llanafan, near Aberystwyth, he was leading once more. But it was not over yet.

Six miles from the end of the Gartheniog stage, north of Machynlleth, a driveshaft broke. On a two-wheel drive car, of course, it would have meant instant retirement. Vatanen, albeit with reduced power, was able to continue to the end of the stage, where he emerged in second place, one second behind Mikkola.

Hannu was ready to drive flat out and make the most of any weakness which the driveshaft failure may have brought about on the Peugeot's transmission. Unfortunately, a thrilling climax was lost when a wastegate on the Audi chose that moment to jam. It could not be fixed and the subsequent loss of power meant Mikkola was helpless as Vatanen, his car now repaired, set the fastest time on the remaining six stages.

'As far as I'm concerned,' says Terry Harryman, 'winning the RAC Rally was absolutely fantastic. It ranks as the second most satisfying result after winning the Safari, which is something else again. But, having said that, if the RAC Rally result had come first, then perhaps it would be the best. Anyway, it was a great achievement and I rate it more highly than victory in, say, the Monte Carlo Rally.'

Peugeot had beaten Audi by a mere 41 seconds after 533 miles of flat-out motoring (four of the stages had been shortened). The rest, led by the Toyota of Eklund and Dave Whittock as they struggled in the wake of this titanic battle, were 17 minutes behind. The results sheet said everything about Peugeot's intentions for 1985 and the stunning power and grip generated by the latest Supercars. And the performance graph would rise more steeply yet.

Wheels Take Wings

Slowly at first, but gradually gathering momentum, the old order would change during 1985. Audi had won the manufacturers championship for three years in succession, but in the light of three wins on the trot at the end of the previous year Peugeot looked set to knock the Quattro off a platform on which it had balanced, somewhat precariously, since 1981. It seemed obvious, too, that Ari Vatanen would take the drivers title as he pleased.

Certainly, there appeared to be nothing wrong with those predictions when Vatanen won the Monte Carlo Rally at the end of January. He had beaten Rohrl's Quattro Sport in treacherous conditions while overcoming an eight-minute penalty after an elementary but potentially disastrous management error by Terry Harryman when he checked in early at a control.

The forecast seemed even more secure when Vatanen led Blomqvist's Quattro Sport all the way in Sweden. Then Ari stopped reading the script. In Portugal, an error of judgement saw the Finn ask too much from a car hobbled by a puncture as he chased the Quattro of Walter Rohrl and Massimo Biasion's Lancia 037.

Biasion, the single entry from Lancia as the team concentrated on development of the four-wheel drive Delta, dropped back when the rally switched from tarmac to gravel. Rohrl then developed mechanical trouble six stages from home and the event was won by Timo Salonen.

It may have been a slightly fortuitous victory for the bespectacled Finn but it marked an increasing confidence as he settled into his role as anchor-man with Peugeot Talbot Sport. Indeed, he was to be the team's only survivor on the Safari Rally, a disastrous event for Peugeot, Audi and Lancia. The Safari was merely maintaining its special reputation, one which Toyota managed to come to terms with in a big way when Juha Kankkunen and Fred Gallagher brought their Celica Turbo home 34 minutes ahead of team-mates Bjorn Waldegaard and Hans Thorzelius.

The joy experienced by Ove Andersson's team in Nairobi on April 8 would not be matched by Renault a few weeks later in Corsica. A win for the Renault 5 Maxi Turbo of Jean Ragnotti and Pierre Thimonier was clouded by a fatal accident which claimed Attilio Bettega, Lancia withdrawing Alen and Biasion as a mark of respect.

Rohrl and Salonen had gone out on the first stage in any case, but Vatanen was to crash at the half-way mark. It is unlikely that Ari would have won but the effects of the accident – his second in succession in Corsica – were beginning to niggle when the teams met again four weeks later in Greece. By the end of the Acropolis Rally, Vatanen's frustration was even more pronounced.

By driving at a beautifully controlled pace, Salonen had won, to move 28 points ahead of Vatanen in the championship. He increased that to 33 points by winning in New Zealand but the difference here was a more subdued and orderly drive by Vatanen into second place. It was a sign that Ari was ready to get back into the swing of things again. He would be his old self in Argentina at the end of July.

Sure enough, Vatanen was fastest at the end of the first stage – albeit by just one second after 16 miles – and he was no longer worrying about his driving, or Salonen, or the championship. Winning was the thing. Three miles into the next stage, a dip in the road almost killed him.

Hammering down a long straight, flat-out in top gear, the Peugeot hit the dip, the tail of the car rising to force the nose into soft ground. That set in motion a devasting series of cartwheels, the Peugeot cavorting down the road for 200 yards or so, bodywork flying in all directions. While the flimsy outside shell broke into a thousand pieces, the passenger cell, protected by a stout steel cage, mercifully absorbed most of the unimaginable forces which were attempting to tear Vatanen and Harryman limb from limb.

Fortunately, Peugeot's helicopter was close at hand and quickly lifted the injured crew to hospital. At first it was thought Vatanen would not live through the night, but his high degree of fitness helped carry him onto the first stage of a long road to recovery.

'The accident happened because there had been several days of rain after we had finished practise,' explains Harryman. 'The water had run across the road and left this soft furrow. There was a bump just before it. We hit that and went nose first into the soft mud – and away we went.'

Harryman was eventually flown home to Northern Ireland where it was discovered he had a broken left shoulder and a fracture in his right hand to add to broken vertebrae. The fact that Salonen had assumed the lead and scored yet another win to more or less tie up the drivers championship almost seemed incidental.

So, too, did the arrival of the latest Audi Quattro Sport, a mean-looking device with deep spoilers and a massive rear wing taken straight from the pages of Formula 1. This car had been entrusted to Blomqvist, who pressed Salonen hard until the engine failed. All was not lost for the German team, however, when an Austrian 'privateer', Wilfried Wiedner, brought an A2 into second place in Argentina to keep Audi's championship hopes alive.

Audi's chances were finally crushed three weeks later on the 1000 Lakes. It was 'Finnish Grand Prix' time again and Salonen joined an elite band by not only winning at home but also by securing the championship for himself and Peugeot Talbot Sport.

The event was also notable for the return of Henri Toivonen, after a five-month absence with a back injury, and Hannu Mikkola, placed on an expensive reserves bench by Audi. Neither driver could hope to tune in immediately to the fast and furious pace, particularly as Peugeot had wheeled out the 'E2', the latest version of their 205 Turbo 16.

Apart from a large black wing wrapped around the rear edge of the roof and a bib spoiler jutting out below the front bumper level, the Peugeot looked much as before, but appearances can be extremely deceptive. Almost every item from brakes to suspension and steering incorporated subtle changes. And a major revision to the engine and its ancillaries saw a leap to over 420 bhp.

The new cars were coming thick and fast now, although for Lancia progress with the Delta S4 had been painfully slow, Alen in particular becoming extremely frustrated by the Rally 037. The Ford RS200 was a long way off but, at long last, the Metro 6R4 was ready for action after a lengthy gestation period on the proving grounds and British national events.

The Metro's appearance had changed considerably since its launch in 1984. For one thing, it had sprouted aerofoils front and rear. It did not look sleek but the Metro, along with the Lancia Delta S4 and the

177

evolution versions of the Quattro Sport and the Peugeot 205, brought a hitherto unknown level of sophistication to rallying – and they would compete against each other for the first time on the 1985 Lombard RAC Rally.

A Road Too Far?

'I think this is going to be one of the toughest yet, Mr. Dave Bloody Whittock has seen to that!' said Malcolm Wilson, clearly not exactly relishing the thought of the Lombard RAC Rally. But his typically forthright reference to the schedule, mapped out by route co-ordinator Dave Whittock, had more than a hint of respect mixed with nervous anticipation. It was like the seconds before you plunge into the sea: you know it will be very cold to start with, but once you get going, the swim will be enjoyable. Although, in this case, perhaps an analogy with swimming the Channel might be more appropriate.

Dave Whittock knew exactly what he was doing. He had, after all, spent many hours sitting in the co-driver's seat and Jim Porter had given the West Country man the opportunity to design a rally in keeping with the tough traditions of the RAC.

'My aim', says Whittock, 'was to make the rally as near to the traditional RAC as I could. In other words, I wanted to make it tougher. It was to be ultra-demanding with as many stage miles as physically possible.

'Mr. Dave Bloody Whittock': a return to tradition.

'As I saw it, on shorter rallies the fastest drivers, who naturally had the most reliable cars, would simply go flat out. Their cars would not let them down and that would be it. I felt that the RAC Rally should be long enough and hard enough for the entire team – everyone, from the tea-maker to the driver – to play their part. The preparation, the planning, the servicing; all these things should be an essential part of a winning team. To me, the RAC is one of the greatest rallies in the world and I wanted to keep it that way at a time when rallies elsewhere were becoming standardised.'

The international brigade, now more accustomed to the 'office hours' format of a day's rallying to pace notes and then a night in bed, were appalled. Timo Salonen, speaking from a position of authority as world champion, roundly condemned the organisers, saying the schedule was far too tough, bearing in mind the requirements of driving cars which had the performance of Grand Prix machines. He was supported by several Scandinavian crews, particularly the Finns.

'I wasn't surprised at Salonen,' recalls Whittock. 'But I was surprised at the rest of the so-called Finnish Mafia joining him in their criticism. Markku Alen said Kielder was dangerous. I told him he should know better than to say a thing like that; you'd think he'd never rallied before. I think the whole affair had been instigated by Salonen – and the trouble was I was torn between everyone. Jimmy McRae and Russell Brookes,

A welcome return to the winner's circle for Henri Toivonen in 1985 after a titanic battle.

for instance, said they had examined the route closely and they didn't think it would be as tough as it seemed.'

Salonen was supported by Jean Todt, who said a secret rally had no place on the international calendar of the Eighties. The remaining aspects of the Lombard RAC – the organisation, the special stages, the behaviour of the spectators – were first class. But a rally without pace notes was asking for trouble.

Others disagreed. It was felt that not all rounds of the championship should be the same and it was the unique challenge of the RAC which made it an event to relish. The question of rallying through the night was not widely condemned either. This was what rallying was all about, said the supporters. As for the organisers, they remained resolute. In any case, the nine hours of competitive motoring were interspersed with $28\frac{1}{2}$ hours of rest time. It was just that little of it would be at night.

So what, precisely, had 'Mr. Dave Bloody Whittock' done to cause such a stir? Nottingham had been chosen for the Rally HQ and the RAC scored another first when they launched competitors straight onto a special stage at the start, rather than providing the usual leisurely departure from a street in the city centre.

The first day, Sunday, was occupied with spectator stages at Wollaton Park, Clumber Park, Chatsworth, Trentham Gardens, Weston Park, Sutton Park and Bewdley. Nothing unusual here. Except, that any indiscretions involving park benches, trees, lion-pens and other sundry items would not be patched up with the benefit of return to Nottingham for a night halt. It was straight onto the main business of the rally after a brief halt at Worcester.

Three stages in quick succession in the Forest of Dean would lead on to four more in South Wales and a three-and-a-half hour rest halt at Swansea. Then it was back to work at 6 am on Monday for the long haul through Wales and another 12 stages before returning to Nottingham at 7.30 pm the same day.

Now the difficult bit. A 10 o'clock departure on Tuesday morning would be the only civilised aspect of the second leg. Over 90 miles of special stages in Yorkshire would lead to a four-hour rest halt at Carlisle. By 3.45 on Wednesday morning competitors would be on their way towards a debilitating run through Kielder and Southern Scotland before staggering back to Carlisle at lunchtime for a welcome break of just $7\frac{1}{2}$ hours.

And just when the weary crews thought they had done with Kielder, they were sent back to deal with the likes of Bewshaugh, Wark, Rooken and Spithope, a journey which would take them into the early hours of Thursday and another visit to the Castle O'er Forest in Scotland before finally taking the road south. A brief halt in Carlisle and then a 6 am re-start before the difficult Lake District stages which would provide the last hurdle on the way to Nottingham for the finish at 3.10 pm.

In all, 2,205 miles, 549 of which would be divided among the 63 special stages actually run (two would be cancelled). It is interesting to note that Whittock had wanted to introduce pace notes to the Sunday stages, but he was eventually overruled. His reasoning is interesting:

'The problem for the competitors is that most of these stages are not on the maps so there is no guidance for the navigator to give to the driver. Yes, I know there are maps issued in the Road Books, but these are not to scale. I felt that with six of seven special stages it would be possible to have practise sessions, three hours or so where they would go through in convoy, twice would be enough, and make notes.

'It's true that the cars would then be travelling faster on the rally itself – but I feel that it's much safer because the crews know where they're going. In any case, any British crew worth their salt will have been to Sutton Park, or wherever, and had a nose around. About a week before the rally, they start putting up the spectator barriers and it's easy to see where the stage goes. Foreigners, who don't have the chance to do this, know it goes on and they don't like it. Not only do they not like it, they *say* they don't like it. I felt that pace notes on these stages would keep everyone happy. But two area organisers said no and that was that.'

Whittock did have his way, however, when it came to unearthing long stages, and at the end of the rally he would be particularly heartened to have Ian Grindrod compliment him on finding stage mileage which he never knew existed. Coming from such an experienced and accomplished co-driver, this would be praise indeed. All told, it was a mind-bending schedule, reminiscent of Jack Kemsley's marathons. Then, of course, the Saabs and Minis had all of 120 bhp.

Timo Salonen, his headlights yellow in the dank morning cloaking Wollaton Park, had 460 bhp at his disposal as the E2 Peugeot set off along the slippery tarmac roads of the municipal park. Hannu Mikkola had 500 bhp to be cautious with as he followed through in the latest Audi Quattro Sport. Then came Markku Alen, dealing with over 450 bhp as he opened an exciting new chapter for Lancia with the Delta S4. Not only did this purposeful device have four-wheel drive, Lancia had the best of both worlds by incorporating a supercharger and a turbocharger in order to extract the maximum from the 1795cc four-cylinder engine at both low and high revs.

Next, Walter Rohrl. A surprising entry this, considering the German driver's dislike of the secret rally, but at least he would gain some local knowledge from Phil Short in the co-driver's seat. Rohrl, in any case, would be kept busy with the experimental automatic gearbox on his Quattro Sport. The gearbox would allow Rohrl to keep his foot on the power (and therefore maintain a high level of turbo boost) while changing up through the gearbox. His left foot, meanwhile, would be free to operate the brake pedal at all times. Starting from rest would be the only occasion when the clutch would be called for. And, with typical efficiency, Audi had built in an override switch which allowed a return to the normal use of the clutch in case of a failure with the new system.

Following Rohrl out of Nottingham were two Toyota Celica Turbos, split by Henri Toivonen's Lancia Delta. Bjorn Waldegaard and Juha Kankkunen did not hold out much hope of repeating their staged dead-heat to win the Ivory Coast Rally, but at least they expected the Toyotas to head the 'two-wheel drive' division. They might even have a chance of tackling the Metros of Tony Pond and Malcolm Wilson, something of an unknown quantity over what would be the first real test of Austin Rover's four-wheel drive machine.

With a 'mere' 410 bhp to play with from the non-turbocharged V6, more or less mounted on the back seat of the stubby little car, Pond and Wilson were hoping that the more immediate response from the normally aspirated engine would be in their favour as they tackled the blind corners. But, could the transmission take the punishment? Would those aerodynamic appendages really work? Wilson felt very confident. The 6R4, he said, would cope with anything 'Mr. Dave Bloody Whittock' chose to throw at it.

Dashing Debutants

Wilson probably did not have time to recall those words when the Metro's bonnet tried to wrap itself around the windscreen on the Serridge stage in the Forest of Dean. That rather startling incident cost Wilson half a minute but problems with the differential two stages later would have a more lingering effect. As Wilson struggled on with front-wheel drive only, this seemed to be the beginning of an inevitable catalogue of failures.

Similarly, a misfire and sundry other minor problems on the Lancias appeared to be the prelude to what would amount to no more than a five-day test session for the Italian team. Alen may have been leading, but when Mikkola gradually forged his way to the front after 14 stages, the rally appeared to be settling down in a predictable fashion. The Lombard RAC was all about reliability and pace; Mikkola and Audi would walk it.

Seven stages later, Mikkola was out. The five cylinder engine had lost its oil pressure, making it two retirements for Audi since Rohrl had literally disappeared when he rolled his car down a steep embankment two miles from the end of the Rheola stage in the Vale of Neath. Salonen had threatened to withdraw from the rally later that night as a protest over the difficult schedule but the Finnish driver was denied the power of his veto when the Peugeot stopped, with no oil pressure, on Hafren.

So with just 20 stages completed and the rally barely 24 hours old, Alen led Toivonen by 82 seconds, with Pond a further 75 seconds behind the Lancias. And the remarkable aspect of the 1985 Lombard RAC Rally was the fact that these three drivers, in comparatively untried cars, would dominate the remainder of the 5-day event. Suddenly, the business of treating the rally as a test exercise had gone out the window. All three were driving as quickly as they dared in wet and frequently icy conditions.

By the time they had returned to Nottingham, Alen led Pond by three minutes with Toivonen a minute behind after a fuel feed problem had intervened three stages from the rest halt.

The order almost changed again at the end of the infamous Dalby stage late on Tuesday afternoon. Alen had arrived at a corner, flat out in fifth gear, and dived into a fire break. It took some time to extricate the Lancia and he was then forced to complete the rest of the 25-mile stage at a slow pace since a rear wheel was threatening to fall off. Pond, meanwhile, had been the fastest through the longest stage on the rally and the gap between the leaders was now 74 seconds, with Toivonen 37 seconds behind the Metro.

A broken differential soon afterwards meant Toivonen had to watch Alen and Pond pull away through Pickering and Cropton, but by the time they had reached Stang Forest, to the west of Middlesbrough, repairs had been carried out and the chase was on, Toivonen setting fastest time over the next three tests. After completing the Falstone stage in the Kielder Forest, Alen led Pond by $2\frac{1}{2}$ minutes and Toivonen was only one second behind the Englishman.

Pond responded by setting fastest time through Yair Hill Forest, near Galashiels, but the furious pace on treacherous roads at a time when the crews were becoming weary, began to tell. Pond lost over a minute when he slid off the Craik stage. Toivonen, on the other hand, was remarkably lucky when he rolled his Delta at Kilburn Hill in the Castle O'er Forest. Not only was the damage slight but the incident cost the

Finn less than half a minute. Alen now led his team-mate by just over three minutes with Pond breathing down Toivonen's neck.

As they made their way into the Kielder complex once more, Toivonen and Pond took it in turns to set the fastest times through Kershope and Bewshaugh. Alen was never far behind, but on the 54th stage, at Wark, he spun. The Lancia was stuck fast and had it not been for a generous act by Kankunnen, when the Toyota driver stopped to help push Alen free, Markku would have been out of the rally.

As it was, he had lost the lead, leaving Toivonen and Pond less than a minute apart. Although suffering from a heavy cold, Pond never gave up. The relentless battle for the lead continued all the way through the Lake District and it seemed certain that something would give; either the driver or the car or both.

Toivonen had not won a world championship rally since the RAC in 1980. He had only driven the Delta S4 for about 30 miles on loose surfaces before the start of the event. The pressure was enormous.

Pond, too, had to measure his speed with the thought that his record on this rally was littered with visits to the scenery. And behind them both came Alen, setting fastest times at Rooken, Spithope and the long Grizedale stage. It was enough to move him into second place but Toivonen was too far ahead. The gap at the finish measured just 56 seconds.

Pond and Rob Arthur, a further 91 seconds behind, had nothing to be ashamed of. They had been overwhelmed by the support from the massive crowd lining the route. The 6R4 had about as much in common with a standard Metro as the tenuous relationship between a jet fighter and a Jumbo jet but, somehow, the British public found a ready identity with the blue-and-white machine.

It had been an absorbing contest and every mile of the route seemed to be etched on the faces of the first three crews as they rolled into Wollaton Park as dusk fell on Thursday afternoon. The next car, the Audi Quattro A2 of Per Eklund, was 26 minutes in arrears with Kankkunen's conventional Celica Turbo another ten minutes behind what had formerly been considered the car to beat. Now, another generation of Supercars had arrived.

Where To Now?

Rallying engineers had appeared to go berserk in 1985. They had acted as though let loose in a magical world unfettered by rules and red tape – which in a sense was true. The products of their creative powers appeared gradually throughout the season and each succeeding vehicle left the observer agog. Each time it seemed the limit had been reached. You could only ask a driver to cope with so much grip and accleration on a special stage, and this was it.

Then a few weeks later, someone would rewrite the definition of a rally car. Whether it was for better or for worse depended on your point of view. But like it or not, this was rallying in the Eighties and we were reminded that drivers' fees were commensurate with the risks.

That was open to doubt. Rally drivers were not receiving anything like the sums enjoyed by their more glossy colleagues in Formula 1. Yet these were racing cars in all but name, and there was hardly an inch of steel barrier or run-off area to be seen. It was not that rally drivers wanted such sanitisation of their sport; merely that due recognition be given to the perils of operating with the tools they had been presented with. There was an unspoken feeling that this Group B monster would suddenly bite back – and then it would be too late.

The Metro 6R4: a racing car in all but name.

13

SORROW AND VERY LITTLE JOY

Into the Abyss

THE VILLAGE of St. Sauveur de Montagut lies in a deep V-shaped valley in the Ardeche. It is early evening on Monday, January 20 1986. As darkness grows, the temperature drops to 5°C but the indications are that it will go no further. There is no sign of ice on the D261, a minor road which climbs away into the trees from the adjoining hamlet of Le Moulinon.

Tonight, a gendarme is positioned at the bottom of the hill. The D261, he says, is closed to normal traffic. Except, that is, for rally cars – and by no stretch of the imagination can a Group B Quattro Sport be called 'normal traffic'.

Henri Toivonen: finger-tip genius.

Walter Rohrl had just emerged from the Audi service area in St. Sauveur. The Quattro had arrived about ten minutes before, after a hard afternoon's work in the mountains to the west of the Rhone Valley. Now it had been prepared in readiness for the 10th stage of the Monte Carlo Rally, and a recent reconnaissance of the D261 confirms that slicks will be in order. The stage will run for 23 miles, crossing the Col de la Fayolle on its way to Antraigues. And the start is just along the road, at the foot of the hill in Le Moulinon.

St. Sauveur is bustling. The normal tea-time traffic of a couple of Citroen 2 CVs and a handful of battered Renault 4s has been augmented by the urgent arrival of the rally and the fast-moving circus of support and service vehicles which accompany it through France. And here's Rohrl, working his way through the main street in a yellow-and-white device which looks and sounds as though it has come from another planet.

The pistol cracks and the surging drone of the five-cylinder turbo reverberates around the street as he accelerates while, at the same time, restraining the Quattro by easing the brakes on and off with his left foot. His hands, meanwhile, are busy swerving the car from side to side as he scrubs heat into the Michelin tyres. With each swing of the wheel, the bulbous, angry form misses the parked cars and on-coming traffic by inches.

This is happening at about 30 mph. It doesn't sound much, but the sensation of crudely-bridled power in such mundane surroundings is

185

overwhelming. Viewed from the back, the massive wing, perched high above the oil coolers and the radiators which fill the boot, blocks any sight of Rohrl and Geistdorfer. The water, seen slopping around in the tanks at back of the rear wheel arches, give some indication of the call Rohrl is about to make on his brakes as he keeps in check the same amount of power which Keke Rosberg had at his disposal when he won the Grand Prix world championship in 1982. The thought of taking this device flat out, at night, on a twisting, narrow mountain road, seems as terrifying as its rowdy presence among the trappings of everyday motoring. It is a stunning display of Group B gone mad.

Half-an-hour later, Rohrl is in Antraigues. His time, the quickest on the stage, has been half a minute faster than that of Massimo Biasion and good enough to move the Audi into third place overall, ahead of the Lancia Delta. On the next stage, La Souche, Rohrl is fastest, and this time he overhauls the Delta of Markku Alen to take second place. The man and his machine are clearly at one. It must be a superb feeling to make such a beast work for you rather than against you. But the observer, watching from another world, can merely speculate on that.

Rohrl's attempts to catch the Lancia Delta of Henri Toivonen are to be largely wasted the following day when a puncture on the Burzet stage costs him six minutes. Toivonen, driving brilliantly despite a leg injury received when he collided with a spectator's car, overcomes a challenge from Timo Salonen's Peugeot to take his second win in succession. Rohrl is fourth behind the similar Quattro Sport of Hannu Mikkola.

We weren't to know it at the time, but the Monte Carlo Rally would mark the swansong of the Audi Quattro Sport and the final chance we would have to publicly applaud Henri Toivonen's finger-tip genius at the wheel of a rally car.

Portugal Pays the Inevitable Price

Toivonen had been confident of victory in Sweden until the engine failed, but trouble of an infinitely more serious nature would arise at the next round of the championship in Portugal.

The behaviour of the crowd had been a worry to the drivers from the moment the Portuguese Rally became a round of the championship in 1973. Each year drivers would complain and editorials would be written about the stupidity of the locals and the effect a fatal accident could have on the sport. As ever, nothing was done to either curtail the suicidal tendencies of the spectators or to avoid the perpetual troublespots.

The worst area was the hillside region of Sintra, situated close to the major population centres around Lisbon. If anything, the lunatic fringe was worse than before and drivers were appalled to find a human wall not only lining the special stage, but frequently forming a barrier across it. Only at the last minute would the spectators part, as though playing an automotive bullfight.

Many did not allow for either the increased performance of the Group B cars or the fact that, in many cases, the sound of their approach was muffled by turbochargers and engines mounted at the rear. Having said that, the accident which occurred could have involved a car from any category.

Joaquim Santos, a local driver, lost control of his Ford RS200 while trying to avoid hooligans making a late retreat from the middle of the road. The car shot into the crowd. A woman and two children were killed and a fourth person died later.

The drivers were not willing to continue the totally unnecessary slaughter; the sport was dangerous enough without this. They held a meeting at a hotel close by the Estoril autodrome and decided not to continue. And still FISA, the sport's governing body, refused to accept the appallng reality of the situation. There was even talk of fining the drivers!

The accident had little to do with sheer speed. It was not an indictment of Group B but, in the tense climate generated by the need to succeed in international rallying, it merely added another turn of the screw.

It was a similar situation to that in the 1975 Spanish Grand Prix, which was run on a stunning but potentially dangerous track in a public park high above Barcelona. The drivers were alarmed to find that the steel barriers lining the circuit had not been mounted properly and many of the bolts were either loose or missing. It did little for their peace of mind and the entire weekend was a series of meetings, protests and boycotts.

But commercial considerations will out on these occasions and the drivers had little option but to race. At the foot of a steep hill a few hundred yards after the start, there was a pile-up as three of the leading cars tangled wheels. The race was halted. There were no injuries and, on a normal weekend, the incident would have been shrugged off as another story to recount at the dinner table.

On this weekend, however, it acted as a stimulant to nervous systems which had become frayed and were close to breaking. There was the unmistakable, but difficult to define, feeling that something dreadful would happen. It did. At the start of lap 26, a car went out of control and flew over a safety barrier, killing four people standing in a prohibited area. Spilt fuel coursed down the hill. Police lashed out with their batons. The pandemonium which ensued was not easily forgotten by those who saw it.

The irony here is that the accident – caused by a rear wing breaking off the car – had nothing to do with the inefficiency of the barriers. But it somehow seemed inevitable. More important, it concentrated the minds, for a while at least, of the hitherto complacent men with the blazers and leather armbands. It would be the same in Corsica on May 3 1986.

Nobody knows the exact reason why Henri Toivonen's Lancia Delta plunged off the road. All that was left was the charred famework as evidence of an immediate explosion which took the life of Toivonen and his co-driver Sergio Cresto.

Toivonen had been a driver of consummate skill, a talent which, up until that fateful moment, he had been exercising to the full as he set the fastest time on 12 of the previous 16 stages. According to those present, he was in devastating form as he put the Delta through its paces on the twisting tarmac. Whether the accident was the fault of the driver or of the Group B car may never be ascertained since no one was present on this remote part of the island. Its effects, however, would be far-reaching.

FISA took their usual course of reacting to events once they had happened and made front-page news worldwide. The stable door was bolted with a series of reforms which would ban Group B at the end of the year and, with more or less immediate effect, introduce shorter rallies with longer rest periods.

FISA, if anything, had overreacted and there was an immediate outcry from manufacturers who, in accordance with FISA's regulations, had built 200 Group B cars which, overnight, had become obsolete. Audi, reasoning that if the Group B cars had been deemed too dangerous now there was no sense in continuing with the same cars until the end of the year, withdrew immediately. The season, already in a sorry state, now fell apart.

Attempting to pick up the pieces of his shattered team, Cesare Fiorio renewed their championship campaign by sending three 037s to take part in the Safari Rally. It was not that the Delta had been scrapped as a result of the tragedy in Corsica but merely that the two-wheel drive 037 would be a more suitable tool in the quest for championship points on this punishing event. Alen finished third ahead of Lancia's main rival, Peugeot, and the Safari was won, once again, by the Toyota Celica Turbo of Bjorn Waldegaard and Fred Gallagher.

It was back to the Delta for the dusty and rough Acropolis Rally, but a turbo failure as Alen made his bid for the lead allowed Juha Kankkunen to add to his earlier victory in Sweden. The two Finns were at it again in New Zealand but Alen never recovered from the shock of meeting a pick-up truck and trailer coming the other way in the middle of a forest stage. He was just as annoyed when team orders in Argentina elected to have him finish second behind Massimo 'Miki' Biasion once Kankkunen had retired.

Next, the 1000 Lakes. A lead of three seconds at the end of the first 2.45-mile stage indicated Alen's intentions. He thrashed the opposition until, towards the closing stages, mounting pressure from Salonen's Peugeot caused Alen to push too far. Driving on the ragged edge, he rolled the Lancia down to third place. With Kankkunen finishing second, Peugeot had wrapped up the manufacturers championship for

Toyota won the Safari Rally and the Ivory Coast—but precious little else in the face of such technically advanced opposition in 1986.

the second year in succession, a magnificent achievement for a team with such a short history.

The Ivory Coast Rally, apart from giving Waldegaard and Gallagher another victory, had no bearing on the championship since Peugeot and Lancia bypassed the trip to West Africa and headed for San Remo. There the sport, climbing from the rock-bottom of Portugal and Corsica, plunged into a steep dive once more when the entire Peugeot team was excluded before the final leg. It was alleged they were running illegal aerodynamic aids on the underside of the car and the row cleared the way for Alen to take a win and close the deficit on Kankkunen. The only plus point of this unseemly row was the added impetus given to the penultimate round of the championship – the Lombard RAC Rally.

Superb British Finale

Judging by the pre-event publicity, it seemed the RAC were about to hold a wake at Bath for four days in November, with the heads and favourite sons of the family in attendance for a final fling of hitherto unseen ferocity. Then, the fond farewells, but few tears, the Group B 'rascal' was to be interred, having carved a memorable if sometimes painful niche in the history of the sport.

But how would the RAC Motor Sports Association handle the necessary arrangements? Bearing in mind the family row just 12 months before, when the boys from Scandinavia could not cope with a 'party' which lasted five days and two nights, it would be necessary to offer a murmur of sympathy, an understanding smile, no rough games after lights out, a minimum of time spent out in the cold, that sort of thing. Yes, this would call for the diplomacy required when world leaders fly to Britain for a State Funeral. And, in this case, many of the foreigners

189

would come not to praise the RAC Rally, but to bury it.

In the end, the organisers had no choice. FISA had decreed that the maximum time in which a rally could progress without a compulsory halt was 12 hours, and each leg had to be followed by a break of at least nine hours. In effect, the rally would stop each evening.

Of course, with the headquarters at Bath, returning to Avon each night would be out of the question. So instead of following the traditional figure of eight loops, the rally ran straight up and down the country, with night halts at Harrogate, Edinburgh and Liverpool. Within the overall total of 1,470 miles, 350 would be stage miles spread over 45 tests; a drastic reduction on 1985.

Jim Porter had stepped down after 14 excellent years and gone off to help run the Ford team. The RAC had selected Malcolm Neill to take Jim's place, the Ulsterman having acted as liaison officer for Nottingham on the previous year's event and before that, as Clerk of the Course for the Circuit of Ireland.

The call for increased control over spectators suited the RAC policy of encouraging the Sunday stages and Neill duly arranged to fill the run to Harrogate with nine visits to public parks and stately homes, a total of 27.29 stage miles.

Under normal circumstances, the drivers would have considered that a waste of time; a warm-up to the main event in Northumbria, Southern Scotland, the Lake District and Wales. But with the total stage distance reduced at the behest of FISA, every mile would count. The drivers would go flat-out all the way.

Anyone who doubted this should have stood in the 3.07-mile mixed surface stage running through Circencester Park. Apart from feeling chilly on this wet and blustery day, they would have seen Markku Alen slide off the road and thump the right-hand side of the Lancia against some trees. The bodywork was replaced, along with a new steering rack and front suspension, but Alen was more concerned about the 25 seconds or so it had cost him. There may have been 1,400 miles to go, but the championship was at stake from the outset and, to make matters worse, Juha Kankkunen had urged his Peugeot through Circencester faster than anyone else to take the lead by six seconds from the Ford of Stig Blomqvist.

This was also an important rally for Blomqvist. Forced to miss his favourite event two years running through no fault of his own, the 1986 season had caused further frustration. The mid-engined RS200, an elegant machine when compared with its rivals, did not appear until the Swedish Rally in February. Blomqvist retired, but his team-mate, Kalle Grundel, suggested that the wait may have been worthwhile as he finished third.

Genuine hopes of doing well in Portugal were ended by the accident, of course, but both Fords threatened to take a sensational victory in the Acropolis until sidelined by niggling problems. After that, Ford announced a virtual withdrawal. The RAC, then, was a last fling – in every sense of the word as far as Stig was concerned, since the relatively underpowered RS200 required every ounce of the driver's skill to make up for the shortfall in bhp.

As for Alen, he had too much power! The Lancia was more than a handful in the tight confines of Trentham Gardens and Chatsworth but, even so, the impatient Finn set fastest time on four stages to move into second place, four seconds behind Kankkunen at Harrogate.

Kankkunen was fortunate to be in the lead. As he tackled Trentham Gardens, the Finn had become aware of several litres of fuel slopping around the passenger compartment of the car. The fumes almost over-powered Kankkunen and his co-driver, Juha Piironen, and despite opening the doors to ventilate the interior, Kankkunen spun shortly before the end of the stage. A fuel cap had not been shut properly but no explanation was given as to how the petrol managed to find its way inside the car. With safety uppermost in everyone's minds, it was a question which was pursued with surprisingly little vigour. But then, of course, no one had been killed.

The cars left Harrogate at 7.30 on a bright but frosty Monday morning. Kankkunen immediately set about consolidating his lead as the real challenge of the RAC Rally lay before him in the forests close by the Pennines and in the Kielder complex.

Through the 17.84 miles of an icy Hamsterley Forest, Kankkunen was six seconds faster than anyone else. His Peugeot team-mate, Timo Salonen, lost 30 seconds and some of his bodywork when he slid off and Blomqvist picked up a puncture which cost the Ford driver almost a minute.

Into Kielder now, with Salonen making up for lost time by setting the pace through Shepherdshield (6.85 miles). As they moved on to Pundershaw, the gap between Kankkunen and Alen was 27 seconds but Markku was more concerned about the challenge coming from within his own team.

Following the loss of Toivonen, Lancia had drafted in Mikael Ericsson, a young Swede more accustomed to less powerful Group A machinery. Thrown in at the deep end, Ericsson did a reasonable job in Greece, New Zealand and Finland with what must have been a difficult car. But it was not good enough for Cesare Fiorio. On the night before the start of the RAC, Ericsson had been told that his services would not be required for 1987. It was a strange time to tell a driver a thing like that. Then again . . .

Since leaving Harrogate, and on stages that he had never seen before, Ericsson had been among the top three times. Now he was just 13 seconds behind Alen and poised to give a thrilling demonstration of both his skill and the performance of perhaps one of the most exciting Group B cars we would ever see.

The Pundershaw stage ran through the Wark forest. Fast and fairly wide by Kielder standards, it nevertheless climbed and fell through the trees, crossing the narrow bridge at Chirdon Burn before rushing up Allerybank, turning left and heading for White Sike and the Little Whickhope Burn at the bottom end of Kielder Reservoir. There, a wet but cheerful marshal was waiting to check them out of the stage and record the times.

After 15.97 miles, Kankkunen was just one second faster than Ericsson. They had averaged 72.13 mph. Alen was another five seconds behind his team-mate and, to put the shattering performance of these Supercars in perspective, the fastest Group A car, the four-wheel drive Mazda of Ingvar Carlsson, was *one minute and 45 seconds* slower than Kankkunen's Peugeot.

Within minutes of completing Pundershaw, they were off again for 15.36 miles of the Bewshaugh stage around Caplestone Fell where the Peugeots and Lancias averaged a mere 62 mph and Kankkunen almost crashed out of the rally.

Charging down a steep slope, the Finn lost control and could have written-off the Peugeot against one of the three narrow bridges on the stage. There was no damage done, but it cost Kankkunen 20 seconds – a serious loss considering that Alen was pushing hard and Ericsson, now just four seconds behind Alen, was continuing his charge.

Before the rally started Alen had talked to Peter Foubister of *Autosport* about his plans.

'Normally on the RAC Rally, I go about 90–95 per cent but when Kielder starts then I only go 70 per cent. I don't know how many times I have been leading the event with everything going well and I get to Kielder Forest and bang! It is all finished. So I go carefully there.'

Clearly, that plan had been abandoned because on the very next stage, Falstone, Alen was fastest! The fact that he was just a couple of seconds behind Kankkunen probably had something to do with it and, by the time they had emerged from Redesdale, the penultimate Kielder stage, Kankunnen led Alen by four seconds with Salonen, fastest through Bewshaugh and Falstone, now third, just one second behind Alen and seven ahead of Ericsson.

The positions changed yet again over the 7.12 miles which made up the Ogre Hill stage, Salonen setting the fastest time to hold joint first place with Alen. Kankkunen was third, three seconds behind. Ericsson, still fourth, was a further seven seconds in arrears.

It was a superb contest, made more difficult by the fact that Malcolm Neill had allowed the minimum of servicing in Kielder. Competitors had been forced to tackle Shepherdshield, Pundershaw and Bewshaugh in quick succession; a total of 38 miles on fast gravel. Choosing the correct tyres had been paramount although, to Alen's chagrin, one or two crafty teams had managed to organise a quick tyre-change in the depths of the forest.

There was obvious relief as the crews emerged from Ogre Hill. The dreaded Kielder was over for another year and now they headed towards Scotland and four more stages before a night's sleep in Edinburgh.

The leader board changed constantly, and by recording the fastest time over the 1.25 miles of tarmac at the Ingliston motor racing circuit, Mikael Ericsson found himself leading the Lombard RAC Rally by two seconds, with Salonen and Alen tying for second place and Kankkunen a further three seconds behind.

'I've never been in a rally which is as close as this,' said Ericsson as he left Edinburgh at 5 o'clock on Tuesday morning. 'I've no tactics for today. You have to go flat out all the way.'

Kankkunen had more or less the same plan as he set the fastest time through Craik Forest to the south-west of Hawick and retook the lead in one bound. Alen responded with the best performance through Castle O'er and, not to be outdone, Salonen had his say on the very next stage when he covered Twiglees in the Eskdalemuir Forest two seconds faster than Kankkunen.

And so it went on. As they moved south, the lead changed hands as though this was a five-lap Formula Ford race at Silverstone. By the time they left Wythop, in the Cumbrian Mountains, the leading four – Ericsson, Kankkunen, Alen and Salonen – were covered by only 16 seconds! Next on the agenda; the Grizedale Forest. Something had to give.

By the time they had done with the 25 miles of flinty gravel roads plunging through the Lake District, the leaders were covered by three-and-a-half minutes.

Once again Grizedale had a hand in rewriting the script of the RAC Rally, and this time it was Ericsson and Kankkunen who limped out with their tails between their legs. Ericsson hit a tree and rearranged the front suspension of the Lancia while Kankkunen had a potentially more serious incident when he rolled the Peugeot. Fortunately his damage was confined to the body panels, although it was later discovered that the chassis had been twisted.

Significantly, the more experienced Salonen and Alen had carved up the Grizedale stages between them and when they reached Liverpool for the final night halt were separated by only nine seconds.

The margin was extended during the first two stages in the Clocaenog Forest in North Wales early on Wednesday morning but Alen went into 'maximum attack' mode and reduced the gap to six seconds as they rushed through Penmachno and Coed-y-Brenin. It was a fascinating duel and yet, cool as you like, Salonen was calmly saying that he would wait until the final three stages of the rally in South Wales before defending his lead.

If Salonen's relaxed announcement ever reached Alen's ears, it would have done little for Markku's anxious demeanour. There was more at stake for Alen of course. Apart from desperately wanting to win the RAC Rally after several attempts, his judgement was tempered with the thought of championship points – or perhaps the thought of losing championship points should he make just one error in the heat of this tingling battle. Now, at least, Ericsson was no longer providing unnecessary pressure even though the young Swede had kicked off the day by setting the fastest times through the opening pair of stages and claiming second fastest on the next two.

Kankkunen, realising he could not hope to make up a three-minute deficit on the leaders – or at least, not while they were driving at such a breakneck pace – eased back slightly. It soon became obvious, however, that Juha was about to become embroiled in yet another neck-and-neck struggle as Tony Pond and Mikael Sundstrom came rocketing up the order after earlier delays. By the time they reached the Dovey Forest, to the north of Machynlleth, Pond was fifth, 16 seconds behind Kankkunen and nine seconds ahead of Sundstrom's Peugeot.

Then a time-consuming puncture sent the Metro sliding down to seventh place. Sundstrom, meanwhile, was keeping pace with the leaders and he had snatched fourth from Kankkunen by the time they left Dovey.

Sometimes the RAC Rally would seem to drag on for days with one place change in the top 20 being cause for celebration among the media. In 1986, it was difficult to know what to write about first.

Bearing in mind that championship points were at stake here, it was perhaps no surprise to find Kankkunen and Sundstrom swapping places after a discreet word in the ear of the young Finnish driver. There would be an unexpected boost for both Peugeot men, however, when Ericsson's excellent drive was brought to a frustrating end through a turbocharger failure on the penultimate stage. Kankkunen was now third; Sundstrom fourth.

But what of the battle for the lead? Over the 5.46 miles of the Myherin stage (reduced in length because of flooding), Alen and Salonen averaged 54 mph to set the joint fastest time, a remarkable achievement at this late stage. They were now nine seconds apart. In years gone by, a lead of nine minutes would have been considered average at this point.

There were three stages remaining and Salonen was as good as his word. Setting fastest time on all three, he increased the gap to 82 seconds and Alen could do little about it. But at least Markku had beaten Kankkunen.

The championship, however, was still undecided, forcing Lancia and Peugeot to trek all the way to the United States to compete in the Olympus Rally. A win for Alen gave him the title, but only for the time being. An FIA Appeal Court would then rule that the Peugeots should not have been disqualified from the San Remo Rally. Thus, Juha Kankkunen was champion after all. Pity the poor soul who had to break the news to Markku. It was messy and unsatisfactory but, in some ways, it was an appropriate end to a year which had brought much sorrow and very little joy.

Timo Salonen and Seppo Harjanne: may the best men win.

In the meantime, the British enthusiasts had witnessed a thrilling demonstration of everything that the Group B Supercars had to offer. There had been battles up and down the field and, at the end of the day, the best man had won.

Yet there was a feeling of relief as the rally reached a safe and satisfactory conclusion on a chilly Wednesday evening at Bath. The new rules, calling for a shorter rally in the interests of safety, had the reverse effect. No longer could a driver pace himself. To win, Salonen had set the fastest time on 14 of the 45 stages. Alen accounted for 16. Neither driver had been hanging about. They may have had longer in bed, but during the relatively brief periods when at the wheel they pushed themselves to the limit in conditions which ranged from ice to mud.

But who could say that this was *safer*? Certainly, it was dramatic. Yes, everyone was talking about the thrill of the chase and the star quality of the men who drove these potentially lethal monsters. But they said very little about the rally itself. The organisation had been exemplary. But the revised format had trimmed down the Lombard RAC Rally to a pale shadow of its former self. It had been a good rally. But it had not been a great one.

14

KEEPING THE SHOW ON THE ROAD

The Fixer

'Competitors should remember not to make a noise by rushing about
unnecessarily on the lower gears and generally making a nuisance.'
Autocar. December 1931.

THAT PLEA, made on the eve of the London to Gloucester Trial, holds
good today. The Lombard RAC Rally would not move an inch without
the support and cooperation of the local communities scattered around
Britain. For three or four hours each year, they must put up with a
multicoloured, bustling circus disrupting rural calm. If the locals are
upset, the complaints land on the desk of Malcolm Neill. And, if the
aggrieved parties are not satisfied, then it is the rally which will suffer.

A considerable number of bucks stop in Neill's ground floor office
in Belgrave Square. As Clerk of the Course, Malcolm receives the brick-
bats as well as the bouquets and he spends most of the time ensuring
that the former are thin on the ground. Like painting the Forth Bridge,
as soon as one rally has finished, preparations begin for the next. In
fact, a little priming is usually done sooner than that.

When the prizes are presented, an announcement is made concerning
the venue for the following year's rally. Neill, therefore, has been hard
at work during the preceeding few months sifting through the appli-
cations and examining the amenities available in each town or city.

'Our first priority is to find a clean, smart-looking town, something
with a bit of history,' says Neill. 'But the most important thing is that
the council, or whoever the ruling body may be, must *want* to have
the rally and they must be willing to help cut through the red tape.
That can cover anything from helping foster a good working relationship with the police to closing roads and speaking to parking wardens!

'We need a suitable scrutineering venue; a large hall, a place where
the job can be done as well as having room to lay on a bit of a show.
We need a town with about 2,500 beds, ranging from four-star hotels
to guest houses.'

196

Marshals ; without them there would be no rally.

Once the hub of the rally has been established, the route can be planned. There was a time when Jack Kemsley would spread a map of the British Isles before him and more or less go where he liked. Today, the hands of the Clerk of the Course are tied by bureaucratic tape supplied by the sport's governing body, FISA.

In the wake of the tragic accidents in 1986, FISA clamped a limit on the special stage mileage and specified a minimum number of hours for rest periods. The RAC, in any case, are restricted to using private land and forestry commission roads, a limitation which makes the route predictable.

'It means,' says Neill, 'that the rally boils down to the basic format of a spectator day on private land on the Sunday, followed by the serious work in the forests from day two to day four.

'We are then looking for between 100 and 120 stage miles in the forests each day, followed by an overnight halt. We find this is the most satisfactory format we can run under the present restrictions on stage mileage and under the restrictions placed on us by the forest roads which we can and cannot use.'

At this point, Paul White, an experienced co-driver, begins his work as Route Co-ordinator. Between them, Neill and White will initiate an organisational structure which will eventually number 12,500 people, none of whom will be paid. You either like rallying or you don't!

The Route Co-ordinator's first task is to speak to the RAC Regional Organisers and discuss the possibilities of routing through the areas that Neill wishes to take the rally.

'I am really limited to four or five areas of forest that we can use in this country,' says Neill. 'We've got Yorkshire, Kielder, South Scotland, the Lake District, North Wales, Mid Wales and South Wales. If you put that lot together, we now have too many stage miles, so one block of forests will be dropped each year. In 1986, it was Yorkshire, for example.

'So if, say, Chester is being used as the rally headquarters, then it's obvious that you would use North Wales because it is close at hand. Mid-Wales is not far and the Lake District is only 90 minutes up the motorway. That leaves you with Kielder and Yorkshire to build up the bulk of your stage miles. Mapping out the route is a relatively straight foward business.

'Our philosophy is that the Sunday run demonstrates the sport to the public at large; it's a promotional day and not rallying as such. Once we are away from that, the idea is to try and have concentrations of maybe 40 or 50 stage miles all in one wallop. That way we get a good period of four or five hours of active rallying.

'Once that is done, the availability of roads means that there is no way you can continue in that area. So, rather than filling in with the odd little stage, we prefer to go up the main road and into the next block of forestry land available to us and get in another 50 or 60 miles. It can be frustrating, however, when you can't get, say, a six-mile section of road and that can ruin the entire plan for a day. The whole thing simply won't join together properly.'

The use of forestry land is crucial to the success of the RAC Rally. Paddy Hopkirk urges his Sunbeam Rapier through a special stage in 1961.

The Regional Organisers, who are responsible for the running of club rallies in their areas, work closely with the foresters in any case and they will know which roads are available. Paul White will then ensure that the requirements and standards of an international rally – vastly different from those of a national event – are applied.

The RAC enjoys a good working relationship with the Forestry Commission, who accept rallying as part of their policy. Not only does this ensure that the forests are used for leisure purposes, but the sport also generates income for the commission.

In July 1976, there were questions in the House over the 'punitive increases in the Forestry Commission charges-per-mile'. John Davenport, then representing the RAC, reminded Hector Munro, the Opposition Spokesman on Sport, that in 1965 the Government had expressed its concern over the control of rallying and the RAC had co-operated by encouraging rally organisers to get the sport off the public roads.

Davenport argued that the 270 per cent rise in forestry charges during the previous 14 months was making the task difficult and Mr. Munro promised to take the matter up with the Forestry Commission. The most recent rise at the time – from 26p to 40p per car, per mile – was never rescinded.

In 1977, the Forestry Commission earned £36,000 from the RAC Rally and, in October 1980, the rate increased to 60p per car, per mile – plus VAT of course! In 1987, a revised payment structure saw the RAC spending £149.50 per mile, regardless of the number of cars.

'The forestry people really have come to accept us now,' says Neill. 'They have become accustomed to the sport and they will literally build special roads for us. We can only use a certain type of forest road and they prepare these roads knowing that the rallies will be using them.'

Neill, meanwhile, has been forming a Working Group made up of the Regional Organisers and senior officials from various fields, such as rescue and results. Their aim, through the process of delegation, is to organise each area of responsibility according to the framework laid down and report back. It is important that the various departments work on a consistent basis in order to avoid problems such as those encountered on the 1961 RAC Rally and recorded in *Autosport*:

> 'The two final stages were noted for very bad sign-posting and the rather disorganised marshalling, in contrast to the rest of the Rally. Arrows in these sections were placed on top of the corners and many drivers "wrong slotted", including Erik Carlsson (who nearly collected Pat Moss in a head-on accident when retrieving the route) and Peter Harper who lost sufficient time to drop him from second to third place overall. We can but hope that next year marshals' instructions will be that much clearer to avoid a repetition of the frayed tempers so near the end of an otherwise excellent event.'

The modus operandi is passed down the line as the Regional Organisers appoint Stage Commanders who, in turn, select sector marshals responsible for choosing the humble but vital marshals lining the stage. Each region will have a Staffing Officer, a secretary, a Safety Officer, a Medical Officer and various other specialists underlining the point that the Lombard RAC Rally is more or less a large company with small offshoots.

Once the organisation is under way, the Clerk of the Course will visit each region during the summer and hold a forum to put his point of view and, more important, field any complaints, questions and worries. And, alongside that, Malcolm Neill will organise a training programme.

'The most important point to get across,' stresses Neill 'is that this is a World Championship rally and not an extension of a British national event. There is a very big difference. I'm not saying the difference is right or wrong because we are merely conforming to FISA's wishes. But we must make sure that everyone understands the FISA procedures as opposed to the RAC "Blue Book" procedures which they are more familiar with.

'It is something we are expanding on every year and, in 1986, I completed thousands of miles attending training sessions. For 1987, we decided to have a major training weekend with all the senior officials coming together under one roof – for the first time, ever. That way, we were able to pass along the line the basic principles, such as the pass structure, rally safety, the way to operate a control, how to fill in the time cards and so on.'

Towards the end of July, a check of the entire route will be carried out, during which time the Road Book is prepared and details of the special stages finalised. The Clerk of the Course will see the route at first hand, making modifications he may think necessary. It will also provide him with a mental picture which he may need to call upon should trouble arise in the field while he is based in the Rally Headquarters.

At this stage, alternative routes are planned in the event of a problem such as the flooding which occurred in Wales on the final night of the 1986 rally. Then, a pre-planned diversion was brought into play and the rally barely broke its stride. Compare that with the chaos in Scotland in 1971!

The work load in the offices of the RAC Motor Sports Association in Belgrave Square rises sharply once the regulations have been issued and entries begin to arrive. Each entry, on average, represents about 50 phone calls, be they from the team manager, the sponsors, or from the competitor's local newspaper.

Training sessions start at the beginning of September and, from that point on, RAC officials are working flat out. Then, three weeks before the rally is due to start, the Clerk of the Course will call a Crisis Meeting. A list of outstanding items is drawn up and, as Neill says pointedly, 'no one leaves until there is a line drawn through each item.'

The final drama, one which seems unavoidable despite careful planning, is sorting out the hotel rooms at rally headquarters. There are never enough, it seems, but the Clerk of the Course is more fortunate than most since he will lay claim to his room six days before the rally starts!

You would think that the period leading up to the start would be ulcer-generating material. According to Malcolm Neill, however, if the job has been done properly, there should be few problems.

'If you've got it right, then the organisation should pass out of your hands about two or three days before the event is due to start. The rally should just "happen". If people like Paul and myself are working flat out right up to the start, then we've done it wrong! Bearing in mind the responsibility you have concerning the correct application of the rules and regulations, you have got to be preparing yourself mentally during this period. You can't afford to be rushing around doing things which should have been taken care of five or six weeks before. It is a case of seeing that everything that has been planned actually happens.'

Meanwhile, the best laid plans . . . . The Clerk of the Course is largely at the mercy of the weather. It is a paradox that rain and ice can add to the quality of the event. But snow is a different story simply because anything in excess of three inches appears to throw Britain into chaos. The country grinds to a halt, dragging the rally with it.

The Clerk of the Course will also be on the lookout for a 'personnel malfunction'; in other words illness or some such causing the absence

FORD SERVICE : LOMBARD R.A.C. RALLY 1986   PAGE 4

NO.	LOCATION	FIRST CAR	CREWS	FROM PREVIOUS POINT			NOTES
				MILES	TIME	ROUTE	
13	BEFORE SS7 Crossroads Service Station, Ollerton roundabout (A614) 120/651675 P61 - 2	16.50	T3	75	3.30	A452, A461, A5, A38, Derby, Mansfield, A6075.	Tyres for: SS7 (Tar) Fuel : check 15L in tank
			E1	75	2.00	A50, A516, Derby, A38, Mansfield, A6075	SERVICE TIME: 12 MINS.
14	AFTER SS7 Ranby Service Stn. on A1 2m. N of A57 roundabout (Esso) 120/647805 P64 - 3/4	17.30	S3 S4	90	3.00	A5, A38, Derby, Alfreton, M1 junc. 30, Worksop, A620, A1 (immed. after junc.)	Fuel: 35L
			E2	25	1.00	A617, M1 junc. 29 to 30 Worksop, A6020	SERVICE TIME: 10 MINS.
15	BEFORE SS8 Hartley Motors (Ford Dealer) on Leeds ring road, opposite Asda. 104/361347 P68 - 2	18.30	T4	125	4.00	A5, A38, M1, Leeds, Exit City on A64 to ring road.	Tyres for:SS8 (mixed) Fuel : check 30L in tank
			E1	55	1.20	A1, A1(M), A63	
			E3	120	3.30	A50, Derby, A38, M1 Leeds & A64 to ring rd.	SERVICE TIME: 10 MINS.
16	AFTER SS8 A.T.S. Tyre Depot on A61 2m. S of Harrogate, 500 yds. N of Spacey Houses (pub) 104/310516 P73 - 1 (off route)	19.10	S2	77	3.00	A6, A624, Glossop, A628, M1, Leeds, A61.	Tyres for:SS9 (mixed) NOT MUCH TIME!!
			S1 T1	135	4.00	A50, Derby, A38, M1, Leeds, A61	
			E2	60	1.20	A1, A63, Leeds, A61.	SERVICE TIME: 3 MINS.

of a key figure. There is also the threat of a communications breakdown as Malcolm Neill explains.

'Each special stage is covered by radio contact with the regional headquarters, which is manned by the Regional Organiser. These places are carefully selected – it could be a caravan on top of a mountain – and we put telephone lines into that base so that they can maintain contact with the Rally Headquarters in Bath, or wherever it may be.

'So, if there is a breakdown in communications, that can be a problem simply because the Clerk of the Course does not know what's going on. But, if the Regional Organiser is doing his job and effectively running the rally at that time, he is as competent as anyone in Rally HQ and he should be able to sort out the problem. But, even so, when you are waiting in the quiet of a hotel many miles from the action, the deadly silence can be a bit worrying!'

There is also the question of a serious accident. The organisers will follow a set routine in dealing with any incident and, of course, each stage will have at least one doctor in attendance. The Clerk of the Course will be kept informed of latest developments which, as Malcolm Neill said before, should follow a pre-arranged pattern, provided everyone has done their homework. It is also important that the Rally Headquarters know what is going on in order that a statement can be issued through the Press Office.

The RAC have frequently been startled by the effects of the rapid

A small part of the detail planning is illustrated by the service schedule produced by Jim Porter and Ford for the 1986 Lombard RAC Rally.

spread of gossip through a forest at the dead of night. A simple fracture at the scene of the accident can emerge as a fatal injury with several spectators thought to be on the critical list. It is the job of the Clerk of the Course to liase closely with the Chief Press Officer and put a stop to rumours before they get out of control.

Spectator control is a major worry and, in many ways, it is a sign that the RAC Rally has become a victim of its own success. Early photographs of the rally show a mere handful of spectators. Now, if it was not for the use of stately homes and public parks, the forests on a Sunday would become totally unmanageable. As it is, there are enough problems during the week in the more popular stages in Wales and the Lake District. The Stage Commanders, however, have the power to cancel a stage should they feel that the hazard caused by a lack of co-operation from the spectators is too great. Indeed, the Dyfnant stage was abandoned in 1985 for that precise reason; an action which the Portuguese would have been well-advised to follow a few months later, thereby avoiding the predictable accident which helped bring rallying into disrepute.

Anxious to avoid similar trouble in 1986, the RAC and Ford initiated a campaign designed to educate the casual spectator. Artist Jim Bamber produced a series of cartoons highlighting the dangers and, judging by the behaviour of more than one million spectators, the scheme was a success.

The Peacemaker

'As a marshal at a time control in Wales, I feel I must protest in the interests of rallies in general, against the very noisy driving of some of the competitors.

We were installed in a narrow street, in a small Welsh town, and the din made by a number of the cars in getting away from this control was appalling, so much so, that it woke the local magistrate who, accompanied by a posse of police, descended upon us, and demanded to know what was going on.

It was explained to him that this was the RAC Rally, etc., and it appears this was the first he or the police knew about it. No one had told them the competitors would be passing through the place, or that there would be a control in it. This gentleman was much put out, and rightly so.

Later in the night, three very large policemen approached and told us bluntly that hardly any competitors were stopping at the Halt sign at the local crossroads, and they proposed to "pinch" the very next one who did not do so.

To do this, they fetched another large policeman out of his bed and put him on duty at these crossroads. He had already done his spell of duty, and to say he was cross is to put it mildly. We, therefore, in addition to all our other duties, trying to keep warm, etc., had to warn each competitor what lay in store for him, or her.'

S. A. Cooke, writing to *Autosport* in March 1955, had a valid point.

If such a letter were to appear in the correspondence columns these days, the RAC would be surprised and appalled.

Each town and village visited by the rally will be carefully scrutinised by the Regional Organisers. They will be sniffing out possible trouble spots and, once again, prevention rather than cure will be the criterion. Without sensitive and carefully thought-out public relations work, the Lombard RAC Rally simply would not survive in the 1980s. There would be more than a magistrate and a couple of large policemen paying a call at Belgrave Square.

Malcolm Neill explains the preparatory work. 'Leaflets are widely disributed; they will be posted in the church halls and pubs in the affected areas so that everyone knows that the rally is coming through. It is also neccessary to inform the local schools, the local dairy and, of course, the local police. Quite often you will find that the school will close simply because the school bus will be unable to get through the spectator traffic; the dairy will change the times of their milk collections and deliveries, and in somewhere like the wilds of Yorkshire, there may not be a morning post that day because it is not practical to send a van into the thick of the rally traffic.

'That sort of disruption is acceptable once a year because, wherever the rally goes, it brings money. The hotels, garages and shops benefit. And, in most forest special stages, we lay on spectator parking and one third of the income raised by the car parking is donated to local charities. In total, charities benefited to the tune of about £10,000 in 1986. And, of course, there is the general curiosity generated by a major rally. People on, say, Fylingdales Moor don't see a lot of international stars coming past their door every day . . . .

'Of course, there are problem areas from time to time and we rely a lot here on the co-operation of the local police. If there has been a problem the previous year, then I will pay a visit to the police and try and straighten things out and make the peace. But, considering the disruption the event must cause the general public, there are very few letters of complaint at the end of it. And each letter that we do receive is answered and the complaint investigated.'

A considerable portion of the rally's image is projected by the competitors themselves. The organisers set a 30 mph average on the public roads linking the special stages and, should the the police report a competitor to the organisers for either speeding or commiting a traffic offence, then exclusion from the rally will follow. That is a strong measure which needs little amplification. It will also, hopefully, prevent letters such as the following missive from a Mr. F. A. C. Barnard of Tonbridge, published in March 1955 (a particularly bad year, it seems).

Before the advent of special stages, the organisers made sure competitors kept to the prescribed route by mounting a series of secret checks. The Morgan of Pauline Mayman clocks in at a control in 1959.

'A rally driver passed me a short while ago, "driving" a white Triumph TR2 in a built up area. Whether he had just bought the car, or was just full of contempt for the lesser motorists, I shall never know. But he went down the street at about 45 m.p.h., weaving in and out of unsuspecting buses and cars, like a snake through grass.

Now there has been quite a lot said of late about competition drivers' road manners, and until seeing that duffle-coated madman, I dismissed the allegations of those who said that all rally drivers should go to ****! But now I'm not so sure. It seems a shame to earn the sport a bad name by these ill manners.

There may be protests that an average speed has to be maintained regardless of other traffic. If this is so, then the organisers of events should make it possible for non-competing drivers to get out of the way first, perhaps by having loud speaker cars preceding the herd!

Better still would be the lowering of the average speed. Don't let's have the police intervening with protests of indignant citizens.

Stop now, before it's too late.'

Well, clearly it was not too late and Mr. Barnard's point was taken. There may no longer be duffle-coated madmen stampeding the herd but the letter illustrates how a moment's foolishness can tarnish the reputation of the entire rally.

The Financier

While examining the practical side of his rally, Malcolm Neill will also be translating the details into pounds and pence. It costs £500,000 to run the Lombard RAC Rally. The budgetary responsibilities are onerous, as Neill explains:

'The rally must run at a profit so we must work out how much we can spend on items such as training. And, if we can't afford these items then we have to find the funds to pay for them from somewhere else. Once the budget has been set, you must stand by it. If you can't, you must let it be known fairly quickly rather than wait until after the event!

'And talking of money, the periferal sponsorship is obviously important. Sponsorship must be arranged for the spectator stages and that gives us a useful income for things like the marshals' training. We require a computer company to assist with the results and that has been arranged with Olivetti for the last few years. Also, photocopying equipment is required and Rank Zerox have helped us for some time now. The amount of paper which is raised during the rally is phenomenal.

'But one of the biggest jobs is the printing beforehand. The Road Book is in two parts of around 150 pages each. There is all the necessary paperwork, arrows, marshals' tabards. It comes to around £70,000; it's quite unbelievable. So, managing a print budget like that calls for good housekeeping. There's a lot of money to be saved there if you get it right.

'But, over and above all that, of course, is the contribution from Lombard. They are very good in that they allow us to have this peripheral sponsorship because you can't sell the Lombard RAC Rally to someone else! And yet Lombard don't object to Olivetti and the software company, Eastman Stuart, advertising in the back of the Road Books, and so on.'

The link between Lombard and the RAC Rally represents one of the longest-running sponsorship contracts in motor sport. The association began in the 1950s when Lombank, a small finance house, arranged credit plans for members of the Royal Automobile Club.

Lombank gradually became involved with the rally and, in 1959, they financed the printing of the road books and time cards, the company's commitment eventually taking on a more tangible meaning for competitors with the presentation of useful gifts and the awarding of team prizes.

As the RAC Rally grew in stature in the early 1970s, Lombank rose to the upper echelons of the motoring finance business and, in 1971, a merger with a subsidiary of the National Westminster Bank produced Lombard North Central, a powerful and influential conglomerate which, happily, was poised to step in when the RAC Rally ran into trouble in 1974.

The abrupt withdrawal of support by the Daily Mirror left the RAC in a quandry. In an interview in *Autocar*, Derek Darwent, manager of 'Special Events' in Lombard's Promotion Department, explains how the sponsorship deal was reached:

> 'It was one of those chance conversations which always seem to occur in business. John Lewsey, who not only worked in the Mirror Group, but also ran the results service of the rally itself, mentioned to us that the Mirror were about to withdraw, and were we interested?
>
> We *were* interested, and in a matter of only two or three weeks, I think, we signed up our first deal with Belgrave Square. It was going to be a much more substantial deal than we ever had before, so we agreed that the event should become the Lombard RAC Rally.'

The first agreement covered a three-year period and the liason was so successful that another three year deal was stuck in 1976. Lombard were spending £70,000 per annum on the rally but their involvement went beyond the injection of cash.

The rally represented a marketing and publicity exercise. There was the growing impression that Lombard *was* rallying. Under the heading 'Rally Gear', small display advertisements offered Lombard RAC Rally jackets for £12.50, 'all in the officially approved design'. It was an extension of a self-generating publicity machine which had been set in motion by Bob Evans, head of Lombard's promotional services division.

Evans, operating with Nick Brittan, a motor sporting entrepreneur with a sharp eye for detail to match Evans's boundless energy, set about placing the media operation on a more professional footing to match the increasing importance of the event itself. Previously, this had been handled by Phil Drackett, an affable RAC Press Officer whose congenial manner matched perfectly the more relaxed mode of covering the rally in the Fifties and Sixties.

In 1958, *Autocar* had noted that the RAC Rally had received very little coverage: 'It was very difficult to get news. There was one column inch and a short report on the BBC on Saturday'. The arrival of support from 'The Sun' and the enterprising journalism of Barrie Gill made Fleet Street sit up and take notice and Evans and Brittan were about to awaken interest once more.

A pre-event news service spread the word nationally as well as creating interest among regional newspapers by concentrating on local drivers. Television stations were massaged and cajoled and the press office adopted a more professional image in keeping with the increased activity. Derek Tye, who worked on the RAC Rally for the first time in 1966, recalls the early days:

'There would be just one phone in the press office and the information would be very slow in coming through. But the journalists didn't expect more than that at the time. It seems very leisurely when you compare it with the banks of computer monitors and rows of constantly ringing telephones today. Nowadays, the media people expect you to have full information about half an hour after the cars have gone through a special stage in deepest Yorkshire. Twenty years ago, you might – just might – get a top ten about three hours later.'

Today, of course, the use of cellular phones allows the immediate relay of special stage times to rally headquarters and the instant analysis and dispersal by computer. A decade or so before, Graham Robson, when not involved with team management, lent the organisers an experienced hand.

'Until the late Sixties,' recalls Robson, 'there was no liason between the field and headquarters. It was not uncommon to find the results in certain far-flung regions running 24 hours late. Jack Kemsley devised a system of two teams out in the field to co-ordinate the results. This would literally involve hedge-hopping from control to control, collecting times and phoning them through every three or four hours. There was no such thing as facsimile machines then! To help competitors, we would display the latest positions on boards at various points along the route. It wasn't perfect – we were often hours out of date – but it's all there was. In fact, when the rally was on the road, the headquarters staff used to get bored. I remember, in 1971 during all that snow, I was based in Perth and I couldn't get a peep out of Rally HQ in Harrogate all night. They'd all gone to bed!'

In those days, the press office would close for lunch and, of course, shut down for the night. Evans and Brittan changed all that.

'We recognised the need to smarten up the entire press operation,' recalls Evans. 'We talked to the press and asked them what they needed – we still do, in fact, because we are continually trying to improve the service. In 1976, we had the press officers wearing uniforms for the first time. There were lots of jokes about the lads looking like redundant airline pilots – but it was all part of the way in which the rally was *presented*. If the operation looked right, then it gave the rally – and Lombard – credibility. And if we weren't providing the service required, then we made sure it was available the following year.'

Evans's work went beyond the press room in rally headquarters. The start and finish area, apart from having Lombard identification prominently displayed, was re-arranged to not only give the public a better view of the cars but also to allow cameramen a more orderly environment in which to work. And, with the advent of the Sunday stages, Lombard took over sponsorship of one stage as means of spreading, not only the corporate image but also the appeal of the rally itself as they entertained guests and generally made full and active use of their involvement. The success of the operation was such that, in 1982, Lombard committed themselves to spending over £1m on the rally during the following five years. By 1988, the words Lombard and Rally will be as synonymous as Stocks and Shares.

Roger Clark and Chris Serle: in at the deep end.

The Book Keeper

In 1981, BBC Television recorded a series of programmes called 'In At The Deep End'. Each week, their reporters would tackle professional tasks which, previously, they knew nothing about. In November of that year, Chris Serle sat beside Roger Clark and attempted to navigate the former British Champion through the Lombard RAC Rally.

It was a shattering experience for the broadcaster. The rally lasted for four days. After the first six hours, Serle's haunted look said everything about the importance of the co-driver's role. The man was mentally exhausted. And there was another 30 hours to go before the first night halt.

Serle considers it to have been one of the most difficult assignments in the series. 'I hadn't realised it was such a complex job,' he says. 'There was also this terrible responsibility which you have to bear knowing that Roger Clark's success or failure depends on you. I had heard about the Monte Carlo Rally and so on, but I had no idea that this sort of thing was going on. I really think the navigators are the unsung heroes of the sport. They are due a lot of respect.'

Respect, when it comes, is earned the hard way. The navigator is the travelling office manager who receives very little of the limelight. When a rally car is at a standstill and the driver is being interviewed, his front-seat passenger is invariably poring over paperwork, deciding how long it has taken them to get thus far, how much time they have to spare, where they must go next and how long it will take them to get there. Do they have enough fuel to do it – and what sort of mood is the driver in?

These days, the term 'co-driver' is a misnomer since the driver does most of the work at the wheel. It wasn't always so, as John Davenport recalls.

'When I first drove with Simo Lampinen in 1964, I was pretty green. We started from a hotel at London Airport and the first stage was down the road at Bagshot. After that, it was a fairly long run down to the second stage in North Devon.

'Simo brought this blanket and pillow along and I remember thinking that was very nice of him to consider the comfort of the navigator. We came out of the Bagshot stage and he said, "Okay, boy, its all yours". And with that, he got into my seat, put the back rest down, wrapped himself up in the blanket and off he went. So there I was, navigating while handling a car I had never driven before!'

Davenport would have had a fair idea of the route in any case since the navigator's first job, once the RAC have released details a few weeks before the start, is to plot the route onto Ordnance Survey maps. This is, in effect, a back-up since the competitors are supplied with a Road Book giving precise details of how to move from the end of one special stage to the beginning of the next.

'I think the maps are rather more than a back-up,' says Terry Harryman. 'It gives you a feel for the event. Road Books are all very well, but until you mark it on a map, the composition of the entire rally does not fall into place. And once you see where the road sections are leading, you are almost certain to know which piece of forest they will be using for the stage itself. So, from experience, you can then remember a lot of what lies ahead and plan accordingly. It helps give you confidence.

'In 1986, I was driving a chase car for Peugeot on the RAC. We spent some time marking the route on the maps and, once that was done, I found I was able to drive about 98 per cent of the way without consulting the map.'

On rallies other than the RAC, the navigator will reach for his pace notes once the start of the special stage has been reached. The stage in question will have been covered by the crew, usually in a road car since the stages in Europe are on public roads which are only closed for the rally proper. During this first practice run, the driver will dictate what he sees – or, to be more precise, what he wants to *hear* later – while the navigator will jot this down in a special short-hand. The stage will be covered two or three times, with the necessary amendments being made to the notes. Thus, on the rally itself, the navigator will call out the notes, giving the driver a picture of what lies over the blind brow and around the next corner. The reconnaissance is a boring and tedious procedure – but crucial to success.

The process is taken a step further on rallies such as the Monte Carlo where snow and ice can be encountered and where road conditions are changing by the minute. Once the driver and navigator have reconnoitred the stage, their pace notes are photocopied and given to an ice note crew. It will be their job to drive over the stage minutes before the road is closed and underline the sections of the notes where snow and ice are to be found – or, *likely* to be found judging by the rapidly falling temperature registered on a thermometer strapped to the car used by the ice note crew. The notes are then handed back to the driver and co-driver when they arrive at the beginning of the stage. Apart from warning the driver of the hazards which lie ahead, a more accurate choice of tyres can be made thanks to the work of the ice note team.

None of this is possible on the RAC Rally. Practice is expressly forbidden (with the exception in 1987, of the spectator stages) and the drivers must tackle the special stages 'blind'. The navigator, therefore, is comparatively idle while the driver does his work. The organisers help by placing arrows at key points and the co-driver can confirm what the driver sees by calling out the indicated direction of the road.

In 1986, the crews were supplied with Ordnance Survey maps showing each special stage, with potential hazards marked. Thus, the co-driver could read the road from the map although, by and large, it remained a matter for the driver's reflexes. In any case, some drivers prefer to get on with the job without an excessive flow of advice from the passenger seat; others like as much information as possible.

The co-driver's work starts in earnest once more at the end of the stage. He is responsible for the time card and its marking by the official. The co-driver will, of course, have had his stop-watch running during the stage and he will check this against the result of deducting the time given for starting the stage from the time registered when the car crossed the flying finish. The control where this is done is between 100 and 300 metres from the flying finish and, if the co-driver disagrees with the time entered on his card, he must sort it out there and then. Changes can not be made once the car has left the area.

It is the accumulation of times taken to cover the special stages which determine the result, the winner obviously being the driver who has completed the stages in the fastest time overall.

There is slightly more to it than that, however. There will be a target time set for the journey from the end of one special stage to the beginning of the next (based on a 30 mph average on the open road; 50 mph on motorways). The purpose here, is to *maintain* these easy average speeds. A competitor will be subject to a heavy penalty if he arrives too early. Similarly, he will be allowed up to 30 minutes lateness. After that, he is out of the rally – unless the lateness is waived by the Clerk of the Course for reasons such as unavoidable traffic jams en route.

Adhering to these tight schedules is the strict responsibility of the co-driver. Should he book in too early – as Terry Harryman did on the 1985 Monte Carlo Rally to earn an eight-minute penalty – then the finger is pointed at the front passenger seat.

'There is *no* tolerance shown,' says Harryman. 'You can do everything perfectly, month in and month out, and not a lot is said. But one mistake and you're seen as an incompetent. If the driver should go off, however, well that's seen as part of his job!'

At regular intervals, servicing is permitted and it will be the co-driver's job to ensure that the work is carried out without impinging on his time schedule. Rally mechanics work at an unbelievable pace but the navigator, in consultation with the team manager, must decide whether there is time for, say, a rear axle change or some other comparatively lengthy job. Then, it's back in the car, out with the road book and off to the start of the next stage.

The co-driver lives by his watch. He is a walking alarm clock for the driver, even before the rally starts. It will be his responsibility to check the time they are due at their car and he will inform the driver and check that he arrives on time.

In 1974, the organisers of the San Remo Rally decided at the last minute to bring the start forward by one hour. The teams were informed in the prescribed manner and everyone arrived on time. Everyone, that is, except John Davenport and Henry Liddon, two of the most experienced co-drivers in the business. It meant that Davenport and Liddon, plus their drivers Simo Lampinen and Jimmy Rae, were unemployed for the rest of the weekend.

'I had made an error of monumental proportions,' recalls Davenport. 'I had received and signed for a circular in three languages which said that a list of cars and crews accepted after scrutineering would be posted, with their start times, at wherever the rally headquarters was.

'Now, as far as I was aware, the rally still started at 20.01. The posters all around the town said 20.01 – but that's no excuse. We knew that there were no no-starters in front of us and it never occured to me to go and check that our start time was anything other than 20.06.

'Lancia, in any case, were staying in two different hotels and they had their team briefing in the other hotel. But, because I had written all the service details and things like that, I didn't bother to go to the briefing because I knew what was going to be said. Or, I thought I did. That's when the team manager brought up the changed starting time!

'So there we were, ambling out of the hotel, thinking we had plenty of time, when the irate call came through from the starting area. I just could not believe it.

'It brought home the inescapable fact that no matter how experienced you are, every piece of paper has to be scrutinised with the eagle eye of a lawyer and nothing which can be checked or cross-checked should be assumed correct.

'In some rallies, you can start late in a case like that. But, on the San Remo, there were various technical reasons why you had to start on time. I wish the ground could have opened up . . . .'

Davenport's error illustrates that the driver will do (within reason!) exactly what he is told. Which explains the stoney silence in Roger Clark's Escort when Chris Serle directed him the wrong way down a motorway at the end of their first day together on the 1981 Lombard RAC Rally. The extra 24 miles each way must have seemed like 124 miles to Serle.

'Before we went wrong,' explains Serle, 'I wanted to stop the car and sort it out. But Roger was chivvying me along and we came to this roundabout and, well, he made a suggestion and I thought, 'okay, you know best'. When I finally discovered that we had gone the wrong way, he was . . . . er, not pleased. He's not a man to suffer fools gladly and I think he was trying hard to think of something to say as a means of consolation. He ended up saying absolutely nothing!'

The Motivator

The driver and his navigator are a kind of automotive husband and wife team. The co-driver will know exactly when to keep his mouth shut; he will pick up the first signs of anxiety in his driver and quell them with some well-chosen words of comfort and reassurance; he will notice immediately when the driver is edging unnecessarily beyond his personal driving limit and gently persuade him to adopt a more circumspect pace. The co-driver is, after all, just as interested in winning as his mate in the next seat and a chilly atmosphere in the car is potentially more serious than the frosty exchanges between husband and wife at the breakfast table.

Above all, though, there must be trust. The driver must believe the instruction to take the next blind corner absolutely flat; the co-driver must have complete faith in his driver's ability to do just that without throwing them both over the edge. The slightest hesitation from either partner can sow the seeds of doubt which can germinate into a destructive distrust.

Ask any co-driver why he does this thankless task and it becomes apparent there is no easy answer. They say it is enjoyable; a challenge. But there is more to it than that. There is a sense of achievement from being organised enough to help a driver hurl the car down a narrow twisting road faster than anyone else, with neither party making a mistake. The co-driver's skills on the RAC Rally are diluted by the secret nature of the event but, none the less, he is part of a team. Roger Clark recalls his working relationship with Jim Porter.

'He knew exactly what he was responsible for; you knew he would do it – and do it well. That was the sort of confidence you could have. You could go to the start of an international and know that *all* of the book-keeping for the left-hand seat had been taken care of. I knew he would give me the answers I wanted, when I wanted them. When you're driving, it's usually so noisy in the car, you don't talk socially. Jim and I are quiet and I don't talk when I'm driving anyway so, apart from instructions, there was no socialising. We were well matched in that way.'

And yet it is still difficult to fully understand the motivation necessary to persuade co-drivers to strap themselves into the front passenger seat. To the enthusiast, denied the thrill of sitting in a rally car, the answer may seem obvious. It must be *exciting*. It is. But the novelty soon wears off.

The flip side of the coin can sometimes be absolutely terrifying. To illustrate the point, and to pay tribute to the work of the driver and his co-driver, I unashamedly quote from *Rallycourse 1984–85*. Mike Greasley, a former co-driver, perhaps truly understands the rally scene better than most journalists. Certainly, on the evidence of the following passage describing the final night of the 1984 San Remo Rally, he can transmit his thoughts onto paper with a rare sensitivity which sums up the more unpleasant side of a glamorous business;

'By any standards it was a foul evening. The rain had started at tea time. It was not a gentle drizzle, but an unrelenting torrential downpour. San Remo was awash. There wasn't a soul on the streets. Darkness had come prematurely that Thursday. The gutters were raging torrents. Such was the ferocity of the downpour that the rain bubbled back up from under the manhole covers. If it was so bad at sea level what could it be like in the mountains above the seaside resort?

It was a question which Ari Vatanen and Walter Rohrl had asked themselves. Instead of relaxing, they had gone into the hills. Despite weeks of practicing, the pace notes would have to be checked one more time, Terry Harryman and Christian Geistdorfer laboriously reading them back. It was a wise precaution. The twisting, narrow tarmac roads which made up the final eight stages of the San Remo rally were awash, not only with rain but mud.

There was no let up. It was still raining as hard by the re-start a few hours before midnight. Now there was thick swirling fog and cloud to add to the misery, a ferocious wind succeeding in uprooting trees. It was a night on which the imagination could run wild, the mountain hamlet of San Romolo taking on a macabre, eerie appearance as yellow arc lights from service vans cut a swathe through the clawing mist . . .

. . . . San Romolo was crucial. It came at the end of the longest stage of the event; nearly 29 miles of asphalt which are difficult enough on a clear, sunny day, let alone such a tempestuous night . . . .

. . . As midnight approached the wind dropped, the cloud vanished and the open tap in the heavens was at last shut. A few minutes into the new day and the Peugeot (of Vatanen and Harryman) eased its way through the San Romolo crowd and into the chained-off PTS service area. In the harsh lights, Vatanen and Harryman sat for a minute inside the car, the engine switched off. The strain showed on

Ari's young face. The uncompromising lights picked out his wet hair, and emphasised the glittering streams of sweat which ran down his cheeks. With his overalls open to the waist, he looked as if he had been through an experience which he was in no hurry to repeat. Harryman sat quietly, shaking his head slowly from side to side. When Ari made for the small PTS camper van and the comforting attentions of his wife Rita, Terry wandered around the car. His wife Anne was also on hand, anxious to do what she could. Now the strain showed more on the faces of the wives.

Lighting yet another cigarette, and finally agreeing to take some secret potions from the team doctor, Terry was sufficiently relaxed to talk about the experience. He said: 'Nothing can explain just how bad it is. You just can't know unless you've been through it.'

The first 12 miles had been hidden in thick fog, and although it cleared, only to come back again, the conditions were at best treacherous. It hadn't been raining, but the roads were still criss-crossed with torrents of water which had brought down all sorts of mud and debris from the mountain sides. The cars seemed to be out of control more often than in control, both Vatanen and Rohrl reporting huge aquaplaning slides which went on for an eternity.

One moment out of many stuck in Harryman's mind. At the end of a twisty section, the Peugeot went wild. Despite four wheel drive, there was no grip whatsoever, Ari unable to do anything as they slid for most of the distance, the perspiring Finn just able to regain control as the left-hand bend approached. There, at least, was some armco, but for most of this alarming moment there had been nothing to stop them flying off the mountain into oblivion. Walter reported an equally alarming moment at the same point, his Quattro Sport completely sideways for 80 metres.

'I'll tell you how bad it was,' said Terry, who by now didn't need to explain any further. 'During that stage Ari reached over three times and gently squeezed my knee. He hasn't done that for a long while – it's his way of saying it won't be long before it's over.'

Terry Harryman and Ari Vatanen: mutual trust.

Drivers

Ian Appleyard

A Jaguar dealer who enjoyed great success with an XK120 (Registration NUB 120). Won the RAC rally twice and a rare *Coupe d'Or* on the Alpine Rally. Invariably partnered by his wife, Pat, Appleyard's driving was a blend of fast, precise skills on the open road and a delicate touch on the speed tests which dominated the RAC Rally at the time.

Peter Harper

Despite sterling work with the Sunbeam Tiger, Peter Harper will always be associated with the Rapier. His RAC victory in slippery conditions in 1958 demonstrated a flair and precision which, sadly, were not rewarded with even more victories on international events at home and abroad.

The Morley Brothers

Don and Erle Morley epitomised the gentlemanly days of the RAC Rally in the late Fifties. Spearheading the works BMC effort, the dissimilar twins (Don was short while Erle was over six feet tall) earned international recognition for their efforts in the Austin Healey but they never won the RAC Rally, third in 1960 being the best result for the Suffolk farmers.

Erik Carlsson

A giant of a man in every sense of the expression. Despite the nickname 'Pa taket' (on the roof), the burly Swede's performances with the little Saab two-strokes were blindingly quick and hugely successful. Won the RAC three times in succession to become a rallying legend.

Pat Moss

An outstanding driver who thoroughly deserved to win the RAC Rally – but missed by the narrowest of margins. Following the family tradition (as a sister of Stirling), Pat Moss possessed a natural gift which earned a brilliant victory in the 1960 Liege–Rome–Liege. Came closest to winning the RAC in a 'Big Healey' by finishing second in 1961. Won the Ladies Prize eight times.

Tom Trana

Won the RAC Rally in 1963 and 1964 in Volvos. Won the Swedish and Acropolis rallies on his way to becoming European Champion in 1964. Moved to Saab in 1967.

Paddy Hopkirk

As familiar a name in British households as Stirling Moss yet the Ulsterman never won the RAC Rally. Drove works Standard-Triumphs and Rapiers before becoming synonymous with the BMC Mini-Coopers. Gained world-wide recognition by winning the 1964 Monte Carlo Rally and went on to enjoy success on many of the European internationals.

Rauno Aaltonen

With Timo Makinen, the first of the 'Flying Finns'. Victory on the RAC Rally in 1965 was part of a remarkably consistent record on the British event, typical of such a great thinker and theorist on rallying. European Champion in 1965.

Simo Lampinen

The results do not reflect the enormous respect which the rallying world holds for this talented and courageous Finn. Started rallying in 1961 after recovering from polio four years previously. Won the 1968 RAC Rally for Saab. Drove for Lancia and victories with the Fulvia on rough events such as the Morocco Rally indicated the ability to pace himself intelligently.

Harry Kallstrom

Won the RAC Rally in 1969 and 1970 at the wheel of a Lancia Fulvia. In the Scandinavian tradition, fast on loose surfaces and, later in his career, the Swede concentrated on events which called for endurance. 1969 European Rally Champion. Now driving trucks in Sweden.

Stig Blomqvist

Out of the car, a mild-mannered, quiet Swede. On the move, extrovert and extremely fast. Made his name with the two-stroke Saab and won the 1971 RAC Rally. Became a front-wheel drive specialist and was able to easily make the conversion to four-wheel drive. Won the RAC again in an Audi Quattro in 1982 when not constrained by team orders. 1984 World Rally Champion.

Roger Clark

The top British driver for more than a decade. A superb natural talent earned 'Albert' two victories in the RAC Rally (1972 and 1976) and second places in 1973 and 1975. Clark's ebullient sideways style will always be associated with the Ford Escort, a forgiving car which helped the Leicestershire driver earn a largely accident-free reputation.

Timo Makinen

A supremely gifted driver, equally at home in the Mini Cooper, the Austin Healey or the Ford Escort. Relentlessly pursued victory in the RAC Rally with the Healey but he was to enjoy an impressive hat-trick with the Escort, partnered as always by Henry Liddon. The fastest, if not always the most successful, driver of his time.

Bjorn Waldegaard

Like Hannu Mikkola, an extremely fast but safe driver. Thoroughly professional and adaptable. Won the RAC Rally while driving for Ford in 1977 but put up mesmerising displays in a variety of cars ranging from a Porsche 911 to a Lancia Stratos and a Toyota Celica. Has won virtually all of the major international events. World Rally Champion in 1979.

Hannu Mikkola

The man to beat, year in, year out. Unreliable machinery let him down on a number of occasions but, when the car and the support matched his professional standards at the wheel, Mikkola would invariably be running at the front – be it in an Escort or a Quattro. Won the RAC Rally in 1978, 1979, 1981 and 1982, the year he won the World Championship.

Henri Toivonen

Rallying lost a driver of exceptional flair when Henri Toivonen was killed during the 1986 *Tour de Corse*. The Finn came to prominence when he hurled his Chrysler Sunbeam into ninth place on the 1978 RAC Rally. Two years later, he won the British event, beating Mikkola fair and square. A move to Lancia in 1985 brought his second win on the RAC and victory on the 1986 Monte Carlo Rally indicated what might have been.

Tony Pond

An established member of the international rally scene for several years. A force to be reckoned with on the RAC Rally, the Englishman's best result being third place in 1985 when he challenged the works Lancias during a magnificent international debut with the Metro 6R4.

Timo Salonen

Despite finishing third for Nissan on the 1979 RAC Rally, the Finnish driver's early performances did not give a hint of what was to come. Joined Peugeot in 1985, almost as a back-up for Vatanen, and won the World Championship. Won the 1986 RAC Rally.

Ari Vatanen

The exhuberance of the Finnish driver took some believing when he arrived on the British scene in the mid Seventies. Won the British Championship in 1976. Took second place on the RAC in 1981, the year he won the World Championship for Ford. Won the RAC Rally in 1984. A bad accident in Argentina kept him away from rallying but he returned to exercise his remarkable skills by winning the 1987 Paris–Dakar.

Markku Alen

Arguably, *the* most exciting driver of the current generation. Finnish by birth but almost Italian by nature after a long period spent rallying for Fiat/Lancia. Innumerable wins on the 1000 Lakes but, to his great regret and that of his British fans, Alen has never won the RAC Rally despite some spectacular performances.

Russell Brookes

Made his international debut on the 1968 RAC Rally but outright victory has eluded him to date despite a string of placings in the top four. Best result was second place in 1979, the same year he became British Open Rally Champion. Won the home championship again in 1985, a suitable tribute to such a determined professional.

Jimmy McRae

A triple winner of the British international championship and five-times winner of the Circuit of Ireland. Outclassed cars and a lack of international exposure have restricted a great all-round talent. Best result on the RAC Rally; third in 1983 (Opel Manta).

Walter Rohrl

A most serious-minded and thoroughly professional driver, underlined by four wins in succession – in four different cars – on the Monte Carlo Rally. World Champion in 1980, the lanky German driver has an open dislike for the secret nature of the RAC Rally, his best result being 5th in 1974.

Juha Kankkunen

Regardless of the politics surrounding the outcome of the 1986 World Championship, the Finn was the sensation of the season. First came to prominence in Britain with a stirring drive in an Opel Manta GTE in the 1982 RAC Rally. Won the Safari Rally for Toyota at his first attempt in 1985 and switched to Peugeot for his championship year before moving to Lancia in 1987.

Results

1932

341 starters, 312 finishers.
Starting points: Bath, Buxton, Edinburgh, Harrogate, Leamington, Liverpool, London, Newcastle and Norwich. Finishing point: Torquay. There was no outright winner although Col. A. H. Loughborough was unofficially acknowledged as finishing first based on his performance in the tests at the end of the event. The best results in each class were:
Class 1 (Cars over 1,100cc)
1 Col. A. H. Loughborough (Lanchester)   315.00 marks
2 J. Mercer (Daimler)   303.37
3 G. F. Dennison (Riley)   301.47
Class 2 (Cars up to 1,100cc)
1 V. E. Leverett (Riley)   291.31
2 R. St G. Riley (Riley)   288.17
3 G. H. Strong (Standard)   285.29
Ladies' Prize: Lady de Clifford (Lagonda).
Team Prize: MCC 'D' Team

1933

340 starters, 308 finishers.
Starting points: Bath, Buxton, Glasgow, Harrogate, Leamington, Liverpool, London, Newcastle and Norwich. Finishing point: Hastings.
No official outright winner.
Class results:
Class 1 (Cars over 16 hp)
1 T. D. Wynn-Weston (Rover)   244 marks
2 D. M. Healey (Invicta)   244
Class 2 (10 hp to 16 hp)
1 Miss K. Brunell (AC Ace)   253
2 C. M. Anthony (Aston Martin Le Mans)   246
Class 3 (up to 10 hp)
1 G. Dennison (Riley 9)   251
2 F. R. G. Spikins (Singer 9)   246
Ladies' Prizes:
Hon. Mrs. Chetwynd (Ford), Miss K. Brunell (AC), Miss D. C. N. Champney (Riley).
Team Prize: Riley Motor Club.

1934

384 starters, 351 finishers.
Starting points: Bath, Buxton, Glasgow, Harrogate, Leamington, Liverpool, London, Newcastle and Norwich. Finishing point: Bournemouth.
No official outright winner.
Class results:
Class 1 (over 16 hp)
1 T. D. Wynn-Weston (Rover)   160 marks
2 H. Hillcoat (Ford V8)   158.6
Class 2 (10 hp to 16 hp)
1 S. B. Wilks (Rover)   159.6
2 F. S. Barnes (Singer Le Mans)   159
Class 3 (up to 10 hp)
1 F. R. G. Spikins (Singer Le Mans)   161.6
2 J. Harrop (MG)   160.2
Ladies' Prizes:
Mrs. R. M. Harker (Sunbeam), Mrs. K. E. Wilks (Rover), Miss J. Astbury (Singer).
Team Prize: Singer.

1935

281 starters, 241 finishers.
Starting points: Buxton, Edinburgh, Great Yarmouth, Harrogate, Leamington, Liverpool, Llandrindod Wells, London and Torquay. Finishing point: Eastbourne.
No official outright winner. No class winners declared.
Gold, silver and bronze prizes presented.

1936

274 starters, 252 finishers.
Starting points: Blackpool, Bristol, Buxton, Glasgow, Great Yarmouth, Harrogate, Leamington, London and Newcastle.
Finishing point: Torquay.
No official outright winner but eight class winners.
Class 1 (open cars, up to 8 hp)
N. E. Bracey (MG)   74.2 marks lost
Class 2 (closed cars, up to 8 hp)
C. E. A. Westcott (Austin Seven)   129
Class 3 (open cars, 8 hp to 14 hp)
A. H. Langley (Singer Le Mans)   66.8

Class 4 (closed cars, 8 hp to 14 hp)
A. G. Imhof (Singer Le Mans)   72.2
Class 5 (open cars, 14 hp to 20 hp)
C. G. Pitt (Frazer-Nash BMW)   72.2
Class 6 (closed cars, 14 hp to 20 hp)
J. L. Finigan (Frazer-Nash BMW)   75.8
Class 7 (open cars, over 20 hp)
F. R. G. Spikins (Spikins-Hudson)   67
Class 8 (closed cars, over 20 hp)
S. E. Sears (Bentley)   73.2
Ladies' Prizes:
Open cars – Miss J. Richmond (Triumph).
Closed cars – Miss M. Wilby (Armstrong-Siddeley).
Team Prize: Singer.

1937

192 starters, 184 finishers.
Starting points: Bristol, Buxton, Harrogate, Leamington, London and Stirling. Finishing point: Hastings.
No official outright winner.
Group 1 (open cars, up to 10 hp)
H. F. S. Morgan (Morgan 4/4)   930.2 marks
Group 2 (closed cars, up to 10 hp)
B. W. Fursdon (Wolseley 10)   928.0
Group 3 (open cars, 10 hp to 15 hp)
J. F. A. Clough (Riley Sprite)   937.4
Group 4 (closed cars, 10 hp to 15 hp)
A. L. Pearce (Triumph Vitesse)   934.8
Group 5 (open cars, over 15 hp)
J. Harrop (SS100)   943.0
Group 6 (closed cars, over 15 hp)
D. Impanni (Frazer-Nash BMW)   935.4
Ladies' Prizes:
Open cars – Viscountess Chetwynd (Ford)
Closed cars – Miss S. Bradley (Triumph).
Team Prize: SS Cars.

1938

237 starters, 231 finishers.
Starting points: Glasgow, Harrogate, Leamington, London and Torquay.
Finishing point: Blackpool.

218

No official outright winner.
    Group 1 (open cars, up to 10 hp)
    G. H. Goodall
(Morgan 4/4)   914.4 marks
    Group 2 (closed cars, up to 10 hp)
    B. W. Fursdon
(Wolseley 10)   908.4
    Group 3 (open cars, 10 hp to 15 hp)
    C. M. Anthony (Aston
Martin)   921.6
    Group 4 (closed cars, 10 hp to 15 hp)
    A. L. Pearce (Triumph
Dolomite)   910.6
    Group 5 (open cars, over 15 hp)
    J. Harrop (SS100)   923.4
    Group 6 (closed cars, over 15 hp)
    D. Loader (Ford V8)   916.4
    Ladies' Prizes:
    Open cars – Mrs. K. Hague (Riley
Sprite)
    Closed cars – Ms. O. Bailey (Rover).
    Team Prize: Riley.

1939

200 starters, 192 finishers.
Starting points: Blackpool, London,
Stratford-upon-Avon and Torquay.
Finishing point: Brighton.
No official outright winner.
    Group 1 (open cars, up to 10 hp)
    G. H. Goodall
(Morgan 4/4)   901.2 marks
    Group 2 (closed cars, up to 10 hp)
    H. F. S. Morgan
(Morgan 4/4)   894.6
    Group 3 (open cars, 10 hp to 15 hp)
    M. H. Lawson (HRG
1500)   909.6
    Group 4 (closed cars, 10 hp to 15 hp)
    G. S. Davison
(Triumph Dolomite)   890.2
    Group 5 (open cars, over 15 hp)
    A. F. P. Fane (Frazer-
Nash BMW)   916.4
    Group 6 (closed cars, over 15 hp)
    H. J. Aldington
(Frazer-Nash BMW)   908.2
    Ladies' Prizes:
    Open cars – Mrs. K. Hague (Riley 12).
    Closed cars – Viscountess Chetwynd
(Ford V8 30)
    Team Prize: Frazer-Nash BMW.

1951

229 starters, 185 finishers.
Starting points: Brighton, Cheltenham,
Harrogate and Skegness. Finishing
point: Bournemouth.
No official outright winner.
General Classification (unofficial):
    1 I. Appleyard/Mrs.

P. Appleyard
(Jaguar XK120)   109.61 penalties
2 P. H. G. Morgan
(Morgan +4)   112.99
3 W. A. G. Goodall
(Morgan +4)   114.55
Ladies' Prizes:
Open cars – Miss M. Newton/Miss A.
Newton (Jaguar XK120).
Closed cars – Miss S. Van Damm/Mrs.
B. Wisdom (Hillman Minx)
Manufacturers' Team Prize: Morgan.

1952

242 starters, 199 finishers.
Starting points: Hastings and
Scarborough. Finishing point:
Scarborough.
No official outright winner.
    General Classification (unofficial):
    1 G. Imhof/Mrs. B.
    Frayling (Allard-
    Cadillac)   183.8 penalties
    2 J. C. Broadhead
    (Jaguar XK120)   185.0
    3 I. Appleyard/Mrs.
    P. Appleyard
    (Jaguar XK120)   186.6
    Ladies' Prizes:
    Open cars – Miss M. Newton/Miss A.
Newton (Jaguar XK120).
    Closed cars – Ms. C. Sadler (Rover).
    Manufacturers' Team Prize: Morgan.

1953

194 starters, 154 finishers.
Starting points: Blackpool and Hastings.
Finishing point: Hastings.
An outright winner declared for the first
time.
    General Classification:
    1 I. Appleyard/Mrs. P.
    Appleyard (Jaguar
    XK120)   29.37*
    2 R. Adams/J. Pearman
    (Sunbeam-Talbot 90)   22.77
    3 G. Imhof/Mrs. B. Frayling
    (Allard J2X)   19.51
    Ladies' Prize:
    Miss S. Van Damm/Mrs. F. Clarke
(Sunbeam-Talbot 90).
    Manufacturers' Team Prize: Jaguar.
    *A figure of merit, based on 11 tests during
the event.*

1954

229 starters, 164 finishers.
Starting points: Hastings and Blackpool.
Finishing point: Blackpool.

General Classification:
    1 J. Wallwork/
    J. H. Brooks
    (Triumph TR2)   416.67 penalties
    2 P. G. Cooper/
    O. L. Leighton
    (Triumph TR2)   435.05
    3 T. C. Harrison/
    E. Harrison
    (Ford Zephyr)   440.50
    Ladies' Prize:
    Miss M. Walker (Triumph TR2).
    Manufacturers' Team Prize: Ford.

1955

238 starters/168 finishers.
Starting points: Hastings and Blackpool.
Finishing point: Hastings.
    General Classification:
    1 J. Ray/B.
    Horrocks
    (Standard 10)   258.1 penalties
    2 H. E. Rumsey/P.
    Roberts
    (Triumph TR2)   462.3
    3 W. K.
    Richardson/J. C.
    Heathcote
    (Standard 10)   559.5
    Ladies' prize:
    Miss S. Van Damm/Mrs. A. Hall
(Sunbeam Talbot).
    Manufacturers' Team Prize: Standard.

1956

213 starters, 165 finishers
Starting points: Blackpool and Hastings.
Finishing point: Blackpool.
    General Classification:
    1 L. Sims/R. Jones/
    A. Ambrose
    (Aston Martin
    DB2)   29.2 penalties
    2 I. Appleyard/
    Mrs. P.
    Appleyard
    (Jaguar XK120)   50.0
    3 Dr J. T. Spare/
    M. Meredith
    (Morgan +4)   54.8
    Ladies' Prize:
    Miss A. Palfrey/Miss A. Jervis (Austin
A40)
    Manufacturers' Team Prize: BMC.

1957

No rally due to petrol rationing as a
result of the Suez crisis.

1958

196 starters, 130 finishers.
Starting points: Hastings and Blackpool.
Finishing point: Hastings.
General Classification:
1 P. Harper/Dr
  E. W. Deane
  (Sunbeam
  Rapier)   652.8 penalties
2 R. A.
  Gouldbourn/S.
  Turner (Standard
  Pennant)   1179.3
3 T. Gold/W. Cave
  (Standard
  Pennant)   1231.4
Ladies' Prize:
Miss P. Moss/Miss A. Wisdom
(Morris Minor 1000)
Manufacturers' Team Prize: Standard.

1959

131 starters, 53 finishers.
Starting point: Blackpool. Finishing
point: London (Crystal Palace).
General Classification:
1 G. Burgess/S.
  Croft-Pearson
  (Ford Zephyr)   32 penalties
2 T. Gold/M.
  Hughes (Austin-
  Healey Sprite)   42
3 M. Sutcliffe/D.
  Astle (Riley 1.5)   43
Ladies' Prize:
Mrs. A. Hall/Miss P. Burt (Ford
Anglia 105E)
Manufacturers' Team Prize:
Standard-Triumph.

1960

172 starters, 138 finishers.
Starting point: Blackpool. Finishing
point: Brands Hatch.
General Classification:
1 E. Carlsson/S.
  Turner (Saab 96)   0 penalties
2 J. Sprinzel/R.
  Bensted-Smith
  (Austin-Healey
  Sprite)   2
3 D. Morley/E.
  Morley (Austin-
  Healey 3000)   2
Ladies' Prize:
Mrs. A. Hall/Miss V. Domleo (Ford
Anglia)
Manufacturers' Team Prize: BMC
Austin-Healey.

1961

150 starters, 81 finishers.
Starting point: Blackpool. Finishing
point: Brighton.
General Classification:
1 E. Carlsson/J.
  Brown (Saab 96)   89 penalties
2 Miss P. Moss/
  Miss A. Wisdom
  (Austin-Healey
  3000)   129
3 P. Harper/I. Hall
  (Sunbeam
  Rapier)   150
Ladies' Prize:
Miss P. Moss/Miss A. Wisdom
(Austin-Healey 3000).
Manufacturers' Team Prize: Sunbeam
Talbot.

1962

157 starters, 102 finishers.
Starting point: Blackpool. Finishing
point: Bournemouth.
General Classification:
1 E. Carlsson/D.
  Stone (Saab 96)   204 penalties
2 P. Hopkirk/J.
  Scott (Austin-
  Healey 3000)   264
3 Miss P. Moss/
  Mrs. P. Mayman
  (Austin-Healey
  3000)   314
Ladies' Prize:
Miss P. Moss/Mrs. P. Mayman
(Austin-Healey 3000).
Manufacturers' Team Prize: BMC
Mini-Cooper.

1963

163 starters, 91 finishers.
Starting point: Blackpool. Finishing
point: Bournemouth.
General Classification:
1 T. Trana/S.
  Lindstrom
  (Volvo PV544)   246 penalties
2 H. Kallstrom/G.
  Haggbom (VW
  1500i)   293
3 E. Carlsson/G.
  Palm (Saab 96)   293
Ladies' Prize:
Mrs. P. Moss-Carlsson/Miss J. Nadin
(Ford Cortina GT).
Manufacturers' Team Prize: Ford

1964

158 starters, 89 finishers.
Starting and finishing point: London
(Kensington).
General Classification:
1 T. Trana/G. Thermanius
  (Volvo PV544)   3510 secs
2 T. Makinen/D. Barrow
  (Austin-Healey 3000)   4631
3 V. Elford/D. Stone
  (Ford Cortina GT)   4860
Ladies' Prize:
Mrs. P. Moss-Carlsson/Miss E.
Nystrom (Saab 96).
Manufacturers' Team Prize: Ford.

1965

163 starters, 62 finishers.
Starting and finishing point: London
(Excelsior Hotel, Heathrow).
General Classification:
R. Aaltonen/A.
Ambrose (Mini-Cooper S)   531 min 23 s
T. Makinen/P. Easter
(Austin-Healey 3000)   534   31
J. Larsson/L. Lundblad
(Saab 96 Sport)   537   18
Ladies' Prize:
Mrs. P. Moss-Carlsson/Miss E.
Nystrom (Saab 96 Sport).
Manufacturers' Team Prize:
Rootes.

1966

144 starters, 63 finishers.
Starting and finishing point: London
(Excelsior Hotel, Heathrow).
General Classification:
1 B. Soderstrom/G.
  Palm (Ford Lotus-
  Cortina)   475 m   15 s
2 H. Kallstrom/R.
  Haakanson (BMC
  Mini-Cooper)   488   50
3 T. Trana/S.
  Andreasson (Volvo
  122)   489   50
Ladies' Prize:
Mrs. P. Moss-Carlsson/Miss E.
Nystrom (Saab Monte Carlo)
Manufacturers' Team Prize:
Not awarded (no finishers).

1967

Rally cancelled owing to Foot-and-
mouth disease in Britain.

1968

96 starters, 32 finishers.
Starting and finishing point: London
(Centre Airport Hotel, Heathrow).
  General Classification:
  1 S. Lampinen/J.
    Davenport (Saab V4)   650 m 34 s
  2 C. Orrenius/G.
    Schroderheim (Saab
    V4)   666 04
  3 J. Bullough/D.
    Barrow (Ford Escort
    TC)   715 08
Ladies' Prize:
Not awarded (no finishers).
Manufacturers' Team Prize:
Not awarded (no finishers).

1969

151 starters, 69 finishers.
Starting and finishing point: London
(Centre Airport Hotel, Heathrow).
  General Classification:
  1 H. Kallstrom/G.
    Haggbom (Lancia
    Fulvia HF)   479 m 17 s
  2 C. Orrenius/D. Stone
    (Saab V4)   483 32
  3 T. Fall/H. Liddon
    (Lancia Fulvia HF)   494 36
Ladies' Prize:
Miss J. Robinson/Miss A. Scott
(BMW 2002).
Manufacturers' Team Prize: Datsun.

1970

196 starters, 67 finishers
Starting and finishing point: London
(Centre Airport Hotel, Heathrow).
  General Classification:
  1 H. Kallstrom/G.
    Haggbom (Lancia
    Fulvia HF)   541 m 50 s
  2 O. Eriksson/H.
    Johansson (Opel
    Kadett Rallye)   544 18
  3 L. Nasenius/B.
    Cederberg (Opel
    Kadett Rallye)   553 18
Ladies' Prize:
Mrs. E. Crellin/Mrs. P. Wright
(Mini-Cooper S)
Manufacturers' Team Prize: Opel.

1971

231 starters, 104 finishers.
Starting and finishing point: Harrogate.

General Classification:
  1 S. Blomqvist/A. Hertz
    (Saab V4)   450 m 47 s
  2 B. Waldegaard/L.
    Nystrom (Porsche
    911S)   454 00
  3 C. Orrenius/L.
    Persson (Saab V4)   460 01
Ladies' Prize:
Mlle M-C. Beaumont/Mlle M. de la
Grandive (Opel).
Manufacturers' Team Prize: Saab.

1972

192 starters, 80 finishers.
Starting and finishing point: York.
  General Classification:
  1 R. Clark/T. Mason
    (Ford Escort RS1600)   410 m 07 s
  2 S. Blomqvist/A. Hertz
    (Saab V4)   413 32
  3 A. Kullang/D.
    Carlsson (Opel
    Ascona Rallye)   419 57
Ladies' Prize:
Mlle M-C. Beaumont/Mlle C. Giganot
(Opel)
Manufacturers' Team Prize: Opel.

1973

198 starters, 91 finishers.
Starting and finishing point: York.
  General Classification:
  1 T. Makinen/H.
    Liddon (Ford Escort
    RS1600)   407 m 08 s
  2 R. Clark/T. Mason
    (Ford Escort RS1600)   412 23
  3 M. Alen/I. Kivimaki
    (Ford Escort RS1600)   415 26
Ladies' Prize:
Miss E. Heinonen/Miss S. Sarristo
(Volvo 142).
Manufacturers' Team Prize:
Not awarded (no finishers).

1974

190 starters, 83 finishers.
Starting and finishing point: York.
  General Classification:
  1 T. Makinen/H.
    Liddon (Ford Escort
    RS1600)   482 m 39 s
  2 S. Blomqvist/H.
    Sylvan (Saab V4)   484 19
  3 S. Munari/P. Sodano
    (Lancia Stratos)   491 55
Ladies' Prize:

Mrs. P. Moss-Carlsson/Mrs. E. Crellin
(Toyota)
Manufacturers' Team Prize: Datsun.

1975

236 starters, 104 finishers.
Starting and finishing point: York.
  General Classification:
  1 T. Makinen/H.
    Liddon (Ford Escort
    RS1800)   360 m 44 s
  2 R. Clark/T. Mason
    (Ford Escort RS1800)   361 57
  3 T. Fowkes/B. Harris
    (Ford Escort RS1600)   366 11
Ladies' Prize:
Miss T. Jensen/Miss M. Brathen (Ford
Escort 1600 Sport).
Manufacturers' Team Prize: Vauxhall.

1976

200 starters, 71 finishers.
Starting and finishing point: Bath.
  General Classification:
  1 R. Clark/S. Pegg
    (Ford Escort RS1800)   362 m 26 s
  2 S. Blomqvist/H.
    Sylvan (Saab 99)   367 03
  3 B. Waldegaard/H.
    Thorzelius (Ford
    Escort RS1800)   367 56
Ladies' Prize:
Miss J. Robinson/Ms. P. Gullick
(Ford Escort)
Manufacturers' Team Prize: Saab

1977

180 starters, 67 finishers.
Starting point: London (Wembley)
Finishing point: York.
  General Classification:
  1 B. Waldegaard/H.
    Thorzelius (Ford
    Escort RS)   501 m 26 s
  2 H. Mikkola/A. Hertz
    (Toyota Celica)   503 49
  3 R. Brookes/J. Brown
    (Ford Escort RS)   511 55
Ladies' Prize:
Miss J. Robinson/Miss D. Selby-
Boothroyd (Ford Escort RS2000)
Manufacturers' Team Prize: Ford.

1978

168 starters, 61 finishers.
Starting and finishing point:
Birmingham.

General Classification:
1 H. Mikkola/A. Hertz
(Ford Escort RS) 527 m 23 s
2 B. Waldegaard/H.
Thorzelius (Ford
Escort RS) 532 41
3 R. Brookes/D. Tucker
(Ford Escort RS) 538 55
Ladies' Prize:
Miss J. Simpson/Miss D. Selby-
Boothroyd (Ford Escort RS2000)
Manufacturers' Team Prize: Ford.

1979

175 starters, 74 finishers.
Starting and finishing point: Chester.
General Classification:
1 H. Mikkola/A. Hertz
(Ford Escort RS) 483 m 38 s
2 R. Brookes/P. White
(Ford Escort RS) 494 07
3 T. Salonen/S. Pegg
(Datsun 160J) 496 22
Ladies' Prize:
Miss M-L. Korpi/Miss E. Heinio
(Ford Escort RS2000)
Manufacturers' Team Prize: Ford.

1980

142 starters, 47 finishers.
Starting and finishing point: Bath.
General Classification:
1 H. Toivonen/P.
White (Talbot
Sunbeam-Lotus) 497 m 33 s
2 H. Mikkola/A. Hertz
(Ford Escort RS) 502 09
3 G. Frequelin/J. Todt
(Talbot Sunbeam-
Lotus) 511 24
Ladies' Prize:
Not awarded (no finishers).
Manufacturers' Team Prize:
Not awarded (no finishers)

1981

151 starters, 54 finishers.
Starting and finishing point: Chester.
General Classification:
1 H. Mikkola/A. Hertz
(Audi Quattro) 510 m 00 s
2 A. Vatanen/D.
Richards (Ford Escort
RS) 521 05
3 S. Blomqvist/B.
Cederberg (Talbot
Sunbeam-Lotus) 523 36
Ladies' Prize:

Miss L. Aitken/Mrs. E. Morgan (Ford
Escort RS2000)
Manufacturers' Team Prize: Lada.

1982

149 starters, 63 finishers.
Starting and finishing point: York.
General Classification:
1 H. Mikkola/A. Hertz
(Audi Quattro) 481 m 46 s
2 Mlle M. Mouton/Miss
F. Pons (Audi
Quattro) 486 03
3 H. Toivonen/F.
Gallagher (Opel
Ascona 400) 486 12
Ladies' Prize:
Mlle M. Mouton/Miss F. Pons (Audi
Quattro).
Manufacturers' Team Prize: Lada.

1983

129 starters, 61 finishers.
Starting and finishing point: Bath.
General Classification:
1 S. Blomqvist/B.
Cederberg (Audi
Quattro A2) 530 m 28 s
2 H. Mikkola/A. Hertz
(Audi Quattro A2) 540 21
3 J. McRae/I. Grindrod
(Opel Manta 400) 552 19
Ladies' Prize:
Miss S. Kottulinsky/Ms. L. Wennberg
(Opel Ascona).
Manufacturers' Team Prize: Audi.

1984

120 starters, 52 finishers.
Starting and finishing point: Chester.
General Classification:
1 A. Vatanen/T.
Harryman (Peugeot
205 T16) 559 m 48 s

2 H. Mikkola/A. Hertz
(Audi Quattro A2) 560 29
3 P. Eklund/D.
Whittock (Toyota
Celica Turbo) 577 07
Ladies' Prize:
Mlle M. Mouton/Miss F. Pons (Audi
Quattro Sport).
Manufacturers' Team Prize: Audi
Sport UK.

1985

155 starters, 62 finishers.
Starting and finishing point:
Nottingham.
General Classification:
1 H. Toivonen/N.
Wilson (Lancia Delta
S4) 572 m 05 s
2 M. Alen/I. Kivimaki
(Lancia Delta S4) 573 01
3 T. Pond/R. Arthur
(MG Metro 6R4) 574 32
Ladies' Prize:
Mrs. L. Aitken-Walker/Mrs. E.
Morgan (Peugeot 205 GTI)
Manufacturers' Team Prize: Opel.

1986

150 starters, 83 finishers.
Starting and finishing point: Bath.
General Classification:
1 T. Salonen/S.
Harjanne (Peugeot
205 T16 E2) 321 m 11 s
2 M. Alen/I. Kivimaki
(Lancia Delta S4) 322 33
3 J. Kankkunen/J.
Piironen (Peugeot 205
T16 E2) 327 16
Ladies' Prize:
Mrs. L. Aitken-Walker/Mrs. E.
Morgan (Nissan 240RS).
Manufacturers' Team Prize: Austin
Rover.

'As to future rallies, it is the generally expressed hope that the R.A.C. will go on, year by year, from strength to strength.' *The Autocar*, 11 March 1932. (Editorial following the first RAC Rally.)

Rally Facts

The Lombard RAC Rally is one of the most labour-intensive sporting events on the calender.

The five-day event requires 12,000 marshals, 200 doctors, 150 timekeepers, 60 staff in rally headquarters, 45 Stage Commanders and 12 Area Organisers.

The computer room at the rally headquarters is operated by Olivetti in conjunction with Eastman Stuart software. Equipment, valued at in excess of £90,000, requires over 100 programmes created specifically in order to cover every aspect of the rally on a minute-by-minute basis.

This information is fed to 33 VDU terminals around the country. Twenty thousand sheets of printout paper are consumed. In the rally headquarters alone, the operation requires more than 1,000 metres of cable.

Rank Xerox provide at least 20 of their latest photocopying machines which consume over a quarter of a million sheets of A4 during the five days. (It is interesting to note that, during the 1986 Lombard RAC Rally, there were only two service calls for the machines which were more or less working round the clock.)

British Telecom install over 100 special 'phone lines throughout the country to service the needs of the information gathering teams, the results service and the world's media. In the rally headquarters in Bath in 1986, British Telecom provided a round the clock team of six operators to staff the telex machines, photo senders, fax machines and specially-installed ISD lines.

In 1986, BBC Ceefax based a two-man team in Bath. They created over 750 'pages' of information during the event.

BBC Radio 'Sport on 2' broadcast 60 reports from their own fully-staffed studio in rally headquarters.

In 1986, the Lombard RAC Rally received six hours of television coverage nationally. BBC

Breakfast TV and TVam provided daily reportage of the rally, TVam sharing their news-gathering camera crews with ITN News, who provided daily coverage in their evening news bulletins.

In 1986, BBC TV devoted four hours and five minutes to daily coverage of the rally, the greatest amount of time they have ever allotted to any motor sport event in this country. Camera crews, riggers, sound technicians and editorial staff numbered 170.

The Lombard RAC Rally was filmed for television coverage in France, Scandinavia, Germany, Italy and Japan.

Over 1,200 press passes were issued in 1986 to assist the provision of news and pictures to 14 countries. A team of 10 press officers was based in Bath, backed up by a mobile crew of three who followed the event round the 1,500-mile route.

The Radio Team, working from a studio in rally headquarters, fed close to 400 reports to 39 local radio stations.

British Telecom Voice Bank served eight separate outlets around the country with reports which were updated five times a day.

Vauxhall/General Motors created their own 'Eventsline' to service their dealers and the public alike with four daily reports of four minutes' duration.

The Times, The Independent, Daily Telegraph, The Guardian, Daily Mail, Daily Express and *Today* carried daily in-depth coverage and pictures of the rally.

On the first day of the 1986 Lombard RAC Rally, 120,000 spectators paid to watch the first nine special stages. The largest single attendance was 18,500 at Trentham Gardens, near Stoke on Trent.

It is estimated that the rally is seen by two million people during the five days.

INDEX

Figures in bold refer to illustrations